FILMING HISTORY FROM BELOW

NONFICTIONS

Nonfictions is dedicated to expanding and deepening the range of contemporary documentary studies. It aims to engage in the theoretical conversation about documentaries, open new areas of scholarship, and recover lost or marginalized histories.

FILMING HISTORY FROM BELOW

MICROHISTORICAL DOCUMENTARIES

EFRÉN CUEVAS

Wallflower
New York

Columbia University Press
Publishers Since 1893
New York   Chichester, West Sussex
cup.columbia.edu
Copyright © 2022 Columbia University Press
All rights reserved

Library of Congress Cataloging-in-Publication Data
Names: Cuevas, Efrén, author.
Title: Filming history from below : microhistorical documentaries / Efrén Cuevas.
Description: New York : Wallflower, an imprint of Columbia University Press,
[2021] | Series: Nonfictions | Includes bibliographical references and index.
Identifiers: LCCN 2021023335 (print) | LCCN 2021023336 (ebook) |
ISBN 9780231195973 (trade paperback) | ISBN 9780231195966 (hardback) |
ISBN 9780231551571 (ebook)
Subjects: LCSH: Documentary films—History and criticism. |
History in motion pictures.
Classification: LCC PN1995.9.D6 C74 2021 (print) |
LCC PN1995.9.D6 (ebook) | DDC 070.1/8—dc23
LC record available at https://lccn.loc.gov/2021023335
LC ebook record available at https://lccn.loc.gov/2021023336

Cover design: Milenda Nan Ok Lee
Cover images: Film stills from *The Maelstrom*, 1997, © Péter Forgács

CONTENTS

ACKNOWLEDGMENTS

This book began taking shape as a specific project in 2017, but it has a prehistory that dates back to 1998, when José Luis Guerín's film *Tren de sombras* sparked my interest in the use of home movies in contemporary cinema. I began developing this interest further during two short stays (in 2000 and 2001) at the Anthology Film Archives, where I enjoyed the hospitality of Robert Haller and Jonas Mekas, and where I began studying the work of the latter in depth— research that served as the foundation for the last chapter of this book. A few years later I would sketch out the connections between home movies, documentary film, and microhistory in an article published in 2007 in the journal *Secuencias*. The book I edited in 2010, *La casa abierta: El cine doméstico y sus reciclajes contemporáneos* (The open house: Home movies and their contemporary recycling), with the support of Documenta Madrid and Antonio Delgado, represented another important step, as although its focus is different, it contains many related elements.[1] Over the years my research has been enriched by other filmmakers and filmographies that have made the exploration of this relationship more complex, leading to presentations at conferences such as Visible Evidence, SCMS, IAMHIST, and NECS, and to various publications, some of which appear in this book in updated versions. Specifically, chapter 1 is partially based on an article published in the journal *Historia Social*, while chapter 2 is based in part on a chapter published in the book *Amateur*

Filmmaking: The Home Movie, the Archive, the Web, and on an article published in *Studies in Documentary Film*, and chapter 7 is based on an article published in *Biography*.[2] I am grateful to these journals and publishers for having given me the opportunity to share my research.

While researching and writing this book, my work has benefited from the contributions of various colleagues with shared interests, through conversations, reading parts of the book, or helping me locate different films. In particular, I would like to thank Robert Rosenstone, Vicente Sánchez-Biosca, Philip Rosen, Stefano Odorico, Anacleto Pons, Deirdre Boyle, and Ohad Landesman. I am also grateful for the support of the filmmakers who gave me access to their films and/or shared their creative processes with me in interviews, especially Péter Forgács, but also Karen Ishizuka, Rithy Panh, Michal Aviad, Mahdi Fleifel, Pia Andell, and the late Jonas Mekas.

I also wish to thank Columbia University, and my host there, Jane Gaines, as it was during my stay as a visiting scholar at Columbia that this project came into being in its current form. Special thanks are also due to Universidad de Navarra for their continuous support for my research through the PIUNA research projects and for the sabbatical they granted me to work at Columbia University. My department colleagues at Universidad de Navarra have been essential travel companions on this journey, especially the members of my research group, Lourdes Esqueda, Julieta Keldjian, María del Rincón, and Carlos Muguiro.

I would like to gratefully acknowledge Columbia University Press for supporting this project, and especially Ryan Groendyk for his advice and support throughout the publishing process. A special mention is also warranted for the translator of the parts of this book originally written in Spanish, Martin Boyd, for his professionalism and rigor.

My deepest gratitude goes, of course, to my family and friends (including the "overlookers," "*alemanes*," and "*mendebalderos*") for having made this journey so much easier. On these occasions, I am always reminded of Joseph J. Rotman's amusing book dedication, which could be paraphrased here as: "To my family and friends, without whom this book would have been completed two years earlier."

FILMING HISTORY FROM BELOW

INTRODUCTION

Film and History

I n 2016 I was invited by Professor Jane Gaines to give a class on Péter
Forgács's film *The Maelstrom* at Columbia University. After the
screening, a student who identified himself as of Jewish descent said
that the film had impacted him more than any other he had seen before
about the Holocaust. This anecdote came back to me sometime later,
when, while rereading the book *History on Film/Film on History*, I came
upon this statement by its author, Robert Rosenstone, about another
Forgács film, *El Perro Negro*: "Of all of the documentaries I have seen on
the conflict [the Spanish Civil War], this is the one that, after years of
study, I find the most startling and provocative, a commentary on the
others and all that I know about the war."[1] It surprised me that for that
student and this researcher, two films based on the home movies of
unknown individuals could be the most convincing representations on
film of these two historical events. What is so special about the story of
the Peereboom family, the Salvans family, or Eduardo Noriega? Or perhaps it would be more appropriate to ask what is so special about Forgács's
way of working with this archival footage that vests these materials with
such historiographical depth, with an approach that can legitimately be
described as microhistorical. Considering Forgács's films from this perspective requires the acceptance of two assertions that are effectively
articulated in this book. The first is that documentaries can record history, that they can investigate the past and contribute knowledge of their

own to complement the work of written history done by professional historians. The second is that there is a type of documentary film that does this with a microhistorical perspective, which in this book will be referred to as microhistorical documentary.

This second assertion constitutes the central theme of this book and is explored more specifically in the first chapter. In this introduction, I therefore focus on the first, of film as a medium for constructing history, and of filmmakers as historians. This is the main thesis that justifies and underpins studies of film and history, a field that has grown considerably since it first emerged as a subject of academic research in the 1970s. Indeed, it has now become a field of study in its own right, with more than one hundred books published in different languages, an association of its own (the International Association for Media and History), and two journals dedicated to it: *Historical Journal of Film, Radio and Television*, and *Film and History*.[2] Further evidence of its growth and diversification can be found in the monographs about film and history studies in the Franco-Italian context by Tiziana M. Di Blasio and in the English-speaking world by Mia E. M. Treacey, which trace its development back to the very earliest days of cinema.[3] It has become something of a cliché for these kinds of studies to cite the brief manifesto published in 1898 by Bolesław Matuszewski, advocating for the establishment of a Cinematographic Museum or Depository where footage documenting historical events could be stored for future scholars, effectively changing cinema ("animated photography") "from a simple pastime to an agreeable method of studying the past."[4] Nevertheless, after the obligatory reference to Kracauer's book *From Caligari to Hitler: A Psychological History of the German Film* (1947), most scholars locate the origins of this field of academic study in the 1970s, with the work of the French researchers Marc Ferro and Pierre Sorlin. The work of these two authors was highly influential thanks to their publications in English, with Ferro's *Cinema et histoire* (1977) translated into English in 1988, and Sorlin's *The Film in History: Restaging the Past* published in 1980.[5] In the English-speaking world, although the British historian Paul Smith edited the influential anthology *The Historian and Film* back in 1976, it would probably be the American Robert Rosenstone who has become the most prominent scholar in the field, with numerous publications since the 1980s, the most comprehensive being his book *History on Film/Film on History*, published in 2006.[6]

Most of the studies by these authors, and by others who have followed in their wake, focus on fiction film, with two traditional lines of research. One line is concerned with the study of "historical films," meaning films that recreate or depict past eras as a central theme of their storylines and not for merely decorative purposes. An increasing number of historians have taken an interest in these types of films, partly for their potential use for educational purposes, but the focus has often been on analyzing their historical accuracy, applying traditional research standards to the depiction of the past offered in these films. Authors like Rosenstone have criticized this approach, which they consider reductionist, as it ignores the fact that historical fiction films—which Rosenstone refers to as "history films"—follow different rules of construction from professional history, without this meaning that they fail to offer valid information on the past.[7] The other line of study examines fiction films as social documents, as Sorlin asserts at the beginning of *The Film in History*, when he defines his object of study as "the cinema considered as a document of social history that . . . aims primarily at illuminating the way in which individuals and groups of people understand their own time."[8] Films are thus considered from the perspective of social and cultural history, as sociocultural artifacts that, beyond their specific storylines, usually convey the dominant axiological framework of their time and place of production. This is also highlighted in another of the seminal works in this field, *American History/American Film*, published in 1979, whose editors, John E. O'Connor and Martin A. Jackson, identify the book's objective as studying each specific film to show "how its visual text as well as the details of its production, release, and reception, relate to the broader historical and cultural questions of the day."[9]

These two lines of research share a primordial interest in mainstream films, as it is these that can most influence our vision of the present time or of past periods (in the case of historical cinema). Sometimes these authors also take an interest in more alternative, independent, or experimental films, where they find different ways of recording history. In this context, it is worth mentioning Rosenstone's interest in filmic modes that reflect a postmodern historiographical approach, which is discussed later in this book, or Antoine de Baecque's proposition of three vectors in the relationship between film and history: reconstruction (of the typical historical fiction film), archive (the film as document, whether fictional or documentary), and interpretation, which is expressed more clearly in the kind of essay film that makes use of montage, like Jean-Luc Godard's film *Histoire(s) de cinéma* (1988).[10]

Notwithstanding their different interests in the study of the relationship between film and history, all these authors agree that filmmakers can record history, that when they examine the past through their films they can be considered historians. There is no such consensus on this point among professional historians, who in many cases continue to believe that cinema—and especially mainstream cinema—has nothing to do with the professional recording of history. However, the notion of the filmmaker as historian is undisputed among scholars of film and history. Robert B. Toplin asserted it clearly as early as 1988: "One of the first tasks for consideration is to recognize producers, directors, writers, and editors for what they have become—historians."[11] Toplin's assertion was published in a forum on film and history in the prestigious history journal the *American Historical Review*, a fact that was considered at the time to be especially symbolic, as it signaled an openness among professional historians to serious consideration of cinema as a vehicle for history. The forum in question opened with an article by Rosenstone, which stressed one of his key ideas: the complementary rather than contradictory relationship between audiovisual history and written history.[12] He would explain this idea more clearly in *History on Film/Film on History*: "This visual form of historical thinking should not and cannot be judged by the criteria we apply to the history that is produced on the page" because it possesses "its own set of rules and procedures for creating works with their own historical integrity, works which relate to, comment upon, and often challenge the world of written history."[13] In short, as he goes onto explain, "to accept film makers as historians . . . is to accept a new sort of history. . . . In terms of informational content, intellectual density, or theoretical insight, film will always be less complex than written history. Yet its moving images and soundscapes will create experiential and emotional complexities of a sort unknown upon the printed page."[14] It is this last idea, which Rosenstone continues to consider mainly in relation to mainstream fiction film, that is the most interesting, as it points to the different level of complexity that films offer in their exploration of the past, as is shown throughout this book. Rosenstone further explores this different form of access to the past achieved by cinema, concluding that "the historical world created by film is potentially much more complex than written text. On the screen, several things occur simultaneously—image, sound, language, even text—elements that suggest and work against each other to create a realm of meaning as different from written history as written was from oral history."[15] This difference in the form of access to the past is what led Hayden White, in the same forum in 1988, to propose a new term for this field, "historiophoty," which he defines as "the representation of history and our thought about it in visual images and filmic discourse."[16] Despite its expressive concision, it is a term that has not been widely adopted in the academic literature.

In his 1988 article White stresses that any objections that may be made by professional historians to the versions of history offered by cinema are questionable, as they seem to overlook the fact that written history is itself a representation of the past, a construction with its own rules of operation. On this point he asserts that "every written history is a product of processes of condensation, displacement, symbolization, and qualification exactly like those used in the production of a filmed representation. It is only the medium that differs, not the way in which messages are produced."[17] Toplin posits a similar idea in the article cited above when he points out that the gulf between filmmakers and professional historians is not as wide as the latter might perceive them. This is also a point that would be reiterated years later by Jennie M. Carlsten and Fearghal McGarry, who observe with a hint of irony that "historians share more in common with filmmakers than they care to concede. In choosing a subject to represent, deciding how to conceptualise it, identifying source materials to illustrate it, and foregrounding key themes to signify its historical significance to a contemporary audience, the historian follows similar methodologies to the filmmaker."[18]

As noted above, studies of film and history focus mainly on mainstream cinema and especially on fiction films. The surprising lack of research on history and documentary film is sometimes explained as being due to the fact that the connection between the two is more obvious and less controversial. While it is true that more exhaustive studies, like the aforementioned book *History on Film/Film on History* or Marnie Hughes-Warrington's *History Goes to the Movies: Studying History on Film*, do include specific chapters dedicated to documentary film,[19] the references to it most commonly deal with informational documentaries.

Such films would fall into the category of expository documentaries, as defined by Bill Nichols, which raises clear problems for those historians skeptical about the ability of film to investigate the past,[20] due largely to the fact that the main function of this type of documentary is to present historical information to a general audience. This usually means that their intended purpose is not to conduct research into the past but rather to disseminate research previously conducted by professional historians. But apart from informational documentaries, the range of documentaries that explore the past is actually quite wide, as is the range of approaches they take: experimental, autobiographical, essayistic, and so on. The most significant cases of such documentaries have been analyzed by scholars in film studies from various perspectives.[21] However, specialists in film and history have rarely studied them. Among the few who have is Rosenstone, who has taken an interest in films such as *El Perro Negro*, *Far from Poland*, and *History and Memory*, as he finds that the postulates of a postmodern history are better reflected in these films than they are in written history.[22]

The microhistorical documentaries analyzed in this book are among the wide range of documentaries that examine the past from their own perspective, and not just with the aim of disseminating preexisting research. They can be understood as bridges between two fields that continue to run along relatively parallel lines, as they combine elements of cinema and of professional written history. These documentaries are constructed with the tools of the filmmaker, with the different expressive layers of sound and image that give them a complexity all their own. Additionally, in contrast to written history, they benefit from cinema's unique capacity to show the places and, in the case of contemporary history, the protagonists of their stories—through archival footage, or, if they are still alive, interviews—which provide access to the past with a powerful emotional charge, reinforced by all the other elements of filmic language. But, at the same time, these films are constructed with strategies and methods also used in written history, in a thorough research process, with the support of witnesses and experts (who may or may not appear in the film) and a detailed examination of archival sources (according special importance to audiovisual archives). Microhistorical documentaries also eschew the omniscient perspective generally adopted in informational documentaries to explore the past via alternative routes that may include questioning the research processes, exposing the constructed nature of the historical narrative, and working with archival sources with a critical approach, conscious of the fact that archives are not mere repositories of the past but the result of a consolidation of historical processes with specific agendas.

Obviously, the methodologies of the microhistorical documentary and written history are by no means identical. Standard written history conforms to specific parameters in its use of sources and its research and writing processes, while microhistorical documentaries construct their discourse on the past with a combination of conventional historiographical tools and creative resources unique to filmic language. Along these same lines, these documentaries do not literally incorporate the modes and methods of microhistory as it has been practiced in its conventional written form. However, the term "microhistorical" is not used here in a metaphorical sense or as if microhistorical documentaries were merely inspired by written microhistory. The application of the term here is best described as analogical (in a classical sense of this term, related to the notion of analogy of proportionality), entailing a common meaning for all the subjects of which it is predicated, while also possessing another meaning specific to each subject. In this sense, the microhistorical status of these documentaries arises from their position within specific parameters, defined by the main features of this historiographical approach understood in its most widely accepted sense. At the same time, these documentaries possess characteristics not present in written microhistory that contribute to their microhistorical status, associated not only with their audiovisual nature but also with other specific features, such as their quality as history of the present, the significant role they give to personal and collective memory, and the autobiographical perspectives that they often contain. It is also important to clarify that the generic category of microhistorical documentary includes films attuned in different ways to this category, as is pointed out throughout this book, resulting in differing degrees to which they may be characterized as microhistorical: from the most paradigmatic case—the films of Péter Forgács—to the most unorthodox—the diary films of Jonas Mekas.

Filming History from Below is divided into seven chapters. The first two explore theoretical aspects of microhistorical film, while the other five focus on individual case studies. Each case study is placed within its historical context sufficiently to clarify its contribution as a microhistorical chronicle of a specific era, nation, or social group, but this necessary contextualization is not intended to constitute an exhaustive analysis of the history of the country or social group in question, as such an analysis is far beyond the scope of this book's objective. Three of these chapters focus on the work of a specific filmmaker (Péter Forgács, Rithy Panh, and Jonas Mekas); the other two deal with explorations of a specific historical event or period from various perspectives. These five case studies have been chosen for their diversity and for the evidence each one offers of the possibilities of the microhistorical documentary form. The diversity is reflected in the countries covered, including the United States, Hungary, the Netherlands, Israel, Palestine, and Cambodia; in the time period represented, from the 1930s through to the first decade of the twenty-first century; and in their varied structures, ranging from collective portraits to autobiographical films to diary films. This book also combines analysis of filmmakers who are well-known among scholars of documentary cinema, such as Forgács, Pahn, and Mekas, and films belonging to a kind of canon, such as *The Maelstrom, History and Memory, The Missing Picture*, and *Lost, Lost, Lost*, with other films that are lesser known outside their specific geographical or social context, such as *Class Lot, Something Strong Within, From a Silk Cocoon, For My Children,* and *A World Not Ours.*

Each chapter focuses on just one or a few films, although occasionally other related films are discussed or analyzed briefly. In total, a close analysis is offered of fourteen films. The practice of close analysis poses the problem of how to describe the different scenes and the filmic strategies used therein, as it is not always easy to avoid descriptions that may be unnecessary for readers who know the film well, and at the same time insufficient for readers who have never seen the film or do not recall it well. To address this issue, for readers with current access to the films, when a specific scene is discussed, the minute of the film where it appears is included.

The common thread in the analysis of these films and filmmakers is the examination of the microhistorical features of each film and the historical chronicle that emerges from their approaches. However, in different chapters I also draw on other methodologies and contributions from related fields to complement this analysis, ranging from studies of autobiography applied to cinema to Michel de Certeau's and Alf Lüdtke's theories of everyday life, Marianne Hirsch's concept of postmemory, and Mikhail Bakhtin's chronotopic analysis. In addition, I have sought to integrate the work of researchers writing in different languages, particularly in English and Spanish, along with significant attention to studies in French, and more sporadically in other languages like Italian or Portuguese.

The chapters presenting the case studies are ordered according to a certain logic. The chapter dedicated to the work of Péter Forgács appears first because I consider it the most paradigmatic case of a documentary filmography with a microhistorical perspective. Conversely, the chapter dedicated to Jonas Mekas and his diary films has been placed at the end because his work is the most historiographically unorthodox, and therefore the most suitable for exploring the creative boundaries of this category of films. However, this criterion has not been applied to determine the order of the other three case studies, as to do so would entail attempting to pigeonhole them artificially within a supposed scale of relevance that would be difficult to justify. Instead, I have simply alternated the cases related to individual filmmakers (third, fifth, and seventh chapters) with those focusing on a historical event or period explored from different perspectives (fourth and sixth chapters).

The first chapter, "Microhistory and Documentary Film," presents the theoretical/analytical framework used for the analysis of the different case studies. Following a brief outline of the features of written microhistory, based chiefly on the work of its most prominent exponents, Carlo Ginzburg and Giovanni Levi, this chapter examines the main features of microhistorical documentaries (shared with written microhistory): an exploration of the past with a reduced scale of observation; a prioritizing of human agency; the use of narrative structures; and a conjectural appropriation of archival sources, which are usually limited because the focus is generally on individuals outside of public history. The chapter also includes an examination of the contributions offered by everyday life studies—with a brief outline of theories by Simmel, Benjamin, and Kracauer—and an overview of the role of personal memory and autobiographical perspectives, questions that are further explored in subsequent chapters.

Chapter 2 examines the use of archival materials in microhistorical documentaries. It begins with a discussion of the new understanding of archives that has emerged since the archival turn in history and archival studies, which has opened up their use to other disciplines, such as art, photography, and cinema. This serves to contextualize the use of archival sources in this kind of documentary, which obviously focuses more on audio/visual materials. The main singularity of microhistorical documentaries lies in the importance they accord to family archives, with an emphasis on snapshots and, especially, home movies. Audio/visual family archives are therefore the main focus of this chapter, which offers an analysis of their characteristics, proposes three basic modes of appropriation (naturalization, contrast, and historicization), and examines the most common structures found in films based on such archives (the collective portrait and the family history).

Chapter 3 deals with the films of Péter Forgács. This Hungarian filmmaker has produced an unquestionably coherent body of work in terms of both thematic content and style, based on home movies and amateur films that he reuses to construct microhistorical narratives, usually set in Europe between the 1930s and 1970s. To analyze his work, the chapter begins with a brief typology of his films and the historical chronicles they offer. This is followed by an analysis of his three films that most effectively embody a microhistorical perspective: *The Maelstrom*, *Free Fall*, and *Class Lot*. The first of these, perhaps his best-known film, presents the Shoah through the home movies of a Jewish Dutch family, the Peerebooms, contrasted with the home movies of the Reich Commissioner for Occupied Dutch Territories, Artur Seyss-Inquart. The other two films document the life of the Hungarian Jew György Pető, based on the home movies he filmed from the 1930s up to the end of the 1960s: *Free Fall* constructs a narrative in a certain sense parallel to that of *The Maelstrom*, but this time located in Hungary; while *Class Lot* continues the narrative after the end of World War II, focusing now on a microhistorical view of the communist regime established at that time.

The fourth chapter presents a study of documentaries that investigate the incarceration of Japanese Americans during World War II from a microhistorical perspective. It begins with an analysis of *Something*

Strong Within, a film made using the home movies of different Japanese Americans interned in the camps, but without the inclusion of interviews of the home moviemakers or other strategies to identify them individually. The film thus offers a collective portrait of life in this ethnic community under such painful historical circumstances, presenting an atypical variation on microhistory, as the scale of observation is reduced but not focused on a specific individual or family. The other three films analyzed in this chapter do focus on specific families, in the form of autobiographies of the female filmmakers who made them: *A Family Gathering, From a Silk Cocoon*, and *History and Memory*. Of the three films, it is the last that offers the most experimental format, in a complex combination of family chronicle and film essay about the ways of representing the past through audiovisual media.

The fifth chapter again focuses on an individual filmmaker: the Cambodian director Rithy Panh, internationally renowned for his films about the genocide perpetrated by the Khmer Rouge against the Cambodian people between 1975 and 1979. The analysis in this chapter focuses on his most accomplished work on this subject: *The Missing Picture*. The chapter begins with a brief overview of his previous films, *Bophana, S-21: The Khmer Rouge Killing Machine*, and *Duch: Master of the Forgers of Hell*, all of which contain certain microhistorical resonances. The analysis then turns to *The Missing Picture*, which offers a complex palimpsest of temporal layers, visual and sound sources, and historiographical perspectives. The film is dominated by the autobiographical approach of the filmmaker, who as a youth suffered through this terrible period that he now explores from a microhistorical perspective. But Panh adds various layers to this autobiographical portrait to offer a basic narrative on the macrohistorical context, but above all to construct an essayistic discourse that deconstructs the official narrative of the Khmer Rouge and interrogates the role of memory and archives in the construction of history.

The sixth chapter returns to the study of a historical event from different microhistorical perspectives, in this case the Palestinian-Israeli conflict and the narratives of national identity that feed the conflict, from the 1930s through to the present day. The first of the films analyzed, *Israel: A Home Movie*, offers another collective portrait based on home movies, this time of Israel during the decades when small-gauge cameras were in common use. What may initially seem like a typical microhistorical perspective on the past ends up being more ambiguous due to the attention given to portraying macrohistorical events. The other four films are articulated around autobiographical portraits, giving significant importance to the present, from which they interrogate the past of their countries and the future that awaits their families. In the Israeli case, an analysis is offered of the work of two female filmmakers with somewhat parallel life stories: Michal Aviad and Julie Cohen. Aviad's film *For My Children* is an excellent example of the combination of scales and historical temporalities. Cohen addresses similar themes in *My Terrorist* and *My Land Zion*, the latter of which leans toward an essayistic approach. The Palestinian perspective is explored chiefly through a close analysis of *A World Not Ours*, a film in which Mahdi Fleifel deals with the lives of refugees through the specific experience of the Ain el-Helweh camp in Lebanon.

Chapter 7 deals with the microhistorical perspective of Jonas Mekas's diary films, with a special focus on *Lost, Lost, Lost*. The chapter begins with an analysis of the particular features of the diary film as an expressive mode and of Mekas's specific approach to it. This is followed by a brief analysis of *Reminiscences*, and then by a close analysis of *Lost, Lost, Lost*, the Mekas film that contains his most explicit exploration of the past. In this film, the Lithuanian filmmaker offers a chronicle of his process of integration into the United States, from his first years when he was closely associated with the community of Lithuanians who had immigrated to the country after World War II to his progressive integration into the community of independent and avant-garde filmmakers in New York City, which is also documented in his film diaries. Based on a chronotopic analysis that draws on Bakhtinian theory, this study of *Lost, Lost, Lost* offers an opportunity to assess the potential of the microhistorical perspective applied to films with a strong personal stamp that may at first appear to be unrelated to a historiographical approach.

The book concludes with an epilogue that offers a brief reflection on the future of the microhistorical documentary in a context where the technology and the medium itself is changing quickly. Notable among the new developments are interactive documentaries (or "i-docs"), presented on multimedia platforms, with nonlinear structures. Some i-docs offer interesting contributions to microhistory, especially when they involve collective portraits, as do *Hidden Like Anne Frank* or *Jerusalem, We Are Here*. In any case, the future of the microhistorical documentary is difficult to predict, as the digital turn is also significantly affecting the way that historians and archivists work. In relation to family archives, which are key to this type of documentary, the proliferation of photos and home videos goes hand in hand with the uncertainty about their preservation and accessibility in the long term. Nevertheless, it seems likely that the exponential growth of the family archive in the digital era will open up new and exciting possibilities for the microhistorical documentary.

1

MICROHISTORY AND DOCUMENTARY FILM

The proposal of the term "microhistorical documentary" to classify certain films requires a prior contextualization, a task that is complicated by the fact that this book is aimed at researchers of both history and documentary cinema. With this challenge in mind, I begin with a discussion of a related field, everyday life studies (with a brief overview of some precursors to this field: the works of Georg Simmel, Walter Benjamin, and Siegfried Kracauer), which contributes some interesting ideas that inform the subsequent analysis of the case studies. I follow with an examination of a concept that is prima facie more specific, "microhistory," on the assumption that the reader already has sufficient understanding of the field of documentary cinema. After this two-part contextualization, I focus on the definition and main features of microhistorical documentaries, and conclude with a discussion on the relationship between memory and microhistory in autobiographical practice, an approach that is central to a number of the films analyzed in this book.[1]

RELATED CONTEXTS: EVERYDAY LIFE STUDIES, SIMMEL, BENJAMIN, KRACAUER

Everyday life studies is a field located at the intersection between sociology, anthropology, and cultural studies. The connection between the history of everyday life (which, understood in its broadest sense, could also include microhistory) and the sociology of everyday life appears obvious from the outset, but in fact there has been very little real dialogue between these two disciplines. Notable among the very few authors who connect the two fields is John Brewer, who, in his study of microhistory and the histories of everyday life, identifies "the critical cultural theory . . . that runs from Georg Lukàcs, through the Surrealists, Walter Benjamin, Mikhail Bakhtin, Henri Lefebvre and the Situationist International (notably Guy Debord) to Michel de Certeau" as one of the traditions out of which the new interest in everyday life has emerged.[2] The sociologist Juan Gracia Cárcamo also discusses this relationship explicitly, acknowledging that dialogue between the two disciplines is uncommon, despite the fact that the growing interest among historians in these issues has a "more or less direct correlation with the perspectives that have been a source of discussion among sociologists who have taken an interest in the study of everyday life."[3] The rise of social and cultural history has certainly resulted in increasing exploration by historians of approaches like the history of representations, the history of popular culture, and microhistory, which in a way run parallel to the growing interest among sociologists and anthropologists in everyday life, although explicit connections between these approaches are still rare.

It is not my purpose here, in any case, to force synergies but to point to ways in which everyday life studies could reinforce historiographical approaches, specifically those related to microhistorical documentaries. To this end, the work of Ben Highmore—developed in the context of cultural theory—is particularly useful because of his way of framing and studying the most prominent scholars in this field. Highmore examines their work based on three clusters of questions related to aesthetics, archives, and critical practices, which exhibit some interesting parallels with the matters explored in the following chapters. Indeed, archives are the specific subject of the second chapter, mainly due to the prominent role played in this type of documentary by family archives, with their representation of everyday life in contemporary societies. The aesthetic dimension is also very visible in the work of the filmmakers employing a microhistorical perspective, which combines historiographical rigor with a creative approach, using the different expressive techniques of cinematic language to propose a critical practice in film form.

In relation to the first of these three clusters, aesthetics, Highmore foregrounds the way that avant-garde artists "locate and apprehend modern everyday life" and "find forms that are capable of articulating it."[4] Among these forms, he highlights the ones proposed by surrealism and montage, for their capacity for defamiliarizing everyday situations and objects in order to represent them in all their complexities and contradictions: "Aesthetic techniques, such as the surprising juxtapositions supplied by surrealism, provide a productive resource for rescuing the everyday from conventional habits of mind. Similarly, if the everyday is conventionally perceived as homogeneous, forms of artistic montage work to disturb such 'smooth surfaces.'"[5] Echoes of these associations can certainly be seen in Jonas Mekas's work, which is analyzed in the chapter 7, but also, albeit less explicitly, in the films of Péter Forgács or Rea Tajiri. Highmore places the second cluster of questions, related to archives, in relation to the tension between the impossible nature of recording the totality of everyday life and the need to avoid undocumented generalizations. Here he introduces the question of scales of observation that would subsequently become so central to microhistory: the dilemma between "the microscopic levels (most frequently classed as everyday) and macroscopic levels of the totality (culture, society and so on)."[6] In this context, an urgent need arises to make the everyday visible, to rescue it from the oblivion to which the grand narratives habitually consign it. To do this, it is important to understand the everyday as a critical practice and as a form of practical criticism, which is the focus of the third set of questions proposed by Highmore. In this way, everyday life can be brought into the light, inverting the most common modes of representation: "Instead of picturing the world as a drama of significant (and exceptional) events and people, set against a backdrop of everyday life, the relation between foreground and background needs to be reversed."[7]

With this framework, Highmore selects particular authors and themes to offer an overview of everyday life studies. Among these, it is worth commenting briefly here on the contributions of Georg Simmel, Walter Benjamin, and Siegfried Kracauer. All three of these authors published their work before the consolidation of everyday life studies in its more institutional and academic form, which may explain why their approaches are more transdisciplinary, with interesting echoes for historiographical studies of everyday life, as Harry D. Harootunian and John Brewer point out.[8] Brewer actually places all three of them in direct dialogue with microhistory: "[Carlo] Ginzburg's approach can be seen as part of a general concern among students of everyday life for small things and discrete particulars, a preoccupation going back to the brilliant essays of Georg Simmel but also found in the writings of Walter Benjamin and Siegfried Kracauer (whom Ginzburg speaks of as an indirect 'influence')."[9]

Georg Simmel's work spans the late nineteenth and early twentieth centuries and would influence key thinkers in the decades that followed, including Benjamin and Kracauer. Often identified as a forerunner of microsociology, Simmel bases his approach on a vindication of the microscopic scale for studying society. In opposition to classical sociology, concerned with the most visible social structures, Simmel argues for studying everyday interactions "between the atoms of society, accessible only to psychological microscopy, which support the entire tenacity and elasticity, the entire variety and uniformity of this so evident and yet so puzzling life of society."[10] In this microscopic analysis of society, Simmel also discovers a macroscopic dimension, in a clash of sociological scales of observation hinted at already in his early essay "Sociological Aesthetics": "For us the essence of aesthetic observation and interpretation lies in the fact that the typical is to be found in what is unique, the law-like in what is fortuitous, the essence and significance of things in the superficial and transitory."[11] For David Frisby, one of the most renowned scholars of Simmel's work, this emphasis on the fragmentary, the fortuitous, the transitory effectively unites this author with Benjamin and Kracauer in a common approach to their understanding of modernity: "They all sought, as it were, to complete the fragment, indeed to redeem it aesthetically, politically or historically. . . . Simmel's 'fortuitous fragments of reality,' Kracauer's 'insignificant superficial manifestations' and Benjamin's 'dialectical images' or 'monads' all redeemed the smallest, most insignificant traces of modernity in the everyday world."[12]

The focus on the fragmentary appears again in the work of Walter Benjamin, very prominently in his famous unfinished Arcades Project (*Passagenwerk*). Although Benjamin's work actually predates everyday life studies by many years, his ideas are particularly interesting since they are posited in dialogue with his historiographical work and in connection with new forms of representation like cinema. This interest in the fragmentary and the anecdotal is for Brewer precisely what constitutes a clear connection with historian Carlo Ginzburg's proposals related to the "evidential paradigm," which are analyzed below, and which he relates to Benjamin's (and Kracauer's) focus "on ephemera, fragments, anecdotes (the literary form that punctures narrative), 'insignificant details' and 'superficial manifestations' to achieve what Benjamin called 'profane illumination.'"[13] Benjamin's approach is not microhistorical either, but he seems to point in that direction quite clearly when he proposes "to discover in the analysis of the small individual moment the crystal of the total event" or "to assemble large-scale constructions out of the smallest and most precisely cut components."[14]

With these fragments otherwise considered insignificant, Benjamin proposes to construct a dialectical history based on the principle of montage. Herein lies the importance for Benjamin of the concept of the "dialectical image," in which the historicity of the everyday enters into legibility, as Highmore suggests. Highmore explains Benjamin's dialectical image as a montage of elements, "a collage practice that can arrange the materiality of modernity into a design that awakens it from its dreamscape and opens it out on to history."[15] Harootunian also stresses this connection posited in Benjamin's work between everydayness and history, in the explicit context of his analysis of modernity: "Thus modernity, especially everyday existence and experience, becomes the site where the past is always situated in the present and where differing forms of historical consciousness constantly commingle and interact."[16]

Another interesting aspect of Benjamin's work is the role he assigns to contemporary art and to new modes of representation, such as photography and cinema, in the task of rendering everyday experience visible, giving it a political articulation and transforming it into a historical experience. Benjamin takes a special interest in surrealism, in the work of Charles Baudelaire and Bertolt Brecht, and in cinema. What interested him in cinema was mainly the role of montage, in keeping with the importance he gave to this concept in his interpretation of history.[17] But his reflections on cinema sometimes take on unexpected suggestions of a microhistorical sensibility, as can be seen in his essay "The Work of Art in the Age of Mechanical Reproduction":

By close-ups of the things around us, by focusing on hidden details of familiar objects, by exploring common-place milieus under the ingenious guidance of the camera, the film . . . extends our comprehension of the necessities which rule our lives. . . . With the close-up, space expands; with slow motion, movement is extended. The enlargement of a snapshot does not simply render more precise what in any case was visible, though unclear: it reveals entirely new structural formations of the subject.[18]

As can be seen in this last sentence, Benjamin was formulating an idea remarkably similar to what Jacques Revel or Paul Ricoeur would propose in relation to the transformations that occur when the scale of observation is changed, as is explained below.

Together with Simmel and Benjamin, another important figure in this context is Siegfried Kracauer, with a similar understanding of everyday life, as Harootunian suggests: "Much as Simmel and Benjamin had done, Kracauer's apparent return to the concrete immediacy of everyday life concentrated on the fragments, the leavings of life."[19] Kracauer's work covers numerous fields, including cultural criticism, sociology, film theory, and historiography. His earliest sociological work already revealed an interest in the study of everyday life, as can be seen in *The Mass Ornament* (1927) and *The Salaried Masses* (1930).[20] Although he was not strictly speaking a professional historian, even in those early years he demonstrated an understanding of reality that comes close to a historical perspective. This is evident in the first of these texts, when he argues, in a proposition with microhistorical resonances, that "the position that an epoch occupies in the historical process can be determined more strikingly from an analysis of its inconspicuous surface-level expressions than from that epoch's judgments about itself."[21]

In the field of film studies, Kracauer's *Theory of Film: The Redemption of Physical Reality*, published later in his career (1960), constitutes a classic work on film realism. As its central thesis, indicated in the subtitle, Kracauer argues that a main function of cinema is to redeem physical, material reality from a lethargic state of virtual nonexistence. He posits a type of filmmaking that reflects what he defines as the inherent affinities of film: the unstaged, the fortuitous, endlessness, the indeterminate, and the flow of life; features that reflect an understanding of cinema in tune with the dynamics of everyday life. He makes this point more explicitly in the final section of the book, when he observes how everyday life is expressed in small random moments, whose texture is captured uniquely on film: "Products of habit and microscopic interaction, they form a resilient texture which changes slowly and survives wars, epidemics, earthquakes and revolutions. Films tend to explore this texture of everyday life."[22]

But Kracauer is not only interesting for this affinity for a kind of microsociology of the everyday but also for his explicit discussion of microhistory, which he outlines in his last book, *History, the Last Things Before the Last*. Published posthumously in 1969, it contains a series of reflections on historiography that had claimed his attention in the last years of his life. Among these were the macro- and microhistorical approaches to the field, explored in a chapter titled "The Structure of the Historical Universe."[23] The content of this chapter is surprising for the intuition and detail of his ideas, which exhibit clear parallels with the propositions of the microhistorians of the 1970s and 1980s, despite the fact that this book went largely unnoticed when it was first published and is not mentioned by any of those historians as an inspiration or influence. Carlo Ginzburg acknowledged this explicitly in 1993: "These posthumous pages . . . still constitute today . . . the best introduction to microhistory. As far as I know they have had no influence on the emergence of this historiographical current. Certainly not on me, since I learned about them with deplorable delay only a few years ago. But when I read them they seemed strangely familiar."[24] Kracauer argues in his book for the importance of microhistory not to illustrate or corroborate macrohistorical perspectives but as a focus of research in its own right that could challenge the assertions of macrohistory. However, rather than suggesting a dialectical approach, Kracauer proposes combining macrohistory and microhistory. To this end, he posits two laws: the law of perspective and the law of levels. According to the first, the greater the distance I take, the more my point of view will influence what I see. According to the second, a conclusion made at one (micro) level cannot simply be exported to another (macro) level, as distortions will inevitably occur.

HISTORY "FROM BELOW": MICROHISTORY

Microhistory, as a specific approach within contemporary historiography, can be located within the broader context of what has come to be referred to as "history from below," which began gaining currency in the 1960s. History from below questioned the traditional approaches that studied major historical events and their protagonists, but also the quantitative approaches that had been in vogue during the preceding decades. The new historiographical approaches emerging under the broad umbrella of history from below foregrounded the everyday lives of individuals and social groups, with a perspective that opened up a dialogue with social and cultural anthropology, disciplines that were also acquiring greater importance in those years. Brewer sums it up clearly:

> A large body of historical writing in the last forty years has made "everyday life," the experiences, actions and habits of ordinary people, a legitimate object of historical enquiry. Anglophone new social history, history written in the context of the new social movements concerned with gender, race and sexual orientation, *Alltagsgeschichte* in Germany, *microstoria* in Italy and post-Annales cultural history in France, all concern themselves with the lives, beliefs and practices of those who had previously been "hidden" from history.[25]

As Brewer mentions here, notable among the new approaches were two that received specific names: the German *Alltagsgeschichte* and the Italian *microstoria*. *Alltagsgeschichte*, the history of everyday life, had its principal exponent and theorist in Alf Lüdtke, responsible for a landmark anthology published in German and English, titled *History of Everyday Life: Reconstructing Historical Experiences and Ways of Life*.[26] The Italian *microstoria* school would have Giovanni Levi and Carlo Ginzburg as its most prominent representatives, each with his own theoretical contributions, and with two landmark works that put the approach into practice: Levi's *Inheriting Power: The Story of an Exorcist* and Ginzburg's *The Cheese and the Worms: The Cosmos of a Sixteenth-Century Miller*.[27] Both these approaches, as Brad S. Gregory puts it, "run parallel to each other and in certain respects overlap."[28] Although they contain certain distinguishing features, they share the same core elements, especially evident between *Alltagsgeschichte* and what Gregory calls "systematic microhistory," a term that he uses to describe the work of Giovanni Levi.[29]

This book focuses on microhistory because it is the approach that has achieved greater international prominence, both in terms of historical practice and historiographical debates. This is evident in the abundance of existing literature published in different countries and languages, beyond the work of Italian microhistorians. In addition to the publications analyzing specific case studies, it is worth mentioning, in the French-speaking world, the book edited by Jacques Revel, *Jeux d'echelles. La micro-analyse à la expérience*; in German, the publications of Hans Medick; in Spanish, the contributions by Anacleto Pons and Justo Serna in Spain and by Carlos Aguirre in Mexico; and in English, Sigurður G. Magnússon and István Szíjártó's book *What Is Microhistory? Theory and Practice*.[30]

It is not my objective to conduct here an in-depth study of written microhistory, but it is necessary at least to identify its main features for the benefit of readers who may be less familiar with this approach. Although it is identified as originating in Italy in the 1970s, because it was there and then that the term was coined, it emerged out of an intellectual hotbed of ideas with different precedents. Celso Medina, for example, traces its origins back to Miguel de Unamuno's concept of *intrahistoria*.[31] However, the British historian Edward P. Thompson, as exponent of the new social history in the 1960s, is often identified as a more immediate forerunner.[32] Thompson is attributed with coining the expression "history from below," which came into widespread use from that moment. Others often mentioned include the American anthropologist Clifford Geertz, who in 1973 introduced the term "thick description" to refer to a "microscopic" observation of the social reality.[33] Brewer emphasizes these connections, identifying Thompson, Geertz's cultural anthropology, and the microhistorians as the three responses that converge to transform traditional historiography: "None of these tactics or moves was isolated or autonomous, and they all shared, to differing degrees, a hostility to overarching narratives and (often even more ferociously) an antipathy to any anti-humanist position, whether structuralist—like that of Thompson's *bête noire* Althusser—or post-structuralist like that of Derrida."[34]

In its most restricted sense, *microstoria* was not really a school or a movement, notwithstanding the fact that it was first associated with a group of authors working in the same period (the 1970s and 1980s) in the same country (Italy). There were important authors in other countries, such as Natalie Z. Davis in the United States, or Emmanuel Le Roy in France, whose book *Montaillou*, published in 1975, is often cited as a precursor to microhistory.[35] But it is in Italy, and specifically in the journal *Quaderni storici* (in the period running from the mid-1970s to the late 1980s) that we can find the most significant contributions to the establishment of what is known today as microhistory. One of the first authors to promote this approach was Edoardo Grendi, who in the period mentioned would propose a historical microanalysis partly inspired by Fredrick Barth's network analysis.[36] Often associated with Grendi is Giovanni Levi, as both adopted approaches closer to social history. Another trend within Italian *microstoria* is related to cultural history, associated with the work of Carlo Ginzburg, who published his well-known book *The Cheese and the Worms* in 1976, although it would not be until 1979 that he would publish a more programmatic article, co-written with Carlo Poni.[37] Despite these two different trends, Italian *microstoria* can be understood as a distinctive historiographical approach, visible in the work of the aforementioned authors in *Quaderni storici* (whose editorial board as of 1978 included Grendi, Levi, Ginzburg, and Poni), and in the "Microstorie" book series by the publisher Einaudi, edited by Levi and Ginzburg from 1981 to 1991. The end of the book series and the differences between these historians has prompted some authors to ask whether microhistory was a fleeting phenomenon or whether it is still relevant today, a question Peter Burke raises in the second edition to *New Perspectives on Historical Writing*, published in 2001.[38] Notwithstanding this debate, microhistory continues to play a role in both historiographical discussions and historical practice; evidence of this can be found in the creation of a new book series by Routledge in 2018 under the name of "Microhistories."

Having established this historical contextualization, what follows is an outline of the main features of microhistorical theory and practice, which will serve as interpretative parameters for the purpose of defining microhistorical documentaries.[39] My intention here is not to delve into the particularities and distinctions of different microhistorical studies but to provide an account of the elements that such studies share. To this end, my authors of reference will be Giovanni Levi and Carlo Ginzburg, as they have been the two most internationally recognized authors in the field, not only for the two books mentioned above, but also for their various theoretical and methodological contributions, many of which have been translated and published in English and Spanish.

The change in the scale of observation is without doubt the most characteristic feature of microhistory. In contrast to historical studies traditionally focused on the macro level, microhistorical research proposes a reduction of scale for the purpose of developing a different understanding of the object of study. As Revel explains, "varying the focal length of the lens is not simply about enlarging (or shrinking) the size of the object caught in the viewfinder, but about altering its form and structure . . . about transforming the content of what is being represented (in other words, the decision about what is actually representable)."[40] Paul Ricoeur also offers an insightful observation on this question when he stresses that this change of scale produces "different concatenations of configuration and causality."[41] The objective here is not to offer particular case studies as "examples" of general theories, but to discover, through a "microscopic" analysis, historical realities that have gone unnoticed in macrohistorical analysis, in order to better explain a particular era.

This objective inevitably brings up one of the most common questions raised in relation to microhistory: its representativeness. For example, in the case analyzed by Ginzburg in *The Cheese and the Worms*, the aim is to determine the extent to which a detailed study of the life of a miller persecuted by the Roman Inquisition can contribute to a better understanding of the popular culture of the sixteenth century. Herein lies the main challenge of microhistory: to propose an alternative pathway to historical knowledge based on the microanalysis of personal and social relations. When writing microhistory, these authors seek to ensure that their analysis will make a significant contribution to our understanding of more general contexts of the society and culture to which their case study belongs. They thus try to avoid what would be mere casuistry (or "incidental analysis," to use Darnton's expression), a tendency that István Szíjártó associates more with some microhistorical practices in the United States.[42] Indeed, it is Szíjártó himself who, to explain the relationship between scales, suggests the analogous application of the concept of the "fractal," which in geometry refers to an object whose basic structure is the same at different scales. The microhistorical case would thus be understood as a fractal whose structure is discovered by historians in their painstaking microhistorical study of an era and which reflects historical issues of a wider scope.[43] This question is also related to Levi's insistence on distinguishing microhistory from local history, to highlight the fact that "the problem of microhistory is always a problem of generalizations."[44] Levi makes this point in relation to his study of the people of Santena in his book *Inheriting Power*: "I tried to see whether certain things, and particularly the land market, for example, studied at the local level, at the micro level, studied with the microscope, might tell us more, might reveal to us the mechanisms that on a larger scale we could never be able to see."[45] Levi stresses the point that he has not written *the* history of Santena, as for him it is not of particular interest. And citing Geertz's famous dictum that "anthropologists study in villages, they don't study villages," Levi concludes that he has written a history *in* those villages, not about those villages.[46]

Closely linked to the vindication of the micro scale is the centrality of human agency, the consideration of the individual as the main historical subject, freely engaging in social relationships, in contrast to more determinist approaches associated with structuralism or quantitative history. Ginzburg and Poni point this out explicitly in their article "The Name and the Game," where they argue for a prosopography from below, a history focusing on "the proper name" (i.e., a specific individual) as a guiding thread for archival research, which would be associated with a study of the subaltern strata of society.[47] Levi stresses this aspect when he rejects the distortions created by quantitative formalization, which "accentuate in a functionalist way the role of systems of rules and mechanistic processes of social change," while ignoring the freedom of action of individual people.[48] By focusing on such individuals, Levi goes on to suggest, microhistory reflects the inconsistencies of normative systems and consequently "the fragmentation, contradictions, and plurality of viewpoints which make all systems fluid and open."[49]

A microhistorical approach also requires an intensive study of available archives, which are not always sufficiently comprehensive, as the issues chosen for study are not the kind of matters that are systematically registered in public archives. However, the lacunae and missing data can sometimes be as eloquent as the documented information. It then becomes necessary to employ conjecture as a method, based on the "evidential paradigm" proposed by Ginzburg in an article in 1979.[50] In this article, Ginzburg compares the historian to a doctor or detective (in the style of Sherlock Holmes) who works with signs or symptoms in order to draw some conclusions. This can give rise to more unorthodox historiographical approaches, as Ginzburg argues with reference to the work of Natalie Z. Davis in *The Return of Martin Guerre*. The Italian historian applauds his American colleague's combination of erudition and imagination, proof and possibility, leading her "to work around the lacunae with archival materials contiguous in space and time to that which has been lost or never materialized."[51]

Microhistorians also advocate the use of narrative structures in writing history, once again in contrast to the strategies used in quantitative and *longue dureé* histories. This idea is consistent with the frequent choice to focus their research on an individual or family, whose history is most appropriately expressed in narrative form.[52] They also often admit the possibility of including the historian's voice in the narrative itself, in what could be described as a metadiscursive strategy, a technique rarely found in older historiographical approaches. Such a strategy is often a response to the need to make the conjectural approach to the sources explicit to the reader, highlighting their fragmentary nature and exposing the way the gaps found in the research are interpreted.

These features have led some to associate microhistorians with postmodern approaches. Their vindication of narrative structures for historical writing, their understanding of archives as fragmentary, and their inclusion of metadiscursive strategies are aspects that could be understood as postmodern, in that they foreground the constructed nature of historical studies, in clear contrast to traditional historiographical approaches and the claims to "total history" of quantitative or serial approaches. This raises a complex question of great relevance to contemporary historiography whose in-depth exploration is beyond the scope of this chapter. In the specific case studied here, both Levi and Ginzburg have dismissed the postmodern label, explicitly stating their rejection of the skeptical or relativist positions often associated with such an approach.[53] Ginzburg is undoubtedly the one who has addressed this question the most directly, in his critique of the theories of Hayden

White. In opposition to a radical constructivist understanding of history, the Italian historian asserts the cognitive dimension of the historiographical enterprise as a legitimate means of gaining access to past realities. However, as Serna and Pons explain in their detailed analysis of this question, the fact that Ginzburg rejects the understanding of history as rhetoric does not mean that he is unaware "that documents are representations and that, for that very reason, the external, what has occurred, what has disappeared, is by its nature irretrievable, but it is not unknowable, because those vestiges, even a single vestige, will enable us ... to allude to that extratextual world, to that presence that the skeptics would deny."[54]

MICROHISTORY AND THE DOCUMENTARY FILM

Having set out the parameters that represent the broadest consensus on the definition of microhistory, the next step is to study how those parameters are reflected in a particular type of documentary that I have defined here as microhistorical. No specific analysis has actually been made in historiography of the relationship between microhistory and documentary film, although it has been explored briefly in relation to the film medium or to fiction films by scholars such as Kracauer, Revel, Davis, Slávik, and Brewer. In his pioneering study of microhistory discussed above in this chapter, Siegfried Kracauer actually mentions Pudovkin and Griffith in an interesting comparison between film and history. Moreover, he posits a combination of macro- and microhistorical scales of observation in the same way that film combines the wide shot and the close-up: "The big must be looked at from different distances to be understood; its analysis and interpretation involve a constant movement between the levels of generality. . . . The macro historian will falsify his subject unless he inserts the close-ups gained by the micro studies."[55]

Some of the best-known microhistorians, such as Revel or Davis, have also made some brief but interesting comparisons between film and microhistory. In *Jeux d'echelles*, Revel considers the importance of the change of scale to gain access to new knowledge in relation to Michelangelo Antonioni's film *Blow-up* (1966), whose protagonist unexpectedly discovers what seems to be a murder plot when he enlarges some photos he has taken of a couple.[56] Davis, on the other hand, refers briefly in her book *Slaves on Screen* to the possibility that fiction film portrays the past in a microhistorical way: "In their microhistories, films can reveal social structures and social codes in a given time and place, sources and forms of alliance and conflict, and the tension between the traditional and the new."[57] However, she does not explore this question or apply it to the analysis of the films she studies in her book.

Among the more recent studies of microhistory, the contributions of Andrej Slávik and of the aforementioned John Brewer are worthy of special note. Slávik acknowledges previous contributions, like those of Revel and even Brewer, to go on to make the somewhat controversial proposition that the essay films of Chris Marker are the best equivalent of Ginzburg's microhistory in the field of cinema.[58] Brewer, on the other hand, identifies neorealism as a clear precursor to Italian microhistory, from which it would take its humanist realism and its rejection of skepticism: "They take their views first and foremost from the Italian neo-realist movement of the immediate post-Second World War era, and more generally from twentieth-century notions of realism derived from literature and film."[59] Brewer asserts that Roberto Rossellini's film *Paisà* (1946) could be considered the first work of Italian microhistory, as it explores the story of Italian liberation during World War II through six episodes set in different regions of the country: "The stories reduce the conflict to a human scale, yet in doing so they undercut or rewrite the positive story of liberation, showing how time's arrow is often diverted. . . . Throughout there is a tension between veracity and verisimilitude, between the patterns of everyday life and the forces of a larger history."[60] This perspective is of special interest because Ginzburg himself made reference to it in an interview he gave in 2014, when he remarked that neorealism constituted a foundational experience for him, particularly the film *Umberto D.* (1952).[61]

The absence of explicit references by historians to the relationship between microhistory and documentary film is perhaps understandable given that documentaries have not traditionally formed part of a shared cultural background like literature or fiction films.[62] Nevertheless, there is no doubt that when studying documentary film, some very interesting parallels with microhistory emerge. At first glance, a possible connection suggests itself between microhistory's interest in history "from below" and the abundant production of documentaries about individuals who are not public historical figures. The list of such films is endless, ranging from the foundational documentary *Nanook of the North* (1927) to more contemporary works like *To Be and to Have* (*Etre et avoir*, 2002), about a small school in rural France. However, it seems more reasonable to associate this documentary trend with anthropology or ethnography rather than with history, as the subjects these documentaries explore are set in the present day of the filmmaker and they rarely include any kind of reflection that could be defined as historiographical, in which the past is featured as an object of analysis. Instead, they would be what are generally referred to as ethnographic documentaries or observational documentaries, two categories which, although not synonymous, share elements in common.

It would be equally inappropriate to posit an association between microhistorical approaches and the kind of historical television documentaries popularized by theme channels like History (formerly History Channel). Without dismissing such a connection outright, it seems rather tenuous, as such documentaries are generally conceived as vehicles for disseminating history, usually understood in the macrohistorical sense, focusing either on past eras or on major historical figures. Because of their informative character, they generally fall into what Bill Nichols has defined as the "expository documentary," with features quite distinct from microhistorical approaches.[63] As Nichols explains, expository documentaries offer an argument about the world, giving the impression of objectivity and of well-substantiated judgments. Their dominant textual mode is the argumentation of an omniscient commentator/narrator, supported by contemporary or archival images, and by testimonies of experts or witnesses.

In contrast to these categories, which have a long tradition in documentary practice, in the 1970s and 1980s new approaches began to appear in nonfiction film that exhibit clearer similarities to microhistorical historiography, reinforced by the fact that their emergence coincided with the dissemination of microhistory itself. The films adopting these new approaches began to question the characteristic omniscience of the traditional expository documentary and often included the research process itself as part of the film, thereby also bringing the filmmaker in front of the camera and breaking the objectivist paradigm popularly associated with documentary film. They also incorporated autobiographical perspectives, in which memory—personal or collective—was a central focus, and they made use of hybrid formats in which the boundaries between fiction and nonfiction, between narrative and essayistic structures, were not always clearly delimited. And they explored new uses of archival footage, with approaches that were more conscious not only of the problems such footage posed but also of its potential, with appropriation strategies that in some cases resembled those used in experimental films.

This creative hotbed has provided the milieu for the emergence of a type of documentary dealing with historical issues that I have termed "microhistorical documentary." Within the flexibility required of any attempt to delimit the boundaries of a creative practice, its specific character places it precisely in between the ethnographic or observational documentary and the expository/informational documentary with a historical subject. As noted in the introduction, it is important to remember that qualifying these documentaries as microhistorical implies positing an analogous rather than a literal translation of the practices of professional written history to documentary filmmaking. Each field is governed by its own strategies and approaches, related to both the obvious differences between written and audiovisual language and the different research strategies employed in each field. As is the case in most historical research, microhistorians base their work on an intensive analysis of the sources they find in archives, and, as they often explore eras prior to the twentieth century, they work largely with written documents. On the other hand, although they also conduct intensive research, filmmakers rely heavily on audiovisual sources and work with them with a more creative approach, in which formal and/or aesthetic questions may be as important as strictly historiographical issues. As was also mentioned in the introduction and is equally true of written microhistories, it is important to note that the documentaries studied in this book exhibit differing degrees of affinity with the most typical features of microhistory, ranging from films whose microhistorical qualities are more paradigmatic, such as *The Maelstrom*, to others whose relationship is looser, such as *History and Memory* or *Lost, Lost, Lost*.

With the foregoing qualifications in mind, it can be asserted that what is referred to here as microhistorical documentary fits within the general parameters of microhistory, as it is usually understood and practiced in contemporary historiography. First of all, these documentaries are characterized by a reduced scale of observation, focusing on specific individuals, families, or social groups, generally of an ordinary or marginal nature, far removed from the big figures and events of public history. However, the objective behind this reduced scale is not to conduct a strictly ethnographic or observational study located in the present of the filmmaker, but to explore the past and to place the "micro" analysis in relation to relevant macrohistorical contexts, thereby making these documentaries historiographically representative in their own right. This is an essential feature of the microhistorical documentary, as it is of microhistory in its differentiation from social and cultural anthropology. In some cases, this representativeness will be quite clear, as it is in *The Maelstrom* or *The Missing Picture*. In other cases, it may not be so obviously foregrounded, but it will emerge through the historiographical tension between the micro- and macrohistorical dimensions that is an indispensable requirement for a documentary to be considered microhistorical. In parallel with its reduced scale of observation and its historical representativeness, these documentaries also prioritize human agency, that is, the analysis of the free action of the protagonists, as a means of understanding more general historical contexts. This feature is particularly accentuated when the films are autobiographical in nature—a point that I return to below.

Microhistorical documentaries and written microhistory also both involve a thorough study of available archives, although documentaries rely especially on audio/visual documents often taken from family archives: home movies, snapshots, and (less commonly) sound recordings. Such sources tend to be rare, especially home movies, which were costly to produce until the popularization of video in the 1980s, and which have also been affected by a lack of concern for their preservation until recently. As is analyzed in detail in chapter 2, filmmakers are thus faced with a task of reconstruction that in some cases is similar to that performed by microhistorians who experience a lack of documents related to their objects of study in institutional archives. Thus Ginzburg's evidential paradigm and its conjectural approach also become important here, because of the need to fill in lacunae and silences, to infer the stories behind the celebratory nature of snapshots and home movies, and to complement these sources with other documentation that can convey their full complexity.

In this task of reconstruction of the past, these documentaries generally employ flexible and innovative narrative strategies. In contrast to the omniscient argumentation of the expository documentary, they offer perspectives that are more limited in terms of their cognitive ambition, due not only to the reduced scale of the object of study, but also to the position of the filmmaker/narrator or the delegated narrators. There is frequent use of structures that combine narrative elements with other more essayistic features, where the filmmaker's voice, either explicitly or conveyed through formal strategies, permeates the discourse more obviously, as can be seen in the films of Rithy Panh, Lise Yasui, or Michal Aviad. In this way, these documentaries reflect Giovanni Levi's suggestion that microhistory should incorporate "into the main body of the narrative the procedures of research itself, the documentary limitations, techniques of persuasion and interpretative constructions," so that "the researcher's point of view becomes an intrinsic part of the account."[64] It would be fair to say that these self-reflexive strategies have been integrated into documentary cinema more naturally than into written history, often openly interrogating the different layers of the past preserved in archives or in the memory of their protagonists, underscoring the constructed nature of the work.

These documentaries also add an affective dimension to their microhistorical exploration that distances them from written history. The film medium offers a range of strategies that underscore this affective dimension, from the sensation of the present moment generated by the audiovisual recording to others like the use of extradiegetic music or, in the case of autobiographical narratives, the filmmaker's voice-over narration. The end result generally contains an unquestionably powerful emotional/affective charge that can bring into play more complex spectator reactions than those elicited by conventional historical narratives, facilitating a stronger level of identification with the stories told. Moreover, it is not unusual for these documentaries to contain a clearly performative dimension that directly appeals to and seeks to engage the spectator.

This is not really so different an approach from that used by microhistorians, who sometimes seek an explicit dialogue with the reader, but the film medium offers tools that can result in a higher level of involvement.

The affective engagement of the microhistorical documentary is also enhanced by the frequent inclusion of testimonies by protagonists and witnesses. This is a direction that microhistorians do not generally take, as their work often relates to eras for which only written sources survive; however, it does connect to another related historiographical approach: oral history. Although microhistorians and oral historians are situated in the same context of social history and are often inspired by an interest in "history from below," there is actually very little dialogue between them. There is also a similar dearth of studies linking oral history and documentary film, with exceptions such as the studies by Michel Frisch or Dan Sipe (who cites Lise Yasui's documentary *A Family Gathering*).[65] But, as can be seen from the cases analyzed in this book, personal testimonies are a key element in most microhistorical documentaries, whether they appear in the form of interviews with the protagonists or through the filmmaker's own autobiographical commentary. Sometimes these interviews form part of the research process but do not end up appearing in the documentary, as is the case in some of Péter Forgács's best-known works. But in most cases, such interviews form an explicit part of the microhistorical narration of the past, as one of the threads used by the filmmakers/historians in their research. Interviewing can even become the dominant research strategy, resulting in a documentary so close to oral history that we might question whether it really should be classified as microhistorical, partly due to its lack of use of archival research. This can be found, almost to the point of being a trend, in certain documentary films from Argentina that review recent history in a tone that could be described as in tune with a microhistorical sensibility: from the immigration stories documented in *Hacer patria* (David Blaustein, 2007) and *Carta a un padre* (Edgardo Cozarinsky, 2013) to the stories of the victims of forced disappearances during the last dictatorship (1976–1983), such as the pioneering film *Juan, como si nada hubiera sucedido* (Carlos Echeverría, 1987) and Nicolás Prividera's *M* (2007).[66]

In view of these structural and formal features, it is worth asking the question—raised previously in relation to the Italian microhistorians—of whether the epistemological approaches of these microhistorical documentaries might be described as leaning toward a postmodernist stance. Robert Rosenstone seems to view it this way when he suggests that the most genuinely postmodern historiography is not being done by historians, but by filmmakers, identifying as a paradigmatic example a film that will be analyzed in chapter 4 of this book: *History and Memory*.[67] However, the postmodern dimension that Rosenstone identifies in these films does not seem to be related to an epistemological skepticism in the Derridian tradition. This can be deduced from the features he points out as postmodern, which range from their capacity "to tell the past self-reflexively" and "make sense of them [past events] in a partial and open-ended, rather than totalized manner" to their way of reminding us "that the present is the site of all past representation and knowing."[68] It is worth questioning the extent to which microhistorians would be comfortable with all the features that Rosenstone describes as characteristic of a postmodern history. But it seems reasonable to assume in any case that microhistorical documentaries fit neatly within the parameters proposed by Ginzburg or Levi for an exploration of new historiographical pathways, without this meaning that they have adopted the epistemological skepticism associated with a certain kind of postmodern sensibility. It seems obvious that filmmakers like Péter Forgács or Robert A. Nakamura view their work not as something epistemologically opaque but as a way of understanding painful historical processes through microhistorical perspectives. Some microhistorical documentaries of an autobiographical nature, where personal memory plays a more central role in the reconstruction of the past, might be more ambiguous in this respect. But this has more to do with the complex relationships between memory, history, and autobiography, discussed below.

MEMORY, AUTOBIOGRAPHY, AND MICROHISTORY

The autobiographical perspective presented in different microhistorical documentaries constitutes an approach generally absent from professional written history. While it is true that over the last century a tradition of historians' autobiographies has been consolidated, these often tend to focus more on the professional dimension of the authors as historians, as Jeremy D. Popkin maintains in *History, Historians, and Autobiography.*[69] In his book *Theoretical Perspectives on Historians' Autobiographies,* Jaume Aurell questions the adoption of an excessively uniform view of this tradition, and proposes an interesting taxonomy that would evolve in line with historiographical trends: from the more humanistic and typically biographical perspectives of the interwar period, to forms closer to the monograph (and *ego-histoires* in France) in the postwar period, and finally to postmodern and interventionist forms in more recent years.[70] But in any case, the content of these works generally turns more on autobiographical/historiographical questions than on the study of periods of recent history based on the author's own personal experience. In the documentary field, however, it is relatively common to find films of a microhistorical nature presented explicitly from autobiographical perspectives. This is not a general trend in autobiographical documentaries, which often take approaches without a historiographical perspective, related more to personal introspection, questions of identity, or sociological concerns; nevertheless, it is a very productive variant for the kinds of microhistorical explorations found in documentary films.

When a microhistorical documentary takes an autobiographical perspective, the interwoven nature of personal memory and public history is placed in the foreground, which in turn points to the complex issue of the relationship between memory and history. A good starting point for considering this relationship could be Paul Ricoeur's assertion that memory is the matrix of history.[71] Memory is personal, but it develops in and feeds on the social or collective dimension. Memory began as oral and therefore generational, associated with lived experience, and it broadened with the introduction of writing—that *pharmakon* that has inspired so much debate from Plato down to Derrida—to become written memory. History feeds off this memory that recalls the past, but in its most common interpretation it is understood as the study and analysis of the traces of the past, applying methods that aim to produce a reliable representation of that past. It is beyond the scope of this book to explore the questions raised by this basic distinction, which Julio Arostegui sums up as the "relationship between *memory* as a permanent representation of experience in the individual mind and in human collectives and *history* as rationalization and objectification temporalized and expounded in a discourse, so to speak, on that experience."[72] Assuming this distinction, we must then ask how it is reflected in microhistorical documentaries with an autobiographical perspective. It is worth clarifying here that the autobiographical should not be automatically equated with the microhistorical, as if the macrohistorical belonged to the public and the microhistorical to the private, which would also include the autobiographical. Such a conclusion would be erroneous not only because there are autobiographical approaches with no historiographical intention, but also because, as various microhistorians have stressed, it is not merely the scope of the study that matters, but the historical knowledge gleaned from applying the "microscope" to the object of study. Having clarified this point, it seems reasonable to assert that in microhistorical documentaries the autobiographical perspective makes personal memory the foundation of the historiographical enterprise, establishing a specific link between lived memory and public history, understanding the latter particularly in its dimension as history of the present.

The starting point is therefore to be found in personal memory in its strictest sense—as a recollection of a lived experience—and in its expression on screen.[73] The representation of that memory poses specific challenges that the best autobiographical films manage to tackle successfully. First of all, they articulate the discourse around the "I" of the filmmaker who remembers, through his or her presence as an autodiegetic narrator and also through his or her physical participation. These films also effectively capture the temporality associated with the mnemonic act, which does not generally involve establishing a strictly physical distinction of time but entails presenting it as a constant flow in which past and present are dynamically intertwined, in the manner of the Greek concept of *kairos*. The past remembered from this perspective is contemplated and interpreted from the present, constructing the kind of complex structure characteristic of Gilles Deleuze's crystal-images.[74] In this sense, the past is not frozen in a time that no longer exists, but continues being affected by the present, as it is somehow recreated when it is invoked, influenced by present knowledge and emotions that vest it with new dimensions.

The exploration of personal memory in the autobiographical documentary also entails its transfer into the public sphere, its conversion into a shared discourse. This explicitly brings into play another of the core issues in the contemporary understanding of memory: the interwoven nature of the personal and social dimensions, of personal memory and social or collective memory. As Geoffrey Cubitt explains, our mnemonic experience "may depend precisely on our ability to articulate what we remember within the linguistic and cultural structures that we share with others, and to negotiate its meanings through social exchanges."[75] It is individuals who remember, but as social beings their memories are influenced by the social and cultural contexts in which they take part; and those memories are in turn shared socially, constructing a collective understanding of memory.[76] This can be observed in autobiographical documentaries, as narratives of identity that filmmakers construct in interaction with their familial and social contexts, and as films that become shared public discourse, contributing to the construction of collective memory.

In this social dimension of autobiographical experience, it is clear that the family constitutes the first and most fundamental context of socialization. This acquires special significance in autobiographical documentaries, as is shown in the cases analyzed in this book. It is also reflected in Jim Lane's proposition of the "family portrait" as one of the basic categories of the American autobiographical documentary.[77] Along the same lines, Alisa Lebow explains that first-person documentaries generally invoke a first-person plural: "Autobiographical film implicates others in its quest to represent a self, implicitly constructing a subject always already in-relation—that is, in the first person plural."[78] It is interesting to note how both Lane and Lebow place the exploration of these family networks in relation to their social and historical contexts, suggesting (without explicitly stating it) a potential microhistorical dimension. In this sense, Lebow suggests that "one encounters a lively, interactive, communicative process with history in these films."[79] And Lane observes that "these family portraits often stand in a tension with an official past that may often be contested in various stories told by individuals."[80] Juliette Goursat is even more explicit in making this connection, as the title of one of the chapters in her book on autobiographical documentary, "Je(ux) d'echelles. Le devenir collectif sous l'angle de l'histoire personelle," creates a play on words out of the title of the book edited by Jacques Revel on microhistory, *Jeux d'echelles*.[81] Goursat highlights the journey from the "I" to the "we" articulated in a series of autobiographical documentaries with a historical approach, including some of the films studied in this book, like Perlov's and Mekas's, although she studies this question much more specifically in relation to Chilean documentaries on the Pinochet dictatorship.[82]

The interaction between personal and social memory also involves specific approaches to the use of archival sources, which in autobiographical documentaries often relies on audio/visual family archives, as are analyzed in more depth in chapter 2. The snapshots and home movies of the family archive are mnemonic objects par excellence, memory supplements as powerful as or even more powerful than writing. This has led authors such as José Van Dijck to affirm that in contemporary culture, memory cannot be separated from its mediated representation, as we increasingly remember through these media. Van Dijck thus proposes the concept of "mediated memory," with which she seeks to negotiate "the relationship of self and culture at large, between what counts as private and what as public, and how individuality relates to collectivity."[83] Indeed, family archives constitute a primary context where the filmmaker's mnemonic work moves beyond the individual "I" into the more immediate social milieu. Moreover, these archives are often related to other activities, like trips, vacations, or public events that explicitly reflect wider social environments within which that mediated memory exists.

It is also worth stressing the importance of family archives for intergenerational memory transmission. Personal memory, as memory of lived experience, covers the biographical arc of each individual, but it expands insofar as we are all receivers of a memory transmitted from one generation to the next. In the last century, snapshots and home movies were added to oral and written transmission, becoming powerful mnemonic anchors in the transmission of memory, as has been explored by scholars like Marianne Hirsch, with her concept of postmemory.[84] Hirsch applies this concept to memories marked by historical traumas suffered by the previous generation, in whose transmission family photographs play a key role. These are memories not experienced personally by the next generation but that still have a strong impact on them. Similar effects are explored in autobiographical documentaries studied in this book, such as *History and Memory, A Family Gathering*, and *The Missing Picture*.

Given their autobiographical character and the time span they cover, these films also fit into the category of "history of the present."[85] This concept, which has been championed by a number of prominent authors, particularly European historians, constitutes something of an oxymoron, given that history is by definition a discipline concerned with studying the past. Here, however, it proves especially useful for studying how the memory of lived experience turns into history, a phenomenon that is very much a part of contemporary societies, as Julio Arostegui suggests, where "the aging of memory is rejected and therefore it is *historicized*, because memory made history is much more permanent."[86] While it is true that any autobiographical project is developed on the basis of a retrospective narrative that aims to reconstruct the personal past and give it meaning, in the case of microhistorical documentaries of an autobiographical nature this retrospective view is explicitly interwoven with the sociocultural contexts that frame it, giving it a historiographical dimension that goes beyond the strictly personal/familiar. Although these documentaries seem to lack the temporal distance expected of the historian, this is precisely where the challenge lies for historians of the present, who, as Henry Rousso explains, "act 'as if' they could seize hold of time as it passes . . . slow down the process of time's retreat and the oblivion that lies in wait for any human experience," thereby giving the present "a substantiality, a perspective, a time frame, as all historians engaged in periodization do."[87] Once again, the dialogue between historians and filmmakers is both complex and rewarding here, as the very nature of cinematic time emphasizes this "presentness." In this sense, Rousso's "seizing hold of time as it passes," which seems to paraphrase André Bazin's idea of photography and film as media that embalm time and rescue it from its corruption, takes on a special meaning in these documentaries.[88] Nevertheless, it is a present that will turn into history when it is subjected to autobiographical retrospection, which in the film medium occurs in the editing phase, explicitly underscored by the autodiegetic narration that verbalizes this retrospective process.

This chapter has offered an exploration of the contexts and general features of microhistorical documentaries, showing how these films fall within the basic parameters of microhistorical practice, with a reduced scale of observation of the past that sheds light on macrohistorical contexts, a central role given to human agency, a conjectural approach to archival research, and a reliance on narrative structures. Films of this kind therefore differ markedly from the informational/expository model of the historical television documentary, but also from ethnographic or observational approaches. Microhistorical documentaries can be distinguished from these approaches largely because of their historiographical purpose, pursued using the tools specific to the film medium, with an analogous, nonliteral adoption of the methods specific to professional written microhistory, which in no way undermines their value as a mode of historical knowledge.

2

THE ARCHIVE IN THE
MICROHISTORICAL DOCUMENTARY

F ollowing the theoretical framework presented in chapter 1, this chapter looks more specifically at the use of archival sources in microhistorical documentaries. This issue is considered first in the broader context of archival appropriation in documentary films, followed by a more detailed analysis of family archives, which are the most important source for microhistorical documentaries, with special attention to home movies.

As a general principle, it could be asserted that documentary filmmakers use archives as a source of information in a manner analogous to the way professional historians do. However, from the outset it is worth highlighting a few aspects unique to documentaries. The first is obvious: as it is an audiovisual medium, although filmmakers may make use of written documents and oral records, they accord special importance to photographic and film records. Second, these archival documents are not merely sources of information but are also included in the film through various appropriation strategies, ranging from expository modes to other more experimental approaches. And third, as these documentaries often deal with relatively recent events, as part of a history of the present, they frequently make use of the testimony of witnesses (or of the filmmaker, in autobiographical narratives) to complement or contextualize the archives.

ARCHIVAL APPROPRIATION IN
DOCUMENTARY FILMS

As an emerging practice of the last few decades, microhistorical documentaries generally approach archives from a perspective that has incorporated the "archival turn" experienced in contemporary historiography. There is no single consensus on the meaning of this term, but it is perhaps best summed up in Ann Laura Stoler's definition of it as a "move from archive-as-source to archive-as-subject" that has resulted in "a rethinking of the materiality and imaginary of collections and what kinds of truth claims lie in documentation."[1] The archival turn has provoked a reconsideration of the role of the archive as an institution and its relationships with power structures (the focus of some of Foucault's and Derrida's well-known theories on the subject), as well as the value of archival documents as historical evidence. This reconsideration has led to a shift away from a static view of the archive to one that considers, as Vicente Sánchez-Biosca suggests, that "an archive is not a neutral repository of material" but "a site of knowledge production."[2] This is a question that has been given increasing attention in archival studies, and which Terry Cook insightfully sums up as follows: "The archive is now seen increasingly as the site where social memory has been (and is) constructed. . . . The record thus becomes a cultural signifier, a mediated and ever-changing construction, not some empty template into which acts and facts are poured."[3] As Marlene Madoff suggests, this has led to a rejection of the fetishization of the archive as a transparent means of access to the past: "Many scholars . . . have come to understand the historical record . . . not as an objective representation of the past, but rather as a selection of objects that have been preserved for a variety of reasons. . . . Whatever the archive contains is already a reconstruction—a recording of history from a particular perspective."[4]

As Cook himself asserts, this does not mean that "everything is adrift in a sea of meaningless relativism,"[5] but that the meaning of archival documents must also be established based on the context of their creation and the subsequent mediations of archival processes. On this point, it is pertinent to consider the arguments of George Didi-Huberman in his book *Images in Spite of All*, where he stresses the value of photographic archives for gaining knowledge of the Holocaust. With this assertion, he initiated an open debate with the filmmaker Claude Lanzmann, who, in his famous documentary *Shoah* and in statements made subsequently, rejected archives in favor of testimony, on the basis that the Holocaust itself was unrepresentable. Following the work of thinkers such as Foucault and Michel de Certeau, Didi-Huberman acknowledges that "an archive is in no way the immediate reflection of the real, but is a writing endowed with syntax . . . and with ideology" and that "the *source* is never a 'pure' point of origin, but an already stratified time, already complex."[6] However, he goes on, this should not lead us to reject the truth of archival documents, and here he cites Carlo Ginzburg, with an argument similar to one already outlined in chapter 1: "Between the excess of positivism and the excesses of skepticism, one must, according to Ginzburg, constantly relearn . . . to see in sources 'neither open windows, as the positivists think, nor walls obstructing sight, as the skeptics claim.'"[7]

This theoretical framework has been expanded and enriched by contributions from other disciplines in relation to archives, in a new manifestation of the archival turn that has opened this field, traditionally the preserve of professional archivists and historians, to other perspectives. As Jeannette Bastian explains, this turn has meant that the "'archive' expanded beyond the text to include memory, witnessing, materiality, performance, art."[8] According to her, "this expansive view of the archive helped construct a conceptual and analytical terrain for discourse in a range of disciplines within the humanities and social sciences,"[9] including art, photography, film, literature, anthropology, rhetoric, and the performing arts. This growing interdisciplinary interest in the archive has specific implications for artistic practices, as has been explored by authors such as Ruth Rosengarten, Anna M. Guasch, and Charles Merewether.[10] For the purposes of this book, the role played here by photography and cinema is of special interest, as they work with the archival materials to expand their meaning, establishing fruitful dialogues between the audio/visual document and different aesthetic, narrative, historical, anthropological, and rhetorical perspectives.

In documentary film, the archival appropriation has a specificity of its own, as the filmmaker is working with archival footage whose indexical link to the present of its filming vests it with a strong truth value for the spectator. But this material is open to interpretation, incorporating new meanings when it is inserted into the narrative or argumentative structure of the documentary. Philip Rosen comments on this question when he points out that documentary "involves a synthesizing knowledge claim, by virtue of a sequence that sublates an undoubtable referential field of pastness into meaning. Documentary as it comes to us from this tradition is not just post facto, but historical in the modern sense."[11] For this construction of meaning, the documentary filmmaker brings the archival footage into dialogue with other expressive tools, ranging from the voice-over narrator to the testimonies of witnesses or experts, the use of extradiegetic music, or ad hoc filming of places and objects. With these and other elements, the filmmaker articulates a structure intended to reconstruct the past, but that transcends the mere transmission of knowledge to include dimensions not normally associated with conventional historiography, like the affective, the essayistic, or the experimental. In this way, documentaries take distinctively historiographical approaches, as Catherine Russell points out in her book *Archiveology*, when she suggests that "film and media artists are uniquely positioned to find and use these tools to produce critical histories and trigger historical awakenings."[12]

Microhistorical documentaries do not make use of the archive in a way necessarily very different from other documentary films, although they do present certain distinctive features, which are analyzed in this chapter. Prominent among these are the types of archival materials they use, which are usually classifiable as marginal, as they do not belong to the official records of public history. In some cases, they can be found in official archival institutions, but more commonly they are found in alternative sites, ranging from a family home to a social or recreational center. The work involved in recovering them has something in common with the work of the archaeologist, a figure with whom filmmakers like Péter Forgács often identify, as is discussed in chapter 3. Emma Cocker also invokes this figure in her analysis of the appropriation of archival footage in contemporary practice. Cocker applies it mainly to the films of Italian filmmakers Yervant Gianikian and Angela Ricci Lucchi, which tend more toward a film essay style, while also containing a historiographical perspective with microhistorical resonances: "The archaeological excavation of buried or forgotten archival fragments within artists' film and video thus has the capacity to serve a dual purpose: it attempts to rescue or recuperate value for lost fragments and write them back into history, at the same time as expose moments of deliberate exclusion within the archive."[13] This idea of recovering marginal archives to "write them back into history" is very much a feature of the microhistorical films studied in the following chapters. However, Cocker suggests that this appropriation generates "a potential disruption of the official order of knowledge in favor of counter-hegemonic narratives capable of producing new (indeed dissenting or resistant) forms of cultural memory,"[14] an argument that would not apply to all microhistorical documentaries, as they do not necessarily contain specifically counter-hegemonic narratives, although they do offer an alternative discourse that can serve as a complement to the dominant public history.

An overview of the microhistorical documentaries analyzed in this book shows that they do use different types of archival documents (public, amateur, family, personal; written, sound, audiovisual), although those belonging to the audio/visual family archive (snapshots and home movies) tend to predominate. Public archives—mainly newsreels and TV news—are used occasionally, on the basis of their more conventional informative nature, to provide a basic macrohistorical context within which the microhistorical narratives can be placed. This is the case, for example, of the documentaries on Japanese Americans incarcerated during World War II, or of those dealing with the Israeli-Palestinian conflict. Sometimes the documentaries seek a deconstruction of this archival footage, especially when it has the quality of propaganda, like the newsreels made by the Hungarian communist regime included in *Class Lot* or by the Khmer Rouge in *The Missing Picture*. In a few cases, footage taken from fiction films may also be used, as it is in *The Missing Picture*, and more significantly in *History and Memory*.

A second type of document appropriated in microhistorical documentaries comes from personal archives, referring in this case strictly to materials related to individuals. Archival literature has been giving increased attention to personal archives, expanding beyond its traditional focus on institutional archives organized according to professional criteria to include materials related to and preserved by individuals, regardless of whether such materials can be found in public archives.[15] However, archival studies do not tend to distinguish between personal and family archives, both of which are generally classified under the first term. While admittedly the boundaries between them are blurry, for this study it seems appropriate to differentiate them, in terms of both their provenance and their content. Snapshots and home movies belong specifically to the category of family archives, as they are made by different family members, represent that family, and are preserved in the family environment. However, diaries and letters are more suitably classified as personal documents, as they are not generally shared with other family members and are preserved privately. Certain official documents, like IDs, are treated here as "personal," based on their content.

Personal documents play an important role in some of the documentaries analyzed in this book. For example, in the opening to the film *From a Silk Cocoon*, the filmmaker shows a box containing key documents belonging to her parents: their birth certificates and the official letters confirming their renunciation and subsequent restoration of U.S. citizenship. Similarly, at the beginning of *A World Not Ours*, the director shows his childhood Palestinian refugee ID card, while in *History and Memory*, Rea Tajiri shows her grandparents' IDs. Of special importance in three films analyzed here are personal letters and written diaries: *From a Silk Cocoon*, *Bophana*, and *Something Strong Within*. The last of these three films includes some brief but highly significant quotes from the diaries of several Japanese Americans who lived in the concentration camps. In *From a Silk Cocoon* the parents' letters and diaries—read in a voice-over—actually constitute the main source of information in the film. A related issue worth raising here is whether the diary films of David Perlov or Jonas Mekas would fall into this personal archive category. As is explored in more detail in chapter 7, in the first stage of filming as film diaries, they would fall into a border territory between what could be defined as documents belonging to a personal archive and what would be more suitably classified as family archive, since the filmed footage often includes family members and friends.

As noted above, the family archive is the most common and specific form of archive used in microhistorical documentary. Following Anna Woodham and colleagues, the family archive is understood here as "an extensive range of objects and documents they [the families] owned which had a connection with past and present friends and family members," including "items such as photographs, certificates, books, letters and recipes," but also "items such as candlesticks, wine glasses, medals, jewelry, [and] souvenirs."[16] In the films studied here, the inclusion of nonphotographic objects is not common, although there are some exceptions worthy of mention for their symbolic importance, like the wooden bird carved by Rea Tajiri's grandmother in *History and Memory*. Among audio/visual family archives—snapshots and home movies—this chapter focuses mainly on the latter, which constitute the specifically audiovisual form of these archives and, therefore, the most widely used. But much of the discussion here about home movies could equally apply to snapshots, understanding both as audio/visual manifestations of a "home mode" of communication, a term originally proposed by Richard Chalfen and picked up by authors such as James M. Moran (who applies it to home videos), Ryan Shand, and Tom Slootweg.[17] In short, this home mode could be defined as a mode of production and reception that includes different audio/visual media (photography, film/video) that represent the everyday life of the family and provide a communicative framework for the intergenerational transmission of family stories.[18] In this sense, "home movies" may also be used as a generic term for the different types of audiovisual records of the home mode, without necessarily distinguishing between the technologies that have been used historically: photochemical (film), magnetic (video), and digital. Obviously, technological developments have resulted in changes to content, style, and viewing habits. Film recording, limited by the length of the reels and by its relatively high cost, was replaced by video, with its reduced time restrictions and low cost, which also brought with it the inclusion of a wider range of possible content. Finally, with digital technology, domestic recordings have multiplied exponentially, but their status as documents and their mnemonic function have given way to their communicative function. As José Van Dijck puts it, the value of snapshots and home movies has shifted from their function as *mementos* to their function as *momentos*, as temporal deictics.[19] Yet despite these developments, a number of common features remain that can still be classified as audio/visual expressions of a single "home mode" of communication.

One last category that should be considered here is amateur film, a type of archival material with its own specific characteristics, despite often being associated with home moviemaking. Home movies have sometimes been labeled as a type of amateur film, and the two terms have occasionally been treated as synonyms, but such a categorization is rather reductive, at least when applied to the decades of use of small-gauge cameras, from the 1920s to the 1970s (the main period of production of the home movies and amateur films used in the microhistorical documentaries analyzed in this book). This is recognized, for example, by authors such as Shand and Slootweg, who offer an insightful means of differentiating them, proposing to refer to amateur films as those made in a "community mode" to distinguish them from the "home mode" that characterizes home movies.[20] "Amateur filmmaking," as the term was understood at least until the 1970s or 1980s, was a practice that sought to imitate professional modes of filmmaking to a certain extent, chiefly by following the main phases of their creative process (preproduction, shooting, and postproduction), but without pursuing a commercial objective. Amateur filmmakers made fiction films, documentaries, or experimental films, presented their productions at festivals and in specific competitions, and in many cases had their own associations to share their projects and develop their skills.[21] Home movies, however, have never sought to emulate professional filmmaking; they are "badly made" films by professional standards, generally projected unedited and without any postproduction. They also have a distinctively autobiographical dimension, as filmmaker, "actors," and audience generally all belong to the same group: the family itself and/or its close circle of friends.[22] Leaving aside for the moment the changes that digital technology and the internet have brought,[23] it is worth clarifying that the boundary between these two film modes was not always completely clear, although generally they can be distinguished based on the filming style and the absence or presence of postproduction work. Charles Tepperman actually proposes a kind of intermediate category that he calls "family chronicle films," made by amateur filmmakers with the usual themes of home moviemaking. But although he does not delve into the distinction between these two modes, his explanation of family chronicle films in fact points to the difference between home movies and amateur films: "In contrast to simple home movie footage, family films by serious amateurs gave shape and structure to the personal relationships and quotidian events that they recorded," exploiting the camera's capacity for recording "as a tool for transfiguring the everyday and reflecting on their place in it."[24]

In the context of microhistorical documentaries, the distinction between the two modes is often significant, especially in films constructed mainly using home movies, as is the case with Forgács's work and with films such as *Something Strong Within* and *Israel: A Home Movie*. These works usually include a small proportion of footage taken from amateur films, some of which exhibits qualities quite close to professional filmmaking, expanding the range of topics and approaches, with consequent effects on both their narratives and their reception. Another interesting variant involves professional filmmakers doing autobiographical projects with a microhistorical dimension, like *For My Children* or *A World Not Ours*, which include domestic scenes filmed by them but intended from the outset for the documentary, resulting in a unique convergence of film practices. Separate consideration is needed for Mekas, whose work is analyzed in chapter 7, who championed home moviemaking as a more genuine approach to filmmaking, a premise on which he developed his own way of making films, which ultimately acquired the status of avant-garde cinema.

FAMILY ARCHIVES FOR A HISTORY FROM BELOW

Family archives, and more specifically their audio/visual materials—snapshots and home movies—have not received much attention from professional historians. In film studies, there has been growing interest in these archives, although research has focused more on their ethno-graphic/cultural dimension—often in the more general context of research on amateur films—than on their use as sources for historical research and their appropriation in contemporary films. Authors such as Patricia Zimmermann or Roger Odin point in this direction, but only incidentally. In the introduction to *Mining the Home Movie*, Zimmermann notes that recent historical research examines the hermeneutic possibilities of home movies, looking at how they "can function as a recorder, an interrogator, a deferral, a condensation, and a mediator of historical traumas that extend beyond the self."[25] She also points out, although without developing the argument, that when such footage is used in contemporary media productions, it is conceptualized "as micro-geographies and microhistories of minoritized and often invisible cultures that are social and highly political."[26] Odin also reflects briefly on the different uses of home movies in contemporary filmmaking, ranging from their use as visual documents of past times to what he considers the most interesting case, the exploration of their contradictions as documents, based on readings as diverse as documentarist, private, emotional, historical, or fictional.[27]

From a microhistorical perspective, it is clear that audiovisual family archives constitute a valuable source for a history from below, since they focus on the lives, cycles, and rites of ordinary "anonymous" families, outside of the official records of public events that are the general concern of traditional archives. While it is true that in the first decades of its existence the technology to make home movies was available only to wealthy families, as early as the 1950s access to the technology had spread to the middle classes in Western countries and continued expanding with the arrival of home video and finally with the incorporation of camera functions into cell phones, resulting today in a universe of ephemeral fragments existing in virtual "clouds." This situation is a long way from Derrida's theory of the archive as a place under the control of the *archons* (an ancient Greek term that originally referred to magistrates who represented the law, and who therefore had the role of guarding documents and the responsibility for interpreting them), as family archives do not generally form part of public archives and are not subject to the scrutiny of professional archivists.[28] It has been only since the 1980s that film archives began collecting home movies, at a time when, paradoxically, this type of footage was growing exponentially thanks to video, which often ended up turning the focus of the preservation efforts onto materials recorded on photochemical film. The contemporary context, with constant recording on cell phones and archiving on personal computers or virtual private servers, has complicated the archivist's task even more, while at the same time raising questions about the future recoverability of these archives.

The domestic nature of these archives also underscores the previously noted underlying duality, especially present in audiovisual documents, of any archival document as both a transparent trace of the past and a construction made of that past. Contemporary studies tend to highlight the quality of the archival materials as constructions that offer only limited access to the past, a view influenced partly by the Foucauldian understanding of the archive as "the general system of the formation and transformation of statements" (related either to events or to things) regulated by laws that determine their subsistence or disappearance.[29] But the audiovisual document possesses an evidentiary force, based on the indexical nature of recorded sounds and images, which triggers a reception that contradicts its definition as constructed discourse. Of special importance here is the line of argument beginning with André Bazin and generally including Roland Barthes's *Camera Lucida* or Susan Sontag's *On Photography*, perhaps best encapsulated in Barthes's assertion that in photography "the power of authentication exceeds the power of representation."[30] This phenomenological view of the photographic image acquires greater force in the case of snapshots and home movies, as their noncommercial nature and their unprofessional formal features give them a surplus of authenticity that underscores their quality as a trace of the past. This acquires a special resonance in the case of images of relatives who have died, which highlights their condition as memento mori, marked by the contrast between the physical absence of the loved ones and their vicarious presence in the images.

Nevertheless, it cannot be ignored that snapshots and home movies are representations, with their own formal and thematic codes. Domestic images conceal as much as they reveal, since they focus on the happy and celebratory moments of life. This could be understood as a kind of falsification of reality, in an excessively reductive interpretation of the home mode of communication. Instead, it would be more appropriate to view them metonymically, as representations that do not claim to deny or disguise the dark times or the sad moments, but that leave them outside the frame by virtue of their very nature. This bias toward the celebratory could also be explained by the fact that, beyond their commemorative nature (marking a birthday or a wedding), such events have a performative dimension that makes them more suitable for recording on film. Another question that might be considered relates to the patriarchal gaze that these kinds of images may be imbued with, as the father was so often the one filming.[31] However, the social evolution of family dynamics and the increasing accessibility of the technology has dissolved this dynamic and its potential bias, progressively turning home movies into an experience shared by all members of the family, in terms of both creation and commentary.

In this context, the definition of snapshots and home movies as historical sources also reveals an evolution of the concept of archives itself. This evolution has run parallel to that of historiography, which has seen the development of social and cultural history and a more open understanding of archives, increasingly including peripheral manifestations like family archives. These prove especially suited to microhistorical research, since it involves a reduced scale of observation and foregrounds human agency. The fragmentary and nonsystematic nature of these archives also fits in well with the concept of the miniature proposed by Alf Lüdtke—in his explanation of the *Alltagsgeschichte*, the history of everyday life—to stress the small scale where "the 'density' of life situations and contexts of action can be made vivid and palpable."[32] Lüdtke proposes creating a collage or mosaic with those miniatures to form societal "patchwork" structures, linking them together in a network of interrelations, thereby addressing the issue of how to apply the knowledge acquired on the micro-scale to larger historical frameworks.[33] Any family archive could be understood as a patchwork that acquires meaning in the most immediate interpretation of the family circle it belongs to, but that also acquires a broader, historiographical value when it is used by a historian/filmmaker to construct a microhistorical narrative. This "family archival patchwork" gives access to the past in its own ways, revealing through its particular stories the social and cultural tapestry of an era: its types of celebrations, religious or secular rituals, leisure habits, and so on. But also, due to the descriptive quality inherent in the image, it can provide valuable information on public spaces, types of housing, styles of dress, and so on, which are expanded to elements of sound as well (forms of speech, soundscapes) with the introduction of home video. One last element that should not be overlooked is the recording of public events by home moviemakers, which can offer perspectives complementary to public records, sometimes becoming the only testimony, as occurred with the famous footage of the assassination of J. F. Kennedy filmed by Abraham Zapruder.

This fragmentary quality of family archives also foregrounds the limitations of their reconstruction of the past, a significant issue in the work of microhistorians, but which in fact affects any historiographical endeavor, as Carolyn Steedman points out: "Historians read for what is not there: the silences and the absences of the documents always speak to us."[34] This issue is actually central in Didi-Huberman's aforementioned book *Images in Spite of All*, which is articulated around the historiographical value of four photographs taken secretly at Auschwitz, directly pointing to his argument that "history is constructed around perpetually questioned *lacunae*."[35] Didi-Huberman actually goes further, presenting these photographs as examples of a "lacuna-image," and at the same time a "trace-image" and a "disappearance-image": "Something— very little, a film—remains of a process of annihilation. . . . It is neither full presence nor absolute silence. It is neither resurrection, nor death without remains. . . . It is a world proliferating with lacunae, with singular images which, placed together in a montage, will encourage *readability*, an effect of knowledge."[36] This idea has a special resonance for microhistorians, who generally work with marginal archives in which the lacunae are even more palpable than they are in institutional archives, leading Ginzburg to propose conjecture as a method based on his concept of the "evidential paradigm," mentioned in chapter 1.[37] The documentaries analyzed here are generally located in this historiographical context, as their main archival sources, family archives, have not been subject to professional preservation and cataloging, and exhibit an obviously fragmentary quality due to both the selective nature of their representations and the nonsystematic organization of their content.

THE FILMIC APPROPRIATION OF HOME MOVIES

All family archival footage undergoes a distinctive change when it is appropriated in a documentary film: what was formerly an archive belonging to a family, to be shown only to family and friends, now becomes public.[38] As Julia J. Noordegraaf and Elvira Pouw affirm, this change makes the attribution of meaning to the family archive "an open and dynamic process, mediated by the various contexts through which the material travels."[39] This issue is also addressed by Jaimie Baron in the wider framework of the appropriation of film archives, when she defines the archival document as an experience of reception based on two criteria: temporal and intentional disparity.[40] Baron suggests that for an archival document to be recognized as such, the spectator must be aware of a temporal disparity between the *then* of the document and the *now* of the making of the film that has appropriated it, a disparity that has to be evident within the film. Additionally, the archival document may also exhibit a disparity of intentions: a difference between the intentions of the original document and the new ones that emerge when it is appropriated in a new film. Baron explores the appropriation of home movies in one of the chapters of her book, pointing out that the most significant disparity of their appropriation is intentional, related to the change from being a familiar/private document to becoming publicly accessible. This may imply a kind of transgression that has become clearer in the times of home video and digital media, since the range of situations filmed has broadened beyond the typical happy scenes of home movies. The author even goes as far as suggesting that our interest in the appropriation of home movies is "fundamentally and unavoidably voyeuristic—offering us the pleasure of seeing something we were not 'meant to see.'"[41] However, the relocation of home movies into the public sphere does not necessarily imply an intentional disparity. There are actually many examples of home movies used in contemporary documentaries that essentially retain their original value. It could thus be argued instead that the temporal disparity is a more relevant factor in the appropriation of home movies.[42] This is especially clear in microhistorical documentaries, particularly in those that take an autobiographical approach, where the presence of loved ones vests the family archive with a singular resonance that relies heavily on the temporal disparity, on the tension between their being here, with us in the film, and far away, alive in their past time.

These differences arising from the twofold disparity of the archival document relate to processes of resignification affecting all archival footage when it is reused in contemporary cinema. Such processes tend to introduce modifications or expansions to their original meanings, resulting from their migration from their original context to a new one, thereby placing them in a new chain of meaning. To study these processes, I adopt a partially modified version of the typology proposed by Rebecca Swender to examine appropriation practices.[43] Swender posits three possible strategies: naturalization, contradiction, and underscoring of conventional specificity. The first, naturalization, happens when the appropriated document keeps its original set of values in the new film, or, as Swender explains, "when the capacity for instability of meaning is deemphasized."[44] The second type of appropriation involves a situation where the document's standard meanings are contested or contradicted. This occurs, according to Swender, when the main text destabilizes the meaning of the original document, exposing its supposed truth claim or adding new context that gives it supplementary meanings.[45] The third type, underscoring of conventional specificity, happens when all the elements of the original footage direct the viewer toward a preferred reading, supporting a particular historical truth claim, regardless of how it is subsequently reused (Swender identifies the Zapruder film as an example of this type).[46] This third strategy is not really relevant to the appropriation of family archival materials, since it would be highly unusual to find family images with a conventional specificity for the general public. I propose instead a different third strategy, which I refer to as historicization, related to the social and historical implications of this type of archival material when it is reused in a new film.

When applying this typology to the use of archival materials in microhistorical documentaries, we can see, first, how they can be incorporated in a naturalized way, retaining their original set of values, usually as visual support for the filmmaker's narrative. An interesting case of such naturalized recycling can be seen in films composed—entirely or mostly—of home movies shot by a relative from a previous generation, with the contemporary filmmaker serving as an intermediary between the family footage and the viewing public. Examples of this can be found in films such as *A Letter Without Words* (1998), *El misterio de los ojos escarlata* (1993), or *La línea paterna* (1994). All three of these cases are very close to what Paul John Eakin has defined in literature as "proximate collaborative autobiography," referring to narratives about some relative or close friend, with two people speaking in the first person, and the authors talking about their own lives while recounting those of their loved ones.[47] In *A Letter Without Words*, this is taken to the point where Lisa Lewenz literally shares authorship of her film with her grandmother, Ella, who shot home movies and amateur films in Germany up to 1938, when she immigrated to the United States.

There are also microhistorical documentaries where the original meanings of the home movies are contested or contradicted. This strategy is most common in cases where they are used while narrating traumatic family events, forcing a contrast between the standard happy scenes portrayed in home movies and the harsh events of the family's past, usually conveyed by a voice-over provided by the filmmaker or interviews with family members. A clear example of this strategy can be found in *A Family Gathering*, while a more ambiguous variant is observable in *Something Strong Within*, involving home movies of Japanese Americans filmed in the concentration camps. Another interesting case is that of the films of Forgács, such as *The Maelstrom* or *El Perro Negro*. In these two films, most of the scenes of everyday life and leisure come from happy periods in the lives of these families before the war. But the interpretation of these scenes through the prism of the tragic fate suffered by the home moviemakers—the Peereboom and the Salvans families, respectively—assigns them a new value that undermines the happy portrait suggested in an initial reading of the images.

The third strategy proposed here, historicization, refers directly to the historical dimension of home movies and snapshots, to their nature as records of past events and times, whether they show public events or bear witness to the ordinary life of a particular community in a bygone era. As Odin suggests, "home movies are sometimes the only records of some racial, ethnographic, cultural, social communities marginalized by the official version of history."[48] The family archive thus becomes a valuable source of documentation for microhistorical perspectives absent from official public histories. To this end, the filmmakers also need to give these materials a historical representativeness, bringing them into dialogue with their macrohistorical contexts in order to underscore their value as historical documents that transcend their more immediate meaning as records of everyday life.

This third strategy can in fact be used simultaneously with either naturalization or contradiction, expanding the layers of meaning that this material acquires in its contemporary reuse. This can be seen, for example, in the previously cited films *A Letter Without Words*, *El misterio de los ojos escarlata*, and *La línea paterna*, all of which generally respect the original meaning of the reused footage but vest it with a new dimension as a document of a past era. In a way, this expansion of meaning is already implicit in the original footage, as the original filmmakers were more aware of their role as witnesses of their time, particularly in connection to public events or to local traditions shot in a more ethnographic style. In the case of *A Letter Without Words*, this historical consciousness comes into the foreground in the footage of the grandmother of the filmmaker, enhanced by quotations taken from her diary and personal letters. In this way, the filmmaker constructs a microhistorical chronicle of Germany between the wars, blending historical processes and family affairs into a single narrative. A more ethnographic approach is revealed in *El misterio de los ojos escarlata*, where Alfredo J. Anzola brings together footage shot by his father, Edgar, in the early decades of the twentieth century, offering a rather unfamiliar portrait of Venezuela, even for its own people. *La línea paterna* is more intimate, but still offers an insightful portrayal of the traditions and social customs of Papantla, the Mexican region where José Buil, the filmmaker's grandfather, lived for many years.

Among the more personal approaches, there are some remarkable films where the sociohistorical context is a prominent factor in the way the filmmakers use their families' home movies, usually because their personal quest leads them necessarily to explore those sociohistorical contexts. One such film is *Yidl in the Middle* (1999), in which the filmmaker, Marlene Booth, reflects on what it was like to grow up Jewish in the postwar years in Iowa, where Jewish people were a very small minority. She uses her family's home movies in a naturalized way, as visual support for her autobiographical narrative. But she goes further, since the home movies become key visual proof of how her family struggled between identification with the community and fidelity to Jewish customs and traditions. The filmmaker summarizes this struggle in the final minutes of the film, where her home movies become the site of convergence of the public and private, the historical and the personal, as she makes explicit in her voice-over: "When I look at them, I see how eager we were to be just as Iowa as possible. Growing up with two distinct sides gave me a unique perspective. . . . I am learning now to see difference and to seek common ground. Maybe that's what it means to be a yiddle in the middle."

A significant historicized tension is also present in the use of family archives in the documentaries analyzed in the following chapters, from the films of Forgács to the documentaries on the incarceration of Japanese Americans or the Israeli-Palestinian conflict. All these films show how documentaries can construct microhistorical narratives through an appropriation of family archives that delves into their dimension as historical sources, while at the same time exploring them with creative perspectives quite distinct from those of conventional historiographical practices.

FROM COLLECTIVE PORTRAITS TO FAMILY HISTORIES

Regardless of the different values and meanings acquired by audiovisual family archives when appropriated in microhistorical documentaries, they are often structured in the films that appropriate them according to two main categories: collective portraits and family histories. The first type, in which filmmakers use home movies to create collective portraits, refers to films that may not at first seem to reflect a microhistorical perspective, as their focus is not on a specific milieu like an individual, a family, or a village, but on settings of a broader scope. However, their historical perspective can still be classified as microhistorical, first of all because their reliance on home movies as their main visual historical sources entails the reduced scale of observation that is so essential to microhistory. Their approach is also clearly in keeping with the patchwork structure proposed by Lüdtke, creating sociohistorical collages with a microhistorical quality.[49] There probably are not many documentaries that belong to this category, but those that do are noteworthy. These include two cases that are analyzed in the chapters that follow: *Something Strong Within* and *Israel: A Home Movie*. Other interesting variations on the model are the French film *Mémoire d'outremer* and the Russian film *Private Chronicles: Monologue*, both of which are analyzed briefly here. These two documentaries straddle the line between macro- and microhistory, as on the one hand they cover extended historical periods (the French colonial period and the final decades of the Soviet Union, respectively), but on the other they make use of home movies as their main archival sources. Both use them in a manner that lies halfway between naturalized and historicized appropriation: they do not attempt to contradict the most obvious values conveyed in the home movie footage, but they do prioritize its status as a sociohistorical document over its nature as a domestic portrait, which is actually blurred by the fact that the footage is never linked specifically to the families represented.

Mémoire d'outremer (1997) deals with the life of French colonizers from the 1920s to the 1960s. Filmmaker Claude Bossion made his film mainly with home movies shot by people living in the colonies, mixing scenes from different countries and apparently organizing them in chronological order (although many of them are not explicitly dated). The soundtrack, however, reinforces the collage effect of the film as a whole by employing very different verbal sources (often unrelated to the images): official reports, encyclopedia entries, personal and official letters, and interviews with some of the actual home moviemakers or the people filmed. The combination of visual and verbal sources from different times and places creates a polyphonic text that seeks a resonance that transcends an ordinary home movie viewing, foregrounding its sketchy and unscripted condition. This condition is identified by Ben Highmore as a key feature in the representation of everydayness, which comes to its fullest when it is characterized by an improvised quality.[50] Highmore points to Impressionist painting as an example of this approach, but it could also be applied to the representation offered by home movies, which similarly combine subject matter and form to capture the unscripted nature of the everyday.

This portrait of colonizers is intended to offer new insights into the history of colonization, related not so much to their macrohistorical context (although some of the verbal sources do provide contextualizing commentary), but to the history of their everyday life. Its chronicle of past times through family archives elicits a mood of nostalgia for a bygone way of life. However, this nostalgic component does not imply a justification of the problematic issues associated with colonization, as Rachael Langford seems to argue. Langford laments the absence of "images of political meetings, demonstrations, bombings, or police actions," which, in her view, results in a depiction of colonialism not "as a struggle, but as a consensual project," and as "a private affair."[51] This interpretation, however, seems to overlook the fact that the film's approach is closely tied to the nature of the visual material used, a misunderstanding also evident in her classification of the footage as "amateur films" and never as home movies. It is true that a few sequences seem closer to amateur filmmaking, such as the harvesting scenes in the region of Souk El Khemis, or the scene showing the Mission Ophtalmologique Saharianne. But most of the sequences would be more suitably categorized as home moviemaking, as they show the activities of the filmmakers' families, like weddings, first communions, hunting excursions, and so on. The film's portrait of everyday life cannot therefore be considered false or fictional, as Langford describes it,[52] because it speaks about colonization from a different perspective, a microhistorical one, through the ordinary situations of the families shown in the home movies. This does not preclude the fact that the film also shows the spectator the differences in social and working conditions between the French colonizers and the African people, thus implicitly revealing the social consequences of colonization through a microhistorical lens.

Private Chronicles: Monologue (1999) constitutes a particularly unique case due to its hybrid nature, based on framing the archival material within a fictional framework. The film offers a portrait of Russian society from the 1960s to the 1980s exclusively through the use of home movies from that period. Arranging the footage chronologically by year (from 1961 to1986), filmmaker Vitaly Manskij selects from a vast collection to offer us the imagined autobiography of a Russian—speaking in a voice-over—born in 1961. Despite this fictional framework, the film succeeds in offering a rather sketchy depiction of Russian society over that period, reinforcing the representation of "everydayness" through the kind of improvised quality described by Highmore.[53] Manskij stresses the hybrid nature of his film by placing his fictional protagonist within a clear historical context, beginning and ending each chapter with a caption specifying the year, accompanied by a photograph, frequently of a major figure in the public history of that period. The overall result is not entirely satisfying because the filmmaker often seems to look for an all-too-perfect match between image and voice-over, thereby dismantling the unsophisticated truth value of home movies and foregrounding the constructedness of the approach. Despite this weakness, the visuals offer a rather surprising portrait of the Russian society of that time, demonstrating how a change of scale can provide new insights into our historical knowledge. This visual portrait undermines the stereotypes that most Western spectators probably had of the Soviet regime, showing parties, dinners, dancing, vacations at seaside resorts, and so on, all shot by home moviemakers using small-gauge cameras, a product typically associated with capitalist societies. These "private moments" are nevertheless intermingled with footage of events more commonly associated with the official public image of the regime, such as the typical Soviet military parades. The overall impression is rather like a collage made with miniatures to form societal "patchwork" structures, evocative of Lüdtke's concept of *Alltagsgeschichte* discussed above.[54]

Private Chronicles: Monologue also shows how home movies can reflect the understanding of everyday life suggested by Michel de Certeau: as a site of resistance against the standardization promoted by the institutional powers. This resistance—a mixture of given inertias and inventive deviations—is to be found, according to Certeau, in how "popular procedures (also 'miniscule' and quotidian) manipulate the mechanisms of discipline and conform to them only in order to evade them."[55] In this context, home movies can clearly qualify as one of the "the innumerable practices by means of which users reappropriate the space organized by techniques of sociocultural production," thereby bringing to light "the clandestine forms taken by the dispersed, tactical, and make-shift creativity of groups or individuals already caught in the nets of 'discipline.'"[56] In *Private Chronicles: Monologue*, this is reflected in the scenes of everyday life, which show little of the orthodoxy appropriate to an official Marxist state. Instead, they resemble scenes familiar to Westernized societies, with their citizens' attachment to habits of leisure and consumerism. They also show a certain clash between private and public spaces, linking the celebration of parties and dancing to private homes, in contrast to the official celebrations that occupy the public sphere.

Apart from these collective portraits, there are a significant number of films that use snapshots and home movies to compose personal and family narratives deeply embedded in their historical contexts. These films usually reflect a microhistorical approach, with an in-depth study of an individual or a family as the route through which a historical period can be understood, expressing the microhistorical goal to offer "a prosopography from below in which the relationships, decisions, restraints, and freedoms faced by real people in actual situations would emerge."[57] This is especially evident in the films of Forgács analyzed in chapter 3. To differing degrees, this also characterizes most of the other films analyzed in this book, particularly *A Family Gathering*, *For My Children*, and *A World Not Ours*.

As the case of Forgács's films demonstrate, the filmmaker's relationship to the home movies does not necessarily have to be autobiographical in order to construct a microhistorical narrative based on a family archive. Other interesting cases of this nonautobiographical approach include the Czech documentary series *Private Century* (*Soukromé století*, 2006), made by Jan Kikl, and the documentary *Y in Vyborg* (*Hetket jotka jäivät*, 2005), by the Finnish filmmaker Pia Andell. *Private Century* is composed of eight 52-minute episodes, made using the home movies of different Czech families filmed between the 1920s and 1960s, complemented with a voice-over narration—usually in first person—constructed on the basis of the memories of the people featured in the footage. The stories tend to focus on the ups and downs of the families, but in at least three of the episodes the family history and public history become more clearly intertwined, attaining a significant microhistorical dimension. Two of these episodes, "See You in Denver" and "With Kisses from Your Love," offer a clearer microhistorical view of Czechoslovakia's communist regime, further supported in the second case by the letters that the father sent from prison. The third, "Small Russian Clouds of Smoke," maintains a kind of microhistorical tension to show a different facet of the country: a portrait of the Russian community living in Czechia, seen through the story of the Popov family. On the other hand, *Y in Vyborg* traces the life of the Ypyä family in Finland from 1939 to 1949. Following the outbreak of war with Russia in 1939, Ypyä's wife and children had to leave Vyborg, and during the war years the couple communicated in letters, but also by making home movies. The filmmaker constructs her documentary using this valuable family archive, piecing together a story with an intense emotional charge that offers an interesting microhistorical perspective on those complicated years in its contrast between the times of peace and of war, and between life in a town far from the conflict and on the front line in Vyborg. The combination of home movies and personal letters also provides an effective balance to its microhistorical narrative, with images focusing on everyday family life (although also revealing the signs of war in Vyborg), complemented with the more intimate story told in the letters (read in a voice-over), focusing on the hardships of separation and war.

Family archives, however, have most commonly been explored in microhistorical documentaries from autobiographical perspectives, as is the case in several of the films analyzed in subsequent chapters, such as *A Family Gathering, For My Children*, and *A World Not Ours*. Filmmakers working with an autobiographical approach often resort to their own family archives of snapshots and home movies in their quest for valuable traces of personal identity. Such an approach possesses a quality that is somehow distinct from nonautobiographical appropriation, where home movies may add a strong sense of authenticity but remain somehow mute, enclosed in their anonymity, preventing us from knowing their stories, especially when they are used as visual illustrations of a macrohistorical narrative. In contrast, when autobiographical filmmakers use snapshots and home movies of their own families, different dynamics are usually generated, beginning with the fact of naming the people in those movies. That deictic act of recognizing the images as their own, usually conveyed through the filmmaker's voice-over, testifies to their real existence in the historical world, placing them in a specific time and place. Their home movies and snapshots thus become "mediated memory objects"—a term proposed by Van Dijck[58]—that help filmmakers travel metaphorically back to their past, to their origins, in what is a necessary step for so many autobiographical endeavors. Such family archives may thus reflect an understanding of the archive as the mediator for the impossible return to the places of origin that Steedman finds in Derrida's *Archive Fever*, where "desire for the archive is presented as part of the desire to find, or locate, or possess that moment of origin, as the beginning of things."[59]

Autobiographical filmmakers look at their own home movies primarily as members of the original audience of the films, their families, participating in the "affiliative look" elicited by family images, as Marianne Hirsch suggests, "through which we [the members of the family] are sutured into the image and through which we adopt the image into our own familial narrative."[60] In this sense, the contemporary recycling of the filmmakers' home movies can be understood as an extension of the very process of home moviemaking, which is not complete until the films are projected and commented on by the family members, creating an ephemeral soundtrack missing from the filmstrip. Now it is the filmmaker who adds that commentary to the soundtrack, setting it down permanently for anyone who watches the film thereafter. This provides the spectators with guidelines for contextualizing the images, enabling them to somehow share the "affiliative look" of the original family. This is in fact one of the biggest challenges for these filmmakers, since they need to provide sufficient justification for their family archive to be part of a public film, so that the spectator does not feel like an intruder, but rather a part of their family, a welcome guest to the family screening.

The use of the filmmaker's own home movies can also give rise to an interesting variation on the concept of "postmemory" posited by Hirsch, as mentioned in chapter 1. Hirsch describes this concept as the relationship of a second generation to powerful and often traumatic experiences that preceded their births, but that were nevertheless transmitted to them so deeply as to seem to constitute memories in their own right.[61] Although she does not explicitly relate her concept to microhistory, her emphasis on family photographs as key documents to fill the generation gap in this process of postmemory suggests the connection is a suitable one. This concept is discussed here mainly with reference to the autobiographical documentaries studied in chapter 4—*A Family Gathering*, *From a Silk Cocoon*, and *History and Memory*—although the traumatic memories recounted in some of these films do not belong strictly to a former generation, since the filmmakers actually took part in the events as children. However, they were in a sense unconscious victims of the traumatic events, and they needed to reach adulthood before they could re-evaluate that traumatic past, aided by the mnemonic link provided by home movies and snapshots.

As has been made clear in this chapter, the main archival sources used in microhistorical documentaries come from the family archive (in most cases home movies). This is a type of archival material that is very well suited to a microhistorical approach, as it involves a reduced scale of observation and makes human agency a central focus. Filmmakers can reuse these family archival documents in various ways to construct their microhistorical narratives, respecting their original meaning or exploring their contradictions, but always emphasizing their value as historical sources for a narrative that provides an alternative or complementary vision of public history. These and other aspects are explored in the different case studies examined in the chapters that follow.

3

PÉTER FORGÁCS'S HOME MOVIE CHRONICLE OF THE TWENTIETH CENTURY

The Maelstrom, Free Fall, and *Class Lot*

A s discussed in chapter 2, the use of audio/visual family archives—and more specifically, home movies—has become increasingly common in contemporary filmmaking, often drawing on their potential as historical sources for microhistorical projects. However, it is rare to find a filmmaker like the Hungarian Péter Forgács, whose oeuvre is made mainly out of home movies (and, more occasionally, amateur films).

Forgács developed an interest in this type of material originally as an archivist. In 1983 he began creating his own collection of Hungarian home movies and amateur films, the Private Photo & Film Archives, with the objective of preserving the visual traces of everyday Hungary. In 1988 he received a grant to make films based on his archive material, which was how he came to make his first documentary, *The Bartos Family*, released that same year. Since then, he has made more than thirty works using home movies and amateur films, most of them feature-length documentaries. Notable among these is the series named *Private Hungary*, comprising fifteen titles, although his filmography also includes films made with footage from other (mostly European) countries. The distinctive nature of his work also lies in the fact that its purpose is not merely informative, nor can it be reduced to a mere compilation of archival footage; instead, it is closer to the work of an *auteur*, who intervenes decisively in the material, both in the visuals and the soundtrack. After more than three decades, his filmography has gained international prominence, with screenings and awards at numerous festivals and museums.[1] He has also aroused the interest of academics, who have published a wide range of writings on his work, some of which are included in the anthology *Cinema's Alchemist: The Films of Péter Forgács*.[2]

Forgács takes a number of different approaches to home movie footage, ranging from the ethnographic to the historical. If we adopt the typology introduced in chapter 2 in relation to the appropriation of the family archive, his use of this footage can be considered somewhere between naturalized and historicized. Many of his documentaries could be understood as cases of "domestic ethnography," with none of the autobiographical connotations that this term has for Michael Renov,[3] but in a sense of its own, as they could be described as ethnographic portraits created out of the footage filmed by the families featured in them, used in many cases without substantially changing their original meaning. Moreover, Forgács's films often include a historiographical dimension, in that they offer an investigation into the past that foregrounds the use of home movies as historical documents. This investigation usually has a microhistorical focus that is more or less explicit, related in different ways to the public history of the period concerned. This is in fact the focus of this chapter: an analysis of the films of Péter Forgács as microhistorical documentaries.

The microhistorical dimension of Forgács's films has not been systematically discussed in any previous studies, or by the filmmaker himself when explaining his work. It is true that Forgács sometimes uses a related term, "private history" (which is referred to in the title of his series *Private Hungary*), as a way of defining his films and distinguishing them "from the 'Grande Histoire,' the notion of public history."[4] This microhistorical concern is also evident when Forgács explains that home movies interest him "because they reveal a level of history that is recorded in no other kind of cinema—a level of history . . . that can show us a great many things about the realities and complexities of history as it is lived by real people."[5] Forgács also points to the key issue of the representativeness of home movies later in the same interview: "These films are full of revelatory moments about how it *was* there. . . . If these revelations of self are then placed in a context where you can sense the whole culture, its history and background, and how particular personalities fit into it, the results become very dynamic."[6] Forgács's observation about the level of history that home movies can reveal brings to mind the point made by Jacques Revel (mentioned in chapter 1) about the change of scale not only increasing "the size of the object caught in the viewfinder" but also altering the shape and framing, changing "the very content of what is being represented."[7] Revel is actually quoted (in a footnote) by Roger Odin at the beginning of his analysis of *The Bartos Family*, although he does not subsequently explore this approach in the rest of his chapter.[8] Ruth Balint and Balázs Varga also associate Forgács's filmography with microhistory, but they do not develop the connection.[9]

To study Forgács's films as microhistory, I propose, first, a two-part overview of his filmography to establish a better contextualization of his work: a classification or typology of his films that identifies his different approaches to history and everyday life, and a brief review of his filmography as a chronicle of the history of the twentieth century. I then undertake a close analysis of the three Forgács films that most clearly display a microhistorical approach: *The Maelstrom*, *Free Fall*, and *Class Lot*.

TOWARD A TYPOLOGY OF PÉTER FORGÁCS'S FILMS

To better understand the historiographical perspective of Péter Forgács's work, it seems appropriate first to categorize the different approaches taken in his feature-length films. This categorization is not intended to be exhaustive or to rigidly pigeonhole his creative projects, and it will be limited to his films based mainly on home movies and amateur films. This is in fact Forgács's most common approach and also the one that generally exhibits a more explicitly microhistorical dimension. In this corpus of films, four basic types or categories can be identified: essay films, domestic ethnographies, collective portraits, and those that can more properly be labeled microhistorical films.

The essay films would include *Bourgeois Dictionary* (1992) and *Wittgenstein Tractatus* (1992), although *Kádár's Kiss* (1997), *A Bibó Reader* (2001), and *Venom* (2016) could also be placed in this category with some qualifications. In the first two films it seems quite clear that Forgács has opted for a format that is not intended to construct a historical narrative but to reflect on the role of small-gauge film formats in relation to non-historical categories. The case of *Kádár's Kiss* is more ambiguous, as the film is characterized mostly by an essayistic approach, although the images are dated chronologically and there are some clear references to Hungary's political history. In *A Bibó Reader* (2001), a reflection on the work of this Hungarian intellectual takes priority over his personal biography. In the case of *Venom*, its more experimental approach also suggests a categorization halfway between essay film and documentary.

The category of domestic ethnography includes films dealing with family histories, with a narrative structure that traces the family's biography, marked by a focus on the family portrait and on aspects of local culture. With some specific qualifications for each film, this category could include *The Bartos Family* (1988), *Dusi & Jenő* (1988), *The Diary of Mr. N* (1990), *The Notebook of a Lady* (1994), *Miss Universe 1929* (2006), *I Am Von Höfler* (2008), and *Picturesque Epochs* (2016). None of these films are completely divorced from the macrohistorical contexts to which their biographies belong, but their main focus is more on personal and family lives, lifestyles and customs, and the everyday spaces (private and public) they inhabited. Public history is therefore not given special attention, although it may occasionally slip through the cracks of the ethnographic narrative, sometimes in significant ways.

The third category is made up of collective portraits. This category includes *Simply Happy* (1993), *Meanwhile Somewhere . . . 1940–1943* (1994), *The Danube Exodus* (1998), *El Perro Negro* (2005), *Hunky Blues* (2009), and *GermanUnity@Balaton* (2011). In these cases, Forgács still works with home movies and amateur films, but, rather than focusing on a family history, he creates group portraits, generational frescoes, or historical collages. The collective nature of these portraits is not per se an obstacle to considering them microhistorical, as was explained in chapter 2; nevertheless, these films do not really take a clear microhistorical approach, although they exhibit some features of such an approach, in terms of both the type of archival material used and their focus on anonymous histories. Perhaps the most borderline case would be *El Perro Negro*, which is articulated largely around the histories of the Salvans family and of Eduardo Noriega, although the film ultimately transcends these two histories to offer a broader overview of the Spanish Civil War.

The fourth category is made up of films that can more properly be described as microhistorical, based on family histories of individuals of no significance to public history, analyzed by Forgács with a historiographical intention that frames them as meaningful to better understand macrohistorical contexts. It is worth considering whether *The Bishop's Garden* (2002) might be included in this category, although as it deals with a public figure in the Hungary of his day, it does not really fit into the "history from below" approach typical in microhistory. A clearer example is *Angelos' Film* (1999), despite the fact that the footage filmed by Angelos Papanastassiou was also intended to reflect events of public history—World War II and the Nazi occupation—in Athens. Finally, the most paradigmatic cases of this category would be the films *The Maelstrom* (1997), *Free Fall* (1996), and *Class Lot* (1997).

PÉTER FORGÁCS, TWENTIETH-CENTURY HISTORIAN

While the degree of the historiographical perspective varies in the different categories proposed above, it is clear that, taken as a whole, Péter Forgács's filmography offers a unique chronicle of twentieth-century history. With a few small exceptions, that chronicle is framed within the period when small-gauge cameras were in widespread use, from the 1920s through the 1970s. The home movies filmed with these cameras do not usually have much meaning for audiences outside the family circle, who would be unfamiliar with most of the people and situations shown in the films. To solve this problem, Forgács provides them with a specific historical context, primarily through interviews with the now elderly home moviemakers, or with other people featured in the footage, often the moviemakers' children. These interviews form an important part of the historical research process, but they are not always included in the films, particularly in his earliest productions, such as *The Bartos Family*, *Dusi & Jenő*, and *Free Fall*. In later films they would appear more often, always as a complement to the archival footage, which continued to serve as the main visual component of the film, as can be seen in *Miss Universe 1929*, *I Am Von Höfler*, and *Picturesque Epochs*.

Forgács's films can be understood as a cinematic variant of a history of the present, a characteristic feature of the microhistorical documentaries analyzed in this book. The "present" in question is a period prior to the immediate experience of the filmmaker, with the exception of the documentaries about the communist era (*Kádár's Kiss*, *GermanUnity @Balaton*, and *Class Lot*), which deal with a period that Forgács, who was born in 1950, experienced himself. This connection with the history of the present is evident in the fact that Forgács's historiographical enterprise is based on the memories of witnesses, which supply a key layer of historical significance to the home movies shown. The domestic nature of these archives clearly points to this historicization of experience which, according to Julio Arostegui, characterizes the history of the present on two levels that can be seen here: "the carryover of the *private experiences* of individuals toward some kind of *public experience*" and the "cognitive construction that enables us to analyze the present reality *qua* history, allowing us to enrich our self-knowledge."[10] This self-knowledge is relative, as the witness's testimony reaches us through the mediation of the filmmaker, who is often not explicit about his dependence on those testimonies for his historical research of the archives. But even so, the preeminence of home movies as mnemonic objects still points to a strong presence of personal and family memory as a foundation for this historiographical enterprise. This echoes Henry Rousso's reflection on the emergence of histories of the present in the last third of the twentieth century, which he describes as "an age of memory," with the result that the "historians of the present time, somewhat more than others, have been confronted with the uncontrolled deployment of that notion [memory], which ultimately subsumed all the other usual forms of relation to the past—history, tradition, heritage, myth, legend."[11]

However, this historiographical dimension of Forgács's documentaries differs from the conventional historian's approach, since his films are made with an explicitly *auteurial* perspective.[12] The most characteristic feature of his approach is unquestionably the habitual use of home movies (and more occasionally amateur films) as visual sources. This footage is sometimes complemented by public archives—both visual (newsreels and other sources) and sound recordings (political speeches, songs, and so on). Forgács creates his historical chronicles out of these archival materials, giving them shape with the painstaking care of a painter or a sculptor, which may be why he considers himself as much a visual artist as a filmmaker. He is meticulous with his editing, combining visual and sound sources and inserting captions that help to contextualize the scenes. The visuals may also undergo different kinds of transformations: alteration of the projection speed, frequent use of freeze-frames to single out the faces of the protagonists, use of tinting to identify where the footage comes from, negative or mirror images inside the frame, split screens with two or more visual sources, and so on. The soundtrack often includes sound effects, although most prominent of all is the use of experimental music. The scores for that music are generally composed by Tibor Szemző, whose contributions Forgács has always considered essential to the creation of his films.

The overall effect clearly goes beyond a conventional historiographical approach and is also quite distinct from the methods of the informative/expository historical documentary, entering territory that evokes some of the elements posited by Robert Rosenstone as postmodern history. Forgács himself seems to point in this direction in at least four of the seven "rules" that guide his filmmaking method, outlined in an interview with Bill Nichols:

> Second: find what is the magic of these unconscious home filmstrips, the magic of re-contextualizing, layer after layer, feel the graphic of each frame. . . .
> Fourth: do not explain, or educate, but involve, engulf the viewer as much possible.
> Fifth: address *the unconscious,* the sensitive, unspeakable, touchable but mostly silent part of the audience.
> Sixth: let the music orchestrate and *rule* the emotional story.[13]

These rules underscore a recurring concern with constructing an experience that goes further than an "objectivist" transmission of historical knowledge to offer an experience that appeals directly to the emotions of the viewers, leaving room to explore what the film offers without guiding them in a fixed direction, with a more open, less totalizing understanding of history.

In this sense, Forgács could be described as an "artist-historian," adopting Miguel Ángel Hernández-Navarro's term, inspired by Walter

Benjamin.[14] According to Hernández-Navarro, certain contemporary artists reveal a decisive interest in exploring history, based mainly on two strategies: 1) telling alternative, fictional, or speculative histories; and 2) discovering parallel histories ignored by the grand narratives, as in the case of Forgács.[15] Indeed, there are a number of Benjaminian ideas explored by Hernández-Navarro that resonate in Forgács's work, in consonance with some of the ideas outlined in chapter 1 related to the connections between Walter Benjamin, everyday life studies, and microhistory.[16] Benjamin conceived of history as an open, incomplete time, active in the present, constructed out of objects and images that acquire meaning through a montage aimed at breaking the continuum of history to activate the latent energy of the objects. Forgács's work can be understood in this way as well, as he works with forgotten home movies and amateur films to rediscover their latent energy as mnemonic objects through his meticulous postproduction work, using them to construct partial but profoundly resonant historical narratives. Moreover, his work as an "archaeologist"—a term that Forgács often uses to describe himself—of home movie and amateur films has an obvious echo in the understanding that Benjamin had of the historian as a collector and ragpicker (*lumpensammler*), someone who works with waste and refuse. In a way, until recently (and in many cases still today) major film archives have considered home movies practically to be "refuse," material that they would store reluctantly or would not consider a priority for cataloging. Forgács's work could thus be understood as a translation to film of that Benjaminian ideal of the historian who collects this film refuse and uses it to construct an alternative history of the twentieth century through montage.

The main focus of this history of the twentieth century is Forgács's homeland, Hungary, but over the years he has expanded it to other European countries, with brief ventures into the Americas as well. In a chronological order that is only approximate (because not all his films offer exact dates for the footage they use), what follows is a brief outline of the time frames and themes he has dealt with in his documentaries, to offer a diachronic view of his work as an artist-historian.

The earliest period explored in a Forgács film can be found in *Hunky Blues,* which is also his only film set in the United States.[17] *Hunky Blues* offers a collective portrait of Hungarians who immigrated to the United

States between 1890 and 1921, based on interviews with twenty-three members or descendants of the immigrant families.[18] To recreate the era visually he makes use of family snapshots and archival footage of various origins from the first decades of the twentieth century, which have no direct relationship to the interview subjects. It could not have been otherwise, as the film deals with a period prior to the development of 16mm cameras, which first became commercially available in 1923, and even then their high cost rendered them inaccessible to that first wave of immigrants. But Forgács is not explicit about the origin of these images, resulting in a certain ambiguity about their relationship to the stories told.

The 1930s constitute the main time frame for several of his films. With footage from this period, Forgács constructs the thematic core of a number of the more biographical episodes in the *Private Hungary* series. This is the case of *The Bartos Family, Dusi & Jenő* (both also using footage from the 1940s and 1950s in their final sections), and *The Notebook of a Lady,* whose archival footage covers events from 1933 to 1944 (juxtaposed with contemporary scenes showing the elderly Baroness Jeszenszky walking through the gardens of the palazzo where she once lived, now shut down and in disrepair). Another biographical narrative from the *Private Hungary* series, *I Am Von Höfler,* begins in 1928 and dedicates much of its footage to those first decades, although it continues through to the 1960s, including a contemporary interview with its now elderly protagonist. A similar case is *The Diary of Mr. N*, two-thirds of which is dedicated to the chronicle of this amateur filmmaker from 1938 to 1943, with the final third continuing up to 1949 and a brief coda in 1967. And outside this series, the film *Miss Universe 1929* offers another biographical portrait, this time set in Austria, with a focus on the 1930s, although it includes an epilogue in the 1970s and a contemporary interview with the home moviemaker.

The 1930s are also the main temporal setting for *El Perro Negro.* The film begins in 1929 with the first films made by the Salvans family, which continue until 1936, when Joan Salvans was murdered. The first half of the film focuses on this family in those years leading up to the Spanish Civil War. The second half focuses on the years of the conflict (1936–1939) using footage by Eduardo Noriega and other archival sources, thus expanding the focus beyond these two filmmakers in an effort to explain the complexity of the war.

Partially overlapping with the years of the Spanish Civil War are other documentaries that focus more on World War II and the Jewish Holocaust, which are perhaps Forgács's best-known films internationally. Of these, the one that begins at the earliest point in time is *The Maelstrom*, which includes images of the Peereboom family as early as 1933 and ends in 1942 or 1943 with their deportation to Auschwitz. *Free Fall* covers a similar but rather shorter period, from 1937 to 1944. The journey of the Slovak Jews to Palestine shown in *The Danube Exodus* took place in 1939, while the second part of the film, the journey of German residents in Bessarabia to the Third Reich, took place in 1940. *Angelos' Film*, which is set in Greece, also covers the years of the war, with a brief prologue set in the years before it. And as its title suggests, *Meanwhile Somewhere . . . 1940–1943*, constructs a collective portrait of the middle years of World War II in Europe. Finally, another episode in the *Private Hungary* series, *Land of Nothing*, begins with a fifteen-minute prologue presenting the everyday life of László Rátz before he was recruited, and then focuses on two years of the war (1942–1943) based on footage filmed by Rátz while he was a soldier in the Hungarian army.

Set in the years after World War II are four films that show different aspects of life and history in communist Europe using the home movies and amateur films made by their protagonists. *Class Lot* continues where *Free Fall* leaves off, presenting the life of György Pető and his wife Eva from 1946 to 1968. Beginning in the 1960s is *Kadar's Kiss*, a collective portrait of Hungary whose found footage is explicitly dated from 1963 to 1971. *GermanUnity@Balaton* traces a period from the 1960s through to the 1980s and is also set in Hungary, at one of its most popular tourist sites, Lake Balaton, although its protagonists are German families from East and West Germany who often used this vacation spot to get together. Also set in these decades, although beginning in the 1950s, is the biographical portrait offered in *Picturesque Epochs* of two painters, Mária Gánóczy and her husband, József Breznay, and their work in the context of communist Hungary.

This brief overview offers an idea of the historical chronicle of the twentieth century that Forgács has constructed over the course of his career, focusing mainly on European countries and limited to the period when small-gauge cameras were in common use. Having established the typology of his filmography and its historical chronology, the following sections present a close analysis of the three films that offer the most canonical microhistorical perspective: *The Maelstrom, Free Fall*, and *Class Lot*.

THE MAELSTROM

In *The Maelstrom* (1997), Péter Forgács offers a microhistorical exploration of the Shoah through the history of the Peereboom family. It could be argued that this film brings together the most paradigmatic features of Forgács's filmography, while also being one of his most complete microhistorical works, offering an original perspective in the extensive filmography about the Holocaust.[19] The extraordinary significance of the Holocaust in contemporary culture may be one of the reasons why this is also Forgács's best-known film, leading many to associate his filmography with the depiction of Jewish families persecuted by the Nazi regime. But, in fact, only four of his films explore such stories as their main focus—*The Bartos Family, Free Fall, The Danube Exodus*, and *The Maelstrom*—although they also appear more incidentally in *Miss Universe* and *I Am Von Höfler*.

The Peereboom home movie collection contains more than four hours of footage shot between 1933 and 1942 (most of it filmed by Max Peereboom), of which Forgács uses thirty-eight minutes. In the other twenty-one minutes of his film, the most important footage comes from the home movies of the family of Arthur Seyss-Inquart, an Austrian who was appointed Reich commissioner for the Occupied Dutch Territories. A few scenes of Dutch Nazis are also included in the film, as well as footage of a Jewish family being forced from their home, images of rough waves crashing against a port (which open the film and justify its title), and six photographs of the Peerebooms. For the soundtrack, Forgács uses the characteristic music of Tibor Szemző, occasionally punctuated by sound effects synchronized with the image. He also inserts public sound recordings on seven occasions: four excerpts from radio broadcasts and three from public speeches (one by the queen of the Netherlands from London and two by Seyss-Inquart).

With these elements, Forgács weaves together a chronicle that Michael Renov describes as being positioned on "the dynamic border between testimonial transcription and aesthetic construction," leading him to characterize Forgács as "at once scribe, witness and poet."[20] Indeed, Forgács makes a film based on an archive that covers a family history cut short by the Nazi persecution, but developed from an auteurial perspective that turns this microhistorical chronicle into a truly moving representation of the Shoah. It is precisely its quality as representative of the Holocaust that gives this documentary its main force, revealing how microhistory can contribute a perspective to our understanding of history by virtue of its reduced scale of observation. In this sense, *The Maelstrom* serves as a highly successful example of a historical "fractal," returning to the interesting analogy posited by Sigurður Gylfi Magnússon and István Szíjártó mentioned in chapter 1.[21] The film could be explained as a fractal of the Shoah insofar as the experience of the Peereboom family—which constitutes its basic structure—was repeated in many other Jewish families, and therefore provides a general understanding of the Shoah. In addition to the change of scale it offers, it focuses on "the proper name" (i.e., a specific individual) as a guiding thread for historiographical research, just as Carlo Ginzburg and Carlo Poni propose, associated with strata of society that do not play a central role in public life.[22] It also gives priority to human agency, conveyed through a narrative-type structure, as a means of access to historical knowledge, which is characteristic of a microhistorical approach.

Forgács constructs this narrative structure with an approach that in some ways resembles a suspense story, gradually introducing the threat that looms over the featured family, until we come to the tragic ending in the final scene. The first part of the documentary (up to 35' [minute thirty-five]) basically focuses on a family chronicle of the Peerebooms from 1933 to 1940. It begins with the parents' silver wedding anniversary, then moves on to vacations on the beach, the in-laws opening a new store, other scenes of outings, Max and Annie's wedding, more vacations, the couple's first child, and the whole family on a trip to Paris. This part of the film also includes scenes of public life filmed by Max, such as Queen Wilhelmina and Princess Juliana's visit, or Juliana's marriage (footage of the princess passing by in her carriage after the wedding).

In this first part of the film, Forgács begins to insert a few visual and sound archival documents related to the Nazi movement, positing a contrast with the Peereboom home movies that increases gradually as the film progresses. Early on in the film he shows scenes from Annie's sports club, while we hear a voice-over of a radio broadcast announcing the Dutch athlete Tinus Osendarp winning the bronze medal at the 1936 Olympic Games (11'). Although this news seems to be included here for its thematic coincidence, Osendarp subsequently became a prominent member of the Dutch Nazi Party and of the SS. Almost immediately after this comes the first scene of footage not related to the Peerebooms, showing activities at a youth camp run by the Dutch Nazi Movement (NSB). Forgács underscores the change visually by giving it a blue tint, which he uses in all the other scenes associated with Nazism, in contrast to the sepia tone of the Peereboom footage.[23] Later, he creates the first explicit clash between the microhistorical context of the Jewish family and the macrohistorical context of the Nazi regime when images of Max involved in some Red Cross exercises are accompanied by a speech by Seyss-Inquart welcoming Hitler to Vienna (26').[24] Shortly after this, a caption informs us of the German invasion of Poland (33'), followed moments later by an elaborate sequence masterfully signaling the turning point in the documentary (35'): Max and Annie are walking through a park with their daughter Flora in a baby carriage; in a voice-over we begin to hear a Nazi meeting and the German national anthem of that era, while the image—with the baby carriage—changes from sepia to blue and a caption announces the German invasion of the Netherlands in 1940 (see figure 3.1). The scene ends with footage in color of Seyss-Inquart and his family at their new Dutch residence, the Clingendael Estate.

The threat is already obvious to the viewer, who will experience the twenty-five minutes that follow with increasing anxiety as the two worlds seem to run parallel to each other, when in reality they are headed for a collision that will be fatal for the Jewish family. In this second part of the film, Forgács continues to weave together an ever-thicker web of clashes that gradually cast the dark shadow of persecution imposed by the Nazi regime in the Netherlands over the microhistorical narrative of the Peerebooms. To do this, he incorporates the reading or the recitative chanting in Dutch of the anti-Jewish laws enacted by Seyss-Inquart (with captions in English summarizing their content) as a key narrative/rhetorical element. The first law mentioned refers to animal sacrifices, regulating the use of anesthetic to minimize their suffering (37'). Meanwhile, on screen

FIGURE 3.1 *The Maelstrom*. The stroller for Flora, the Peerebooms' daughter.

we see images of Max and Annie's little girl in a park, creating a cutting paradox that raises the specter of the dark future that awaits this baby. The first explicitly anti-Jewish law, which defines who is Jewish, is announced moments later (39') over amateur footage showing scenes of a Dutch Nazi Party (NSB) training camp, presenting the threat against the Jewish community more explicitly. Later we hear laws related to the economic assets of Jewish people (44'), the ban on going out in public (50'), the requirement to wear a Star of David (54'), and finally the order declaring what they could take to a "work camp" in Germany (56–58'). We generally hear these laws while the Peerebooms' home movies are on screen, creating a specific resonance with the everyday lives of this Jewish family. In this way, what would otherwise be mundane scenes, such as the shot of children playing in the small yard of a house under the smiling gaze of their elders (50'), acquire a new meaning when a caption tells us that Jews have been banned from going out in public.

Forgács also creates visual associations between the world of the Jewish family and the world of the Nazis, in a complex orchestration that combines parallels and contrasts in this second part of the film. The parallels are obvious enough with the introduction of footage of family scenes of the Seyss-Inquarts, which are juxtaposed with the footage of the Peerebooms. The clearest sequence in this sense (48'–50') is the one that shows Arthur Seyss-Inquart's daughter and her husband feeding their little girl, followed by Max and Annie coming out of the hospital with Jacques Franklin, their newborn second child, which in turn is followed by some scenes of the Nazi leader playing with his little granddaughter. Forgács underscores the parallels between these two worlds on at least two other occasions: when he shows Annie and other people skating in winter in Vlissingen, followed by a scene of the Seyss-Inquart family skating at the Clingendael Estate (43'); and when he juxtaposes a scene of men at an NSB training camp bathing in a river with an image of Annie bathing at the beach (38'). The intimate or everyday quality of these scenes, reinforced by the innocence conveyed by the children of both families, opens a space for a more complex reading of reality, as it presents the human face of the Nazi leaders. Such a depiction inevitably calls to mind Hannah Arendt's reference to the banality of evil in her book *Eichmann in Jerusalem*, not only in the more direct formulation applied by Arendt to Adolf Eichmann, but also more indirectly in the sense that the Seyss-Inquarts' home movies provide privileged access to their family intimacy, showing that "normal," home-loving people were capable of carrying out the Jewish genocide.[25]

The contrasts between the two worlds are repeatedly underscored throughout this second part of the film, bringing the persecution of the Jewish community increasingly into the foreground. Not long after Seyss-Inquart is shown as a loving family man, we hear a speech of his in which he makes his anti-Semitic stance explicit, over images of him and his family playing at his Dutch residence (again linking the micro- and macrohistorical dimensions). Shortly afterward, we are informed of the first impact of the anti-Semitic persecution on the Peerebooms: Max's brothers Nico and Louis are arrested in 1941 in the Koot raids (45'). Forgács presents this—in the only internal flashback in the narrative—with images from home movies already shown earlier of vacations on the beach where both of them can be seen. A little later, after we have been informed of the transfer of all Jews—including the Peerebooms—to Amsterdam, a caption tells us of the deaths of Nico and Louis in Mauthausen. Then, Forgács again contrasts the private register (with Annie feeding her child and putting him to bed) with the anti-Semitic public discourse, this time through an interview with an SS doctor about "ethnic cleansing."

The final scene is drawing near. But first there is a sequence showing SS Reichsführer Himmler's visit to the Clingendael Estate (53'–55'). The main part of this sequence shows Himmler and Seyss-Inquart playing in a doubles tennis match. Here we get a glimpse of something that was already evident in the previous Seyss-Inquart footage: its ambiguous nature as home movie footage. Its subject matter is typical of this type of filmmaking: private family moments or leisure activities like horse riding or playing tennis. But their behavior in front of the camera often looks forced, as if they were being filmed by someone outside the family or as if they had expected that these films would end up being shown outside the family environment. As Ernst Van Alphen suggests, the Seyss-Inquarts know they are part of history as representatives of the Nazi regime, and this means their home movies can be interpreted more as part of a historical time than the personal time normally associated with this type of footage.[26] In other words, the microhistorical dimension that characterizes home movies begins to blur here, placing the footage on a hazy frontier between micro- and macrohistory, paradigmatically represented in this tennis match between two prominent leaders of the regime during the Nazi occupation of the Netherlands.

After a few brief images of Jews in the Amsterdam ghetto, we now come to the final sequence (56'–59'), perhaps the most widely discussed in Forgács's filmography, due to its metonymic power as a representation of the Shoah from a microhistorical perspective: Max, Annie, and her stepmother together in a living room, smiling, drinking coffee, and arranging clothing, with Max and Annie's two children playing next to them, in an innocent scene with no apparent special meaning (see figure 3.2). But the unsettling music of Tibor Szemző and the cold voice-over narration explaining what every Jewish family can take to a "work camp" (summarized in captions in English) produce a clear dissonance with the image. This serves to convey the clash with the original meaning that the

FIGURE 3.2 *The Maelstrom*. The Peereboom family, preparing for their forced departure to a "work camp" in Germany.

Peerebooms had intended for these images, in an interesting variant of the second type of appropriation of home movies discussed in chapter 2. Forgács underscores this dissonance, to the point of openly contradicting the apparently happy and ordinary meaning of the home movie, with three consecutive captions that provide the macrohistorical context. The first expresses the point of view of the Peerebooms themselves, and partly explains why they look so relaxed: "Preparation by Max, Annie and her stepmother for their departure for work camp in Germany." The second relates to the point of view of the spectator, who knows the true nature of the journey they are about to take: "4 September 1942, Franklin, Flora, Max, Annie, and her stepmother are deported to Auschwitz." And the third informs us indirectly of their death with the statement, appearing over a picture of Max's brother Simon and his newlywed wife, that he was the family's only survivor (a caption that thus also reveals who has been the main source of information for this reconstruction of the Peere-booms' history).

The scene possesses a powerful emotional charge that deeply affects the viewer, as this is no impersonal narration of the Holocaust but the death of a "familiar" family, of people with whom we have shared moments of leisure and celebration, and who are now innocent victims of the machinery of genocide. The evidentiary force of home movies constitutes the basis of this striking effect on the viewer, as we are compelled to recognize that what we are watching is not fiction, but the real death of innocent people. At the same time, this impact is intensified by the powerlessness we feel in our situation as spectators, knowing the tragedy looming over the Peerebooms in the present of their home movies, but being unable to help them from our position in the contemporary present. Forgács explains it insightfully when he describes this distance as the force behind the film's dramatic tension: "The time lapse between today—the viewing time—and the past—the film-event time (historic time)—this distance is full of tension. The bridging of two dates . . . is a strong effect, because . . . we are aware of the would-be victims' future, but not able to communicate our knowledge."[27]

This temporal tension is effectively constructed through the combination of the informative and affective elements of the archival images: we know the fate of a Jewish family under the Nazi regime, but it is an affective knowledge that makes us suffer with them right up to the impact of the final scene. This tension constitutes an eloquent expression of the distinction that French theorist Roland Barthes makes between *studium* and *punctum* in his study of photography. In contrast to the informational aspects provided by any photograph (which he labels *studium*), Barthes posits the presence of other elements that leave a deeper impression because of their emotional impact (*punctum*). He also identifies a type of *punctum* that is of special relevance to this case, based on the temporal distance between the present of the archival image and the present of the viewer: "This new punctum, which is no longer of form but of intensity, is Time, the lacerating emphasis of the *noeme* ('*that-has-been*')."[28] To explain his idea, Barthes analyzes a photograph of a convicted murderer about to be executed, taken in 1865:

The photograph is handsome, as is the boy: that is the *studium*. But the *punctum* is: *he is going to die*. . . . I observe with horror an anterior future of which death is the stake. By giving me the absolute past of the pose (aorist), the photograph tells me death in the future. What *pricks* me is the discovery of this equivalence. In front of the photograph of my mother as a child, I tell myself: she is going to die: I shudder, like Winnicott's psychotic patient, *over a catastrophe which has already occurred.*[29]

The Peerebooms' home movie footage, especially this final scene showing them in their living room, constitutes one of the most disturbing examples of this *punctum* that can make us shudder, showing us in their present an innocent family that we know is going to die in their near future. This is why *The Maelstrom* is so persuasive and why its microhistorical portrait of the Shoah may help us to understand the magnitude of this genocide more deeply than an exhaustive study in the tradition of conventional history.

FREE FALL AND CLASS LOT

Péter Forgács adopts a similar approach in *Free Fall* (1996), which consists largely of footage filmed by the Hungarian Jew György Pető from 1937 to 1944. However, this time his protagonist survived the Holocaust and continued shooting home movies from 1946 to 1968—footage that Forgács used to make *Class Lot* (1997). These two films can therefore be analyzed together, as a microhistorical chronicle of Hungary over four decades that were marked by enormous historical changes, with World War II, the alliance with Nazi Germany, and the subsequent communist regime.

The long period covered by György Pető's home movies brings these two films close to what could be categorized as a biography of this Hungarian family, raising the question of the similarities or differences between microhistorical and biographical approaches. Jill Lepore addresses this question with an insightful description of the differences between the two, identifying the following as the most significant: "If

biography is largely founded on a belief in the singularity and significance of an individual's life and his contribution to history, microhistory
is founded upon almost the opposite assumption: however singular a
person's life may be, the value of examining it lies not in its uniqueness,
but in its exemplariness."[30] This connects with the concept of the fractal
discussed above and can be seen clearly in the history of the Peerebooms
told in *The Maelstrom* and now in the history of the Petős told in *Free
Fall* and *Class Lot*. This exemplariness is not incompatible with the fact
that, here again, the individual proper name is a guiding thread of the
historical research, resulting in the kind of prosopography from below
advocated by microhistorians. Forgács himself rejects the classification
of these films as biographies, asserting that his work based on home
movies "is closer to archaeology than to an actual biography."[31] Defining
himself as archaeologist, Forgács seeks to place the emphasis on the fragmentary and incomplete nature of these home movies, and the laborious
task of recontextualization required to render them historiographically
meaningful. This is a task in some ways similar to the one taken on by
microhistorians, with their exploration of fragmentary sources that neces-
sitates the activation of the evidential paradigm posited by Ginzburg.

As in *The Maelstrom*, *Free Fall* and *Class Lot* underscore the importance of everyday life as a historiographical category, using György Pető's
family history to offer an alternative account to the public history of a
particularly troubled period for contemporary Hungary. However,
Forgács does not ignore the public history, which he shows through
newsreels from the era, political speeches, voiceover narration, and so
on. The end result is a masterful balance between the different scales of
observation while still keeping the main focus on the microhistorical
scale. These questions are analyzed below, considering each film individually in order to identify the nuances that Forgács introduces in his
exploration of the different periods they cover: the Horthy regime and its
increasing ties to Nazism in *Free Fall*, and the communist regime in
Class Lot.

Of the two films, *Free Fall* is the one with more similarities to *The
Maelstrom*, as it covers a similar historical period, also uses home movies
as visual source, and has the persecution of Jews and the Shoah as its
main theme. However, there are also some significant differences. In *Free*

Fall, Forgács introduces more explanations of the macrohistorical context, largely due to the need to provide viewers with a basic knowledge of Hungarian history, something that was hardly necessary in *The Maelstrom.* The other most notable difference is the way he conveys the impact of the Shoah on the Jewish families featured in the film. With the Peerebooms, the viewer learns of the death of Louis and Nico quite late in the film, and no information is provided on the fate of the rest of the family until the end. In the case of the Petős, over the course of the second part of the film—through captions and in most cases without a narrative justification other than their appearance in a home movie—the fate of family members and friends is gradually revealed. In narratological terms, this weakens the suspense effect and the consequent emotional tension that Forgács achieved in *The Maelstrom.*[32] Although the habitual use of home movies might suggest that the story is conveyed to the spectator through an internal focalization (the featured families), the tone in *The Maelstrom* is actually marked by the fact that the viewer has extratextual knowledge that the protagonists do not, creating a tension between our identification with the Peerebooms (internal focalization) and our superior extratextual knowledge, closer to the absence of focalization. In *Free Fall,* however, the story moves further away from an internal focalization, as it foreshadows the final fate of most of the protagonists (in many cases, their death in concentration camps) from minute 33 right through to the end of the film, in minute 72. This somehow defuses the vicarious identification that the spectator might otherwise feel with the Petős, with the exception of György and his wife, Eva, whose survival is revealed only in the final minute of the film. The overall tone therefore tends toward an absence of focalization, further accentuated by the greater presence of sequences of macrohistorical contextualization and the sporadic appearance of a voice-over narration with an omniscient character.

Through this narrative approach, Forgács offers a complex articulation of the macro- and microhistorical dimensions, giving *Free Fall* a distinctive profile in its historical portrait of the era. The film begins by introducing György Pető, in a kind of prologue that runs for around five minutes, recounting that he lived in Szeged, that he studied music and accompanied the singing and dancing Rosner Sisters on their tours in the 1930s, that in 1936 he inherited his father's lottery shop, and that in

1937 he bought an 8 mm camera. We are then introduced to his family, through home movies of family gatherings: his brother, Lacy; his sister, Rózsi, and her husband, Lázsló (a lieutenant in the army and not Jewish), and so on. After this prologue, now in the year 1938, Forgács begins providing information on the macrohistorical context of both the different anti-Jewish laws that were being enacted at that time and the main developments in Hungarian history in those years. In the 1930s Miklos Horthy's government gradually began forming closer ties with the Nazi regime, until it finally joined the Axis powers in 1940. Prior to this, Germany had helped Hungary regain part of the territory it had lost after World War I, thanks to the First and Second Vienna Awards (1938 and 1940). In 1941 Hungary declared war on the Soviet Union to support the German invasion, but after their resounding defeat by the Soviet army at the Don River in 1943, they were no longer active in this front and even began secret negotiations with the Allies. Germany ended up imposing a "friendly" occupation of Hungary in March 1944. In October they installed a puppet government, which would last until Soviet troops invaded the country and brought an end to the Nazi occupation in April 1945. The film's audience is informed of the basic elements of these historical developments through captions and public archives (film and sound), with one important exception: the occupation of Košice (Kassa in Hungarian), located in southern Slovakia, in November 1938, as a consequence of the First Vienna Award (10'–12'). This event is shown through footage filmed by György Pető—with a recording of the radio broadcast by a BBC correspondent supportive of the annexation added by Forgács—in a fragment that includes intertitles made by Pető himself, suggesting a production more typical of an amateur filmmaker than a home moviemaker. Alongside this political context, *Free Fall* also traces the evolution of the increasing persecution of the Jewish community in the country as it breaks into the happy everyday world of the Petős.[33] This persecution was expressed in various laws enacted in and after 1938, but always stopping short of collaboration with the Nazi machinery of extermination, until the German occupation of 1944, when, in just two months, with the collaboration of the new government, around 450,000 Hungarian Jews were deported to Auschwitz, where nearly all would die.

Once again Forgács effectively articulates the microhistorical chronicle— in this case woven together using György Pető's home movies—with the macrohistorical context of the era, in another example of a historical fractal that helps explain the history of Hungary in relation to World War II and the Shoah from an original perspective. Unlike *The Maelstrom*, in this film the Hungarian filmmaker presents the contrast between scales of observation very early on. As early as minute 5, a caption announces the first anti-Jewish law, which is also heard in a recitative chanting in Hungarian, followed by or overlapping with an English translation in a voice-over, a strategy that is repeated over the course of the film to inform us of the anti-Jewish legislation.[34] Later on, György Pető's own footage displays this intersection of historiographical scales when he starts working for the Jewish Labor Service in 1940. The Labor Service was created as an alternative for certain communities, including Jews, who were considered by the Hungarian government to be too "unreliable" to serve in the army. In 1940–1941 Jewish Labor servicemen were predominantly involved in building roads or performing earthworks under relatively normal conditions. But the situation worsened when they were sent to the Russian front in 1941, and it continued to deteriorate right up to the end of the war, resulting in the death of many Jews due either to inhumane working conditions or to the open hostility of their supervisors. The image that *Free Fall* gives of the Labor Service, however, provided by footage filmed by György himself in 1940 and 1941, is one of friendly interactions with their bosses and apparently light workloads, with a surprisingly jovial tone. These scenes are actually introduced for the first time (31') in a sequence including their own captions (in Hungarian), beginning with two introductory titles: "Souvenirs of a shoveler," followed by "Some merry moments from the life of the Jewish labor company at Kiszombor." Like the sequence of the occupation of Košice, this footage was subject to some postproduction work, again placing it on the boundary between home movie and amateur film. However, when György is sent to the Labor Service again in 1942, but this time to the Russian front, he does not take his camera, and we are informed of his departure and his fortuitous survival through captions alone; this is also the case when he is recruited for the Russian front again in 1944.

As noted above, around halfway through the film, Forgács also begins to include news of the ultimate fate of György Pető's family and friends, with no specific intradiegetic motivation. The first of these refers to his friend Bandi Karos, who is shown in the footage of the labor camp, over which a caption appears stating that he was shot to death four years later. This dissonance becomes even more intense when the information provided by the captions contrasts against the happy, ordinary present of the home movies, for example, when we see Eva's mother smiling at the meal where the two families are celebrating György and Eva's engagement (46'), while a caption informs us that she died in the Neukirchen camp in 1944. Similar situations are used to tell us of the death or deportation of other friends and relatives, of which the most painful are those related to the children. For example, we see Lacy Pető's young son Janika at bedtime, while a caption informs us that he died when Budapest was bombed in 1944. Shortly after this we are shown György and Eva's newborn son, Andris, in October 1943, beginning a six-minute section focusing on him (62'–68'), which also includes some brief references to public history. The most shocking part of this sequence is a caption telling of the baby's death—a few months later in Neukirchen, in 1944—almost immediately after he was introduced, leaving barely enough time to empathize with his innocent gaze, although we will continue to see home movies of him for several minutes longer (see figure 3.3). *Free Fall* ends with a section for which Forgács no longer uses György's footage (68'–73'); it has the tone of an epilogue and serves mainly to recount the deportation of the Hungarian Jews, with specific information about the Pető family. This section concludes with images of a forest and a caption stating that Eva survived the concentration camp, György returned from Soviet captivity, and they had a daughter after the war.

In short, *Free Fall* is a film very close in formal terms to *The Maelstrom*, as can be seen from its use of home movies and the evocative music of Tibor Szemző, and with a similar microhistorical approach, based on the Pető family archive. Forgács takes on the challenge of constructing this microhistorical narrative while framing it within the complex macrohistorical context of the era, a feat that he achieves with the different layers provided by the archival footage, the soundtrack, and the textual information of the captions.

Class Lot is explicitly presented as a continuation of *Free Fall* right from its first scene, which features the baby who appeared at the end of the previous film, Kati, born in November 1946. With a similar approach, Forgács now constructs a microhistorical narrative of Hungary from

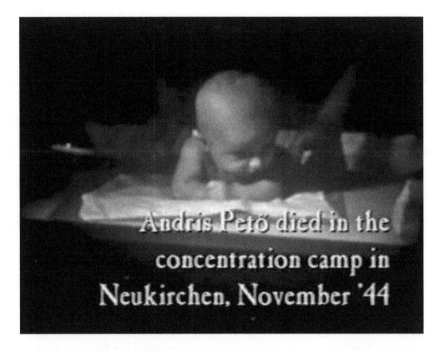

Andris Pető died in the
concentration camp in
Neukirchen, November '44

FIGURE 3.3 *Free Fall*. Andris, the Petős' newborn son.

1946 to 1968, while following the life of György, Eva, and their daughter, Kati. The archive on which this film is based is again the family's home movies, which are generally presented in a sepia tone. However, the film also contains elements that differentiate it from the previous pictures: in narrative terms, it features a more explicit internal focalization on the daughter, with various flashbacks that connect it with *Free Fall*, and the presence on a few occasions of an omniscient narrator; it also posits a more explicit overlap of macro- and microhistorical scales; and, visually, it frequently makes use of different combinations, such as split screens, superimposed images, or inserted images (framed in various ways).

Forgács makes use of an omniscient narrator in certain parts of the film, such as in the first few minutes, in order to provide a brief outline of György Pető's life, or to explain the family's move to Budapest. However, the film tends toward an internal focalization through the daughter, Kati, who to a large extent is the story's guiding thread for two reasons. The first is consistent with the type of archive used, home movies, which follow the daughter's growth, from infancy until she starts college. In addition, Forgács reinforces this internal focalization by including an interview with Kati at different points (a strategy that was not used in any of his previous films), which often turns her into the narrator or commentator of the different historical situations of her family. Nevertheless, the Hungarian filmmaker seems to resist breaking the stylistic unity provided by home movies as the film's visual source, relegating the interviewee to the top right corner of the frame, an unusual choice for a documentary but effective in this film.

The other characteristic narrative element of *Class Lot* is the use of flashbacks, establishing a dialogue with the family's past through the insertion of older home movies (most of which were already included in *Free Fall*). On two occasions (37' and 40'), the film briefly recalls the history of the family's suffering as victims of the Holocaust—through captions, photographs, and home movies—although it does so while maintaining the internal focalization, as it tells this history to explain that Kati found out about those past events in her preteen years. The second occasion could be described as more chilling, because Forgács shows Kati as a baby, in 1946, and then inserts an image of her brother, Andris, in 1943, also a newborn, in his first mention in this film (40'). A caption states that he died when he was one year old in the Neukirchen camp, which, combined with Szemző's unsettling music, vests this scene with a special emotional resonance, particularly for viewers who have not seen *Free Fall*. A similar strategy of juxtaposing time frames reappears on four other occasions in the final part of the film to show the family in different periods sharing the same frame: the mother, Eva, in 1940 and 1968; the daughter, Kati, in 1948 and 1968; and the father, György, in 1941 and 1965, and, later, in 1908 (photograph), 1939, and 1968, which is the last year of the Petős' footage. With this strategy, rarely used before in his filmography, Forgács thus looks back on the past images of this family archive.[35] This serves to link *Free Fall* and *Class Lot* together as parts of the same life journey, thereby underscoring the passage of time and the ability of film to preserve that fleeting past, evoking André Bazin's powerful metaphor of cinema as the mummification of change.[36]

The microhistorical perspective that dominates *Class Lot* is now more deeply intertwined with the macrohistorical context, which is visible mainly through the frequent insertion of newsreels made by the communist regime and captions related to the main events and figures of the period. After the Soviet occupation of Hungary, there was a period of transition during which a democratic system was permitted; but since the pro-Soviet parties received only limited support in the two elections held in those years, starting in 1947 the Moscow-backed government began taking over key positions, restricting freedoms, and persecuting opposition leaders, until finally Hungary became a communist regime in 1949. This evolution of the macrohistorical context is not detailed in the documentary, although certain elements are included that suggest or fill in this information. For example, at the beginning of the film (6') we are shown a fashion parade held in the fall-winter season of 1947–1948, followed by an advertisement for cigarettes, both of which clearly predate the official communist regime. The communist leaders are also presented in various contexts. In the beginning (3') we see the communist leader of the postwar period, Mátyás Rákosi, followed by one of his lieutenants, Ernő Gerő, giving a political speech. Later on (18'), we see Imre Nagy, then prime minister, announcing the death of Stalin in 1953, and shortly after that (23') we are introduced to János Kádár, who is explicitly identified as "communist chief" from 1956 to 1988 (see figure 3.4). Also appearing is Soviet leader Nikita Khrushchev, giving a speech in another visual insert later in the film (36'). What is interesting about these images is that, with the exception of Gerő's speech, Forgács introduces them all as small visual inserts over the Petős' home movies. The clash between macro- and microhistorical scales thus becomes more explicit, also pointing to the resistance of everyday life to political and social systems, a tension that is more pronounced here because the system in question is a totalitarian regime. The theories of Michel de Certeau come to mind again here, and Ben Highmore contextualizes them in a way that seems to highlight the connections with this film's microhistorical exploration more clearly: "The cultures of everyday life are therefore submerged below the level of a social and textual authority. While they tend to remain invisible and unrepresentable, they perform *something like* a guerrilla war on these authorities. . . . This position offers a valuable 'view from below,' and productively foregrounds a range of practical forms of 'resistance' within everyday life."[37]

Forgács's work also reflects this dialectic between the communist political system and everyday life in other scenes where the combination

FIGURE 3.4 *Class Lot.* Summer vacationers at Lake Balaton juxtaposed with Janós Kádár, general secretary of communist Hungary.

of visuals and soundtrack create resonances that amplify the resistant quality of the everyday, often with a touch of parody or irony. An early example of this is found when the home movie footage of the Petős' lottery shop (4') is shown, accompanied by a communist song, which could be interpreted as a threat that would be realized later, when the regime expropriates the business. Another curious scene (11'), perhaps taking the parody slightly overboard, is the one showing a female singer at an official ceremony performing a propagandistic song, with superimposed images of little Kati in home movies filmed by her father. Another contrast with a clearly ironic intention is the sequence showing an official newsreel about the country's agriculture with superimposed images of family vacations: at the lake, by the pool, or traveling by train (24'–26'). The soundtrack reinforces the ironic contrast, as the newsreel announcer's words clash not only with the images, but also with Szemző's music, which in this sequence becomes dynamic and upbeat, in keeping with the Petős' home movies. The same type of music is used in another scene (34'–35'), where the clash of scales acquires one of its most effective expressions in the film: inserted over images in color of Kati playing with a Hula-Hoop is a newsreel of the official May Day parade of 1957 (see figure 3.5). The ambient sound of the parade and the narrator's commentary compete with Szemző's music on the soundtrack, while Forgács emphasizes the young communists' loyal dedication to the party with the caption: "Eternal allegiance!" The image of Kati, engrossed in her control of the Hula-Hoop, thus acquires a metonymic dimension of unquestionable rhetorical power, as an image of the microhistorical resistance against the communist regime.

Class Lot includes many other references to this contrast between scales of observation, with the inclusion of official newsreels on several occasions and references to the popular culture of the era, often linked to György Pető's work as a musician in an operetta company. Overall, the

FIGURE 3.5 *Class Lot*. Kati, the Petős' daughter, juxtaposed with young people marching on May Day.

contrasts and combinations of scales presented by Forgács in this film can be said to offer a clear example of the value of a microhistorical perspective, in that it provides a different kind of access to contemporary Hungarian history, offering a view that nuances and complements the official and critical discourses on Europe's communist regimes of the last century.

Through a close analysis of *The Maelstrom, Free Fall*, and *Class Lot*, this chapter has offered a study of a filmography that is truly unique for its systematic use of home movies (and to a lesser extent, amateur films) as the main visual archive for a series of historical chronicles. While a diverse range of approaches can be identified in the films of Péter Forgács, as has been made clear by the typology proposed above, it is undeniable that many of his films are imbued with a microhistorical sensibility, which has given rise to some of the best examples of the microhistorical documentary form. His films effectively show how a filmmaker can undertake significant historiographical investigations through a creative process that, without abandoning the historian's rigor, offers an emotional understanding that can open up new pathways in historical research.

4

THE INCARCERATION OF JAPANESE AMERICANS DURING WORLD WAR II

Something Strong Within, A Family Gathering, From a Silk Cocoon, and *History and Memory*

During World War II, after declaring war on Japan in 1942, Washington took steps to intern the entire population of Japanese ancestry living on the West Coast of the United States in different camps in remote locations, for fear of the possibility of their collaboration with the enemy. Around 120,000 people were thus subjected to incarceration. Worse still, it was not only first-generation immigrants (Issei) who were affected; nearly two-thirds of those incarcerated belonged to the second generation (Nisei), who had been born in the country and therefore had full rights as U.S. citizens. This controversial decision was accepted by the general public without much protest, due not only to war anxiety but also to the increasing prejudices aroused by the steady growth of the Japanese immigrant population on the West Coast since the mid-nineteenth century. Their forced incarceration in concentration camps,[1] which lasted in most cases until the end of the war in 1945, provoked a profound identity crisis for Japanese Americans, as they were stripped of their property (which they were forced to sell off at a loss) and automatically became suspects (and de facto prisoners) on the sole basis of their ethnic background, a fate that most Americans of German or Italian descent did not have to suffer. After their release, few returned to where they had been living before, and the years of internment were often left out of family narratives, repressed like a nightmare that nobody wished to remember. In the 1970s, the third generation (the

Sansei, children and grandchildren of the victims of incarceration) launched a campaign for redress, culminating with the enactment of the Civil Liberties Act of 1988, which apologized for the internment, admitting that it was based on "race prejudice, war hysteria, and a failure of political leadership." At the same time, beginning in the 1970s, and especially since the 1980s, there has been an abundance of historical studies, literary works, and films about these events.

Numerous short and feature-length documentaries have been made examining this period of history.[2] These documentaries can be considered from various perspectives: on the one hand, they refer to issues of representation of transnational and biracial ethnic minorities, a topic that has been analyzed extensively, including in studies related specifically to Asian Americans and Japanese Americans. On the other hand, since these are often histories with which the filmmakers themselves have a personal connection, these films can also be analyzed from the perspective of autobiographical studies, a field in which the stories of ethnic minorities have offered valuable insights into the history and culture of their time, as Betty Ann Bergland observes: "Because ethnic autobiographies point to the multicultural complexity of the United States, they illuminate the richness and complexity of that culture—the tragedies and injustices as well as the resistance and resilience of its people."[3] Without ignoring this diversity of perspectives, I focus here on these films as history, on the historiographical perspective they offer, with particular attention to those that best reflect a microhistorical approach. A common element that all these films share is their deconstruction of the official narrative that was used to justify the mass internment. They thus posit a countermemory to the official narrative of the era, focusing—as George Lipsitz proposes with reference to a broader context in *Time Passages*—"on localized experiences with oppression, using them to reframe and refocus dominant narratives."[4] Jun Xing expands on this idea in her study of documentaries made by Asian American women about these events: "As an alternative way of remembering and forgetting (rooted in the personal, immediate, and particular), countermemories create an autonomous cultural space for marginalized social groups," calling attention "to the fact that history is multileveled and plural-voiced narration."[5] These countermemories thus reveal a common effort to construct an alternative collective memory of these events, often articulated through personal and family histories. As Rocio G. Davis suggests, "history and family are at the center of many Asian American documentaries as filmmakers use family stories to claim for their forebears and, by extension, for themselves, a place in America's historical and cultural narrative."[6]

It is therefore not surprising that a significant number of the documentaries that explore this period in Japanese American history use microhistorical strategies, including some of the best-known and most effective films portraying these events. For this study, I have chosen four that exhibit clear microhistorical features while at the same time taking distinctly cinematic approaches, showing how a microhistorical perspective can be expressed in different ways in relation to the same historical events. The four films selected are: *Something Strong Within*, based on home movies with no personal connection to the filmmakers; *From a Silk Cocoon* and *A Family Gathering*, both with autobiographical stories that rely heavily on home movies, snapshots, and family letters; and *History and Memory*, halfway between documentary and essay film, and with a more explicit exploration of historiographical issues.

SOMETHING STRONG WITHIN

Something Strong Within was originally made for the exhibition "America's Concentration Camps: Remembering the Japanese American Experience," presented at the Japanese American National Museum in Los Angeles, California, in 1994, although it was subsequently distributed independently as a documentary. This forty-minute film was created by Robert Nakamura and Karen L. Ishizuka based on the home movie collections of nine home moviemakers, all of which were archived at the museum itself. The film begins with a "prologue" that includes explanatory text on the historical context, followed by footage of the forced removal of Japanese Americans in Guadalupe, a small Californian town, filmed by the superintendent of the school district. After this prologue, the title of the film appears, and then, superimposed over home movie footage of one of the camps, we see a quote (taken from the diary of Yuri N. Kuchiyama) that explains the reason behind the title and the project: "Courage is something strong within you that brings out the best in a person. Perhaps no one else may know or see, but it's those hidden things unknown to others, that reveals a person to God and self." The rest of the documentary consists of footage of the internment camps from the nine collections of home movies, with captions occasionally superimposed to provide factual information related to the visuals, as well as another six quotes taken from diaries written by Japanese Americans in those years. The soundtrack features extradiegetic music—except for one scene that includes a sound recording of a Boy Scouts Drum and Bugle Corps in one of the camps—with the frequent addition of sound effects synchronized with the image.

These elements clearly resemble Péter Forgács's approach, analyzed in chapter 3, with his use of home movies and amateur films as his main visual source, as well as the inclusion of on-screen textual information and instrumental music, which also plays an essential role here, as Ishizuka notes: "Music was a critical element and considered the third partner in a three-way artistic collaboration."[7] However, some important differences are observable. The most significant of these is the fact that the makers of this film, Robert Nakamura (director and editor), Karen L. Ishizuka (screenwriter and producer), and Dan Kuramoto (composer), have a more direct relationship with the footage used. All three are Japanese Americans, Kuramoto's family was interned at the camps, and Nakamura himself was actually interned at the Manzanar camp from the ages of five to seven, although this information is not included in the film. Moreover, the filmmakers have strived to the utmost to respect the nature of the different home movies as "collections," generally treating them as independent blocks and indicating their creators at the beginning of each collection. This approach led them to ignore chronological or thematic criteria to structure the film, instead emphasizing the distinctive nature of each collection, visible in the random order of the different scenes, and further underscored by the repetitions that occur from one section to the next. For the same reason, Nakamura does not manipulate the appearance of the images as Forgács sometimes does, but instead respects their original features, which are highly visible in the changes from black and white to color of the original footage.

With these formal features, *Something Strong Within* offers an interesting variation on the microhistorical documentary in its exploration of the forced internment of Japanese Americans. Nakamura and Ishizuka propose a clear change in the scale of observation, focusing on the experiences of families unknown to public history, documented in their home movies and in occasional quotes taken from personal diaries. The filmmakers thus propose a history from below, articulated through the ordinary lives that these families tried to carry on during their years of internment in the camps. However, their approach breaks with the orthodoxy of the more typical work of microhistorians, as here they do not focus on a single family, nor do they attempt to base their documentary on a narrative structure that would in some way reflect the story of its protagonists. There are no interviews with the people shown in the footage—who in some cases were still alive, like Dave Tatsuno—or any other biographical material that might contextualize them. There is not even any attempt to identify individuals when they appear in the images. Instead, the emphasis is on the inherently fragmentary nature of home movies, very much in line with the historiographical approach of Alf Lüdtke and his *Alltagsgeschichte*, mentioned in other chapters. The concept of the miniature posited by Lüdtke for the creation of societal patchwork structures used to construct a history of everyday life is successfully expressed in this film by Nakamura and Ishizuka, who achieve this effect of collage or patchwork with the home movie collections to recount the history of those dark years, with some revealing nuances.[8]

The home movies used in *Something Strong Within* also serve to highlight—perhaps even more clearly than in Forgács's films—the limitations of the available archives that microhistorians generally have to work with. Although this is material preserved in institutional archives (the Japanese American National Museum), it is not as exhaustive as what would be expected of archives related to a public figure. The very nature of home movies, which were always filmed in constrained circumstances due to the costly nature of the materials and processes, is accentuated in this case because such filming was initially forbidden, and even when it was later permitted, it was still being done by people in conditions of incarceration. Moreover, because of the very nature of these archives, the gaps, the lacunae, what has not been filmed, become as eloquent as the filmed footage, in a way triggering Carlo Ginzburg's evidential paradigm, the use of conjecture as a hermeneutic method. This is a strategy reinforced by the filmmakers themselves, who do not attempt to share all the information available on these historical events with the viewer, as might be expected of a conventional historian. Instead, they aim for a more emotional type of engagement: "We created a multi-layered media piece using a palette of home movies that unfolded and played out to an evocative music score with the purpose of inviting the viewer to emotionally get a feel for—rather than intellectually learn about—camp."[9] While it is true that the home movie collections are explicitly attributed to their authors, the documentary offers no information about these individuals other than their names and the concentration camps where they were interned. This constitutes an ambiguous allusion to the human agency characteristic of microhistory because the ultimate aim is to create a collective portrait constructed out of the "miniatures" offered by each of the home moviemakers with their everyday scenes.

This collective portrait contains a profound paradox that gives the documentary a uniquely poignant quality, as it presents the apparent everyday lives of ordinary families who happen to be interned in concentration camps. Many of the scenes shown are similar to those found in any other home movies: scenes in the snow (probably an exotic experience for families from Southern California), children playing games, adults playing sports like baseball or football, or people simply posing for the camera. Other scenes reflect everyday situations but reveal the internment camp setting more directly: people cooking, eating, sewing, or washing clothes, but as groups in collective facilities. Sometimes the home movies explicitly document the location: wide shots of the barracks or the desert or mountain landscape that surrounds them, images of the living quarters, close-ups of the signs indicating the purpose of each building, and shots of the arrival and departure of trains or buses.

This paradox is also reflected in the appropriation strategies applied to the home movies, as this documentary combines all three modes outlined in chapter 2, in a manner similar to Forgács's films. First, they are used in a naturalized way, as there is a clear intention to maintain their original meaning as portraits of the everyday life of these people. Second, the context in which the home movies appear—the film *Something Strong Within*—underscores the dramatic contradiction represented by the home moviemakers' situation of incarceration, giving these images a meaning that is quite the opposite of the positive values of celebration and reminiscing typically associated with home movies. And third, they constitute a historical document of singular importance, as a visual record of a historical injustice. Robert Rosen hints at this combination of approaches when he suggests that the film's most frequently used strategy is dissonance, provoked by a clash of meanings, tonalities, and associations. Rosen identifies the polarity between the indoor and outdoor spaces of the camp as the most expressive of these dissonances:

> On the outside lie the homes and communities that have been left behind, the encompassing context of a free society.... On the inside there are bleak barracks fashioned as homes, fences and guard towers as omnipresent reminders of confinement.... Worst of all are the dissonance-inducing images that bring the inside and the outside together: trucks and trains coming and going, the post office and the shipping dock with their constant flow of objects in and out of the camps, and periodic oblique reminders of the war in the form of Japanese American GIs on leave from fighting at the front.[10]

Indeed, the presence of the Japanese American soldiers provokes the most acute dissonance, particularly bewildering for the contemporary spectator. These were soldiers of the segregated 442nd Infantry Regiment, made up of volunteers and recruits. Nakamura and Ishizuka reflect this very clearly in a sequence showing the Heart Mountain Camp (Wyoming), which begins with a quote by Junji Kumamoto: "In 1944 I was inducted into the U.S. Army. The loyal American part of me welcomed the opportunity to show my loyalty. The rational part of me recognized the irony of being inducted from a concentration camp" (28'). After this quote, we see footage of the camps with a USO dance for soldiers and a parade of boy scouts carrying U.S. flags. This sequence ends with a visit by Sergeant Kuroki (29'–30'), who is welcomed by a large crowd of camp inmates, turning the innocence of these home movies into the most scathing condemnation of the injustice of their incarceration. But the filmmakers also highlight this irony much earlier in the film (5'), when they show home movies of another Japanese American soldier (see figure 4.1). After we see him point to his name on a board with the names of enlisted soldiers, a close-up of the board shows a quote by President Roosevelt, taken from his announcement of the formation

FIGURE 4.1 *Something Strong Within*. A Japanese American soldier from the 442nd Regiment visiting his relatives at Minidako internment camp.

of the 442nd Regiment: "Americanism is a matter of mind and heart. Americanism is not, and will never be, a matter of race or ancestry." Reading this quote on a board located in the Minidako concentration camp effectively produces a dissonance that borders on incredulity for the contemporary viewer.

Looking at the documentary as a whole, the resistance of the Japanese American population in the face of adversity emerges as a central theme. Their innocent smiles as they go about their everyday lives behind barbed wire are disarming and incomprehensible except in the context of collective resistance. Ishizuka expresses as much when she indicates that the goal of the film "was to show the resistance that is inherent in the inmates' conviction to make the best of the situation."[11] It is a goal that is summed up very well in the final quote shown in the documentary, which for the first time is by one of the home moviemakers:

I hope my home movies share with you one aspect of the camp experience—that is the spirit of the Japanese American community. Despite the loneliness and despair that enveloped us, we made the best we could with the situation. I hope when you will look at the scenes of *mochitsuki*, pipe repairing, dining hall duty and church service, you look at the spirit of the people. You will see a people trying to reconstruct a community despite overwhelming obstacles. That, I feel, is the essence of these home movies.

It would indeed be difficult to find a more appropriate way to articulate this everyday resistance to the injustice suffered by Japanese Americans for four years. As we see in *From a Silk Cocoon*, there were protests during this period, which grew when a loyalty questionnaire was issued in 1943, leading to the removal of "disloyal" inmates to Tule Lake, a segregated camp. But *Something Strong Within* focuses on that other, more everyday, kind of resistance, clearly evocative of one of the key concepts posited by Michel de Certeau in his theory of everyday life mentioned in previous chapters. As Certeau and Luce Giard suggest, "everyday practice patiently and tenaciously restores a space for play, an interval of freedom, a resistance to what is imposed (from a model, a system, or an order)."[12] Certeau is not referring to situations like the one suffered by Japanese Americans during World War II, but to the ordinary dynamics of modern societies, whose principles of production seem to have colonized even everyday life. Nevertheless, his understanding of everyday practices as practices of resistance eloquently describes the lives of Japanese Americans in the concentration camps, reflected in the home movies used in this documentary. This is even clearer in Luce Giard's comment on Certeau's work: "Beneath the massive reality of powers and institutions . . . Certeau always discerns a Brownian motion of microresistances, which in turn found microfreedoms, mobilize unsuspected resources hidden among ordinary people, and in that way displace the veritable borders of the hold that social and political powers have over the anonymous crowd."[13] The terminology itself seems to connect, if only by way of analogy, to the microhistorical dimension of *Something Strong Within*, where the borders have turned into physical barriers imposed by an overreaching political power, against which "microresistances" are established by these ordinary people, who fight to maintain their identity and dignity as U.S. citizens of Japanese descent.

FROM A SILK COCOON AND
A FAMILY GATHERING

Other filmmakers have explored the mass incarceration of Japanese Americans to tell of the impact it had on their own families. This was a trend fostered by the Sansei (the third generation), resulting in films such as *Who's Going to Pay for These Donuts, Anyway?* (Janice Tanaka, 1992), *Rabbit in the Moon* (Emiko and Chizu Omori, 1999), and the three that are analyzed below: *From a Silk Cocoon, A Family Gathering*, and *History and Memory*. These films offer evidence of the frequent presence of autobiographical approaches in microhistorical documentaries. As discussed in chapter 1, autobiographical documentaries are not necessarily categorized as historical documentaries, despite the fact that every autobiography is based on a retrospective look on a person's life. To be considered a historical documentary, a film's retrospective look must have a historiographical intention, to explore the past with an aim that goes further than describing the specific experience of an individual or family. However, if these documentaries do engage in a revision of the historical past, they are likely to adopt microhistorical approaches. The autobiographical perspective adds nuances of its own, as it involves the exploration of recent historical periods—a history of the present—that gives the personal and family memory a key role, supported by the use of documents belonging to the family archive and testimonies by the filmmaker's relatives (linking it as well to practices of oral history). This is evident in the documentaries that are analyzed here, *From a Silk Cocoon* and *A Family Gathering*.

From a Silk Cocoon (2005), co-directed by Stephen Holsapple, Emery Clay III, and Satsuki Ina (who was also executive producer, scriptwriter, and narrator), tells the story of Ina's parents, who lived in concentration camps for more than four years, during which time she and her brother were born. Satsuki Ina had worked as a therapist researching the long-term impact of the internment of Japanese Americans (not in her own family, however, as her parents never spoke to her about their traumatic experience), resulting in the production of the documentary *Children of the Camps* in 1999. Shortly after this, her mother died, and she found 180 letters that had been exchanged between her parents while they were incarcerated in separate prison camps, plus a diary that her mother had written in from 1941 to 1946 and a haiku journal that her father had written in almost every day while interned in Fort Lincoln, North Dakota (see figure 4.2).[14] With this documentation, the filmmaker decided to tell the history of her parents, Itaru and Shizuko, a young couple that was sent to an internment camp shortly after they got married, while Shizuko was pregnant. Both took a stance against incarceration and rejected the Loyalty Questionnaire, leading to their internment in the special camp for "disloyals" at Tule Lake, their subsequent separation, and their delayed release in 1946.

FIGURE 4.2 *From a Silk Cocoon.* Flmmaker Satsuki Ina going through her parents' documents, photos, and letters.

From a Silk Cocoon can be understood in some ways as complementary and in others as contradictory to *Something Strong Within*, despite both films taking a microhistorical perspective. First of all, there is a clear difference in the type of archival sources used: in one case, visual archives (home movies) predominate, while in the other, written documents are the primary source. Second, in Ina's film there is a more explicit contrast between the macrohistorical and microhistorical scale, as the letters and diaries provide a chronicle that combines a narrative of the main public events with her parents' private reactions, fears, and anxieties. In this way, *From a Silk Cocoon* is charged with an affective dimension that appeals to the spectator more explicitly, an appeal that is further supported by the music and the poetic force of the father's haikus inserted throughout the film. Moreover, in contrast to the collective portrait of *Something Strong Within*, Ina's film presents an investigation focusing on a young couple, Itaru and Shizuko, underpinned by an explicit narrative structure that recounts their personal lives through the autobiographical voice of their daughter. In this sense, this film is closer to the Forgács's films analyzed in chapter 3, in its dimension as a representative fractal of the collective drama suffered by Japanese Americans. Finally, the storylines and emotional texture of the two films also take different routes: in contrast to the paradoxically ordinary and even celebratory nature of the home movies in *Something Strong Within*, Ina's film offers a detailed chronicle of a perhaps lesser-known aspect of those years: the hardships suffered by Japanese Americans who challenged the injustice openly.

The main distinctive feature of *From a Silk Cocoon* lies in its extensive use of written documents to give the film a microhistorical focus, mainly through the letters written by Ina's parents, her mother's diary, and her father's haikus.[15] The documentary also presents a few very significant official documents: the birth certificates of Ina's parents, who were both born in the United States, their application to renounce their American citizenship in 1944, and the document that gave them back that citizenship in 1959. This documentation contributes to the construction of an incomplete history, which the filmmakers sometimes fill in with brief interventions by an omniscient narrator who refers to some basic aspects of the public history, in a manner that is not altogether effective, as these interventions weaken the microhistorical approach (although because of their brevity they do not distort it excessively). Due to the lack of specific visual sources, the filmmakers often resort to various types of archival footage not related to the family and to frequent reenactments of the scenes described in the letters and diaries, especially in the second part of the film, in a way undermining its dramatic force as they evidence the excessive dependence on written material.

The film also makes use of another valuable documentary source: family photographs from those years. There are only a few of these, but all of them have a strong emotional resonance, especially the ones show-ing the two children in the concentration camps. These photographs stand out as mnemonic objects that physically connect two generations: the Nisei parents subjected to incarceration; and the Sansei children, who experienced it at a very early age, barely suffering the experience consciously.[16] This material connection gives shape to a particular trans-mission of the memory of the events, especially given that in this case the parents kept silent about the period. As Marianne Hirsch argues, family photographs constitute a unique expression of the intergenerational con-nection, bridging separation and facilitating identification and affilia-tion: "When we look at photographic images from a lost past world . . . we look not only for information or confirmation, but for an intimate material and affective connection that would transmit the affective qual-ity of the events. We look to be shocked (Benjamin), touched, wounded and pricked (Barthes's punctum), torn apart (Didi-Huberman)."[17] This more affective and intimate quality of the family photograph acquires a different dimension when it also serves as a means of intergenerational transmission of traumatic memories. This process has been termed by Hirsch as "postmemory," a concept already mentioned in chapters 1 and 2, and which characterizes the histories contained in *From a Silk Cocoon*, *A Family Gathering*, and *History and Memory*.

Postmemory is the mnemonic experience of the second generation, "those who grew up dominated by narratives that preceded their birth, whose own belated stories are evacuated by the stories of the previous generation shaped by traumatic events."[18] Hirsch proposes this new term in response to the need to characterize a process that is not strictly speaking based on personal memories, as this second generation did not take part in the events, yet they experienced them intimately, with a strong affective charge due to an intergenerational family connection, which also separates it from history: "distinguished from memory by generational distance and from history by deep personal connection."[19] Hirsch also emphasizes the mediated nature of postmemory (which is more obvious than in ordinary mnemonic experience), as it is highly dependent on mnemonic objects that connect to the traumatic past, with special value given to family photographs. The autobiographical documentaries analyzed here clearly involve a postmnemonic process, although their approaches do not stray as far from history as might be inferred from a more literal understanding of Hirsch's theory, precisely because of their microhistorical focus. This can be seen in *From a Silk Cocoon*, where Ina tries to learn about and understand the traumatic experience of her parents, exploring their story through a family archive that gives her access to a past imbued with a powerfully personal emotional charge, but without losing the historiographical perspective because it offers a microhistorical understanding of the events portrayed.

The postmnemonic perspective also helps to elucidate the value of the family photographs included in *From a Silk Cocoon*, which otherwise might be deemed secondary records compared to the diaries and letters. Hirsch highlights the importance of this type of archival source in her book *Family Frames* with an observation that is especially apt for this documentary: "Photographs in their enduring 'umbilical' connection to life are precisely the medium connecting first- and second-generation remembrance, memory and postmemory. They are the leftovers, the fragmentary sources and building blocks, shot through with holes, of the work of postmemory."[20] This "umbilical" connection has an added resonance here, because Satsuki and her brother were born in the concentration camps, and the photographs of them as small children in the camps underscore their dependence on the maternal figure (since their father was sent to another camp early on). At the same time, the limited number of pictures available reminds us of their fragmentary nature, their status as leftovers of those distressing years for the Ina family.

Similar issues emerge in *A Family Gathering*, which has nuances of its own, in an effective combination of constituent elements of postmemory, autobiography, and microhistory. The film's original thirty-minute version was released in 1988, written and directed by Lise Yasui, while a second, fifty-two-minute version (the one analyzed here) was produced for television in 1989, directed by Lise Yasui and Ann Tegnell (who is also credited as editor in both versions). The story of the Yasui family has been one of the most widely studied and disseminated cases of the Japanese American experience in the 1930s and 1940s, partly due to the impact of the documentary.[21] Lise Yasui uses in her film an autobiographical perspective to explore the history of her grandparents and their children. In 1905 her grandfather Masuo immigrated to Oregon, where he went on to become a successful businessman in Hood River, as well as something of a leader in the Japanese American community of the region. In 1912 he married Shidzuyo, a young woman from Nanukaichi, his hometown in Japan, and they had nine children. In 1942 they were both sent to concentration camps, where they would spend four years. After that they settled in Portland, but Masuo never recovered from the trauma of internment, and in 1957 he committed suicide. His granddaughter Lise did not learn of his tragic end until her father told her in 1984, while she was in the process of making the documentary.

The intergenerational transmission of a traumatic memory is even more of a central focus here, as is evident from this brief description of the film's storyline. The filmmaker also takes a more active role in this process, as the story is not focused so much on the discovery of a family's past, as in *From a Silk Cocoon*, as on the filmmaker coming to terms with her own identity within her family history. What distinguishes this film from the others studied in this chapter is precisely its articulation around this process of self-understanding, founded on a false premise—her memory of a supposed meeting with her grandparents that never actually occurred—and on her incomplete and superficial knowledge of the traumas suffered by her grandparents and their children during their years of incarceration. In this sense, this is not a typical process of postmemory, as the access to the traumatic memory was consciously blocked by the filmmaker's parents and their siblings through their silence about her grandfather's tragic fate, but also through their creation of an alternative history. The most paradigmatic example of that alternative history would be the home movies her father filmed in the 1950s and 1960s, for which he always provided a commentary that skirted around the tragic moments of the family's past. The documentary is thus presented as another interesting variation on the postmnemonic process, insofar as that process takes shape through the work undertaken by the filmmaker with this film.

The autobiographical dimension of *A Family Gathering* marks the story from the outset, with the filmmaker's "I" at the heart of the narrative—not in a solipsistic way, but as part of the network of relationships constructed around the family, with three generations as the protagonists. This reflects Alisa Lebow's observation, mentioned in chapter 1, that autobiographical documentaries are often constructed "in the first person plural."[22] At the beginning of the film a photograph of Yasui's grandfather appears on-screen, and the filmmaker begins her voice-over narration: "This is my grandfather, Masuo Yasui. Through my father's stories, I knew him as a patriotic American and a self-made man. What my father didn't tell me was that in 1941, five days after Pearl Harbor, my grandfather was arrested and taken away by the FBI. When I discovered this, I wondered what else I didn't know." This family history is thus presented as the framework for her microhistorical investigation. Although Yasui contextualizes it sporadically with references to major events in public history (often illustrated with newsreel footage), the film offers a study of this era on a reduced scale of observation, with a narrative structure that relates the family history of the Yasuis and the trauma they experienced following Masuo's arrest and the family's incarceration. To construct this story the filmmaker's main sources are interviews with her father, Robert, her uncles Homer and Min and her aunt Yuka, her father's home movies, and, to a lesser extent, the letters her grandfather wrote during his incarceration. The use of interviews with the protagonists of the past events once again links this film to the methods and sources of oral history, and to the context of a history of the present, where memory plays a key role in the construction of history because it is still possible to have direct access to witnesses of the events. However, their use here is mainly at the service of the microhistorical enterprise, as the history of the Yasui family is understood as representative of events that affected an entire community, offering a deeper understanding of those dark years in Japanese American history.

The other main source in this documentary are the home movies filmed by Lise Yasui's father, which in a way become the cornerstone of its narrative, even though they are used quite sparingly. These are movies filmed when her father was already an adult in the 1950s and 1960s, with no direct connection to the concentration camp experience. However, for Yasui they constitute the "umbilical cord" that links her to her grandparents, the medium connecting intergenerational remembrance. The filmmaker relies on these home movies to modulate her story, in a strategy that oscillates between a naturalized use and other more symbolic or performative uses. Their naturalized use is made clear practically from the beginning, when we see a home movie of a girl while the filmmaker's voice-over tells us: "This is me in 1959" (see figure 4.3). This is followed by images of her first years on the East Coast, with her maternal family, providing important information about her parents' interracial marriage. Her voice-over specifies this information, but adds another layer of meaning by offering her subjective experience of this multiracial background: "I was raised in Pennsylvania, surrounded by blue-eyed relatives from my mom's side of the family.... As a kid, I thought the only difference between me and my relatives was my Japanese name. I never felt different. This was the only family I knew" (2'). The extradiegetic music provides yet another layer, combining Western piano rhythms

FIGURE 4.3 *A Family Gathering.* Filmmaker Lise Yasui as a child with her mother's family.

with traditional Japanese elements, with the *shakuhachi* (a Japanese flute) and *koto* (a traditional Japanese stringed instrument), composed by a Japanese/African American composer, Sumi Tonooka, whose mother was also interned during the war. As Cassandra Van Buren notes, this musical hybridization functions as an "expression of Yasui's multifaceted experience living in the United States as a woman of half Japanese, half white ancestry," and also of the experience of her father and his siblings, "since they too live under the influence of two different cultural systems."[23]

As the film progresses, Yasui elaborates on this naturalized use of the home movies, underscoring their role as mnemonic objects that give privileged access to the past. But she also contrasts that role with another function given to them by her father, as a barrier to access to her family's traumatic past, a wall made out of the happy present of the domestic scenes. Her voice-over sums this up insightfully: "I expected that one day, my dad would tell me about the traumas of his past, but he never did. Instead he showed home movies. . . . For me, they represented the boundary between the father I knew and the father whose real feelings about his past might always remain hidden from me" (32'). This also serves to highlight the incomplete nature of these mnemonic objects, which conceal as much as they reveal, a problem that takes on special significance given that this film and others made by filmmakers of the Sansei generation, such as Janice Tanaka, Satsuki Ina, and Rea Tajiri, seek to explore these gaps and silences, to bring their family stories back from oblivion. Peter X. Feng identifies these gaps as a common feature of Asian American identity, which, in his words, "is defined not by history, but by gaps in history," because "the absence of information bespeaks a historical trauma that defines Asian Americans."[24] By examining these traumas and the reasons for their erasure, Feng adds, these documentaries "seek identity in the interplay between memory and history; in so doing, they further theorize the relation between family stories and the histories of ethnicity."[25]

For Yasui, her family's home movies actually play a key role in the intergenerational connection, which in a way seems to help her to get around the wall built by her father, as they connect her with her grandparents through a reminiscence constructed in her memory that never actually happened. This memory is presented as a kind of framing device for the film, as it is mentioned at the beginning and at the end, providing a fundamental interpretative key to *A Family Gathering*. The first scene shows home movies of her grandparents with her brother (see figure 4.4), while she recalls in a voice-over the evening that she spent with them in her childhood, before concluding by contradicting her own recollection: "Later, I learned that my grandparents never made such a visit, that I never met my grandfather at all. The memory was one I'd made up, a creation drawn from all the stories I'd heard and the images on my father's home movies" (1'). This "false" memory, illustrated metonymically with several of these home movies, creates the umbilical cord that connects Yasui to her grandparents, establishing a clear postmnemonic bond that acquires its fullest meaning when she learns about her grandfather's full story and his tragic end. In addition, this invented memory gives the home movies a performative quality as memory creators. This might seem to run counter to their more obvious interpretation as providers of transparent access to the past, yet home movies in themselves

FIGURE 4.4 *A Family Gathering.* Lise Yasui's grandparents with her brother.

already have something of a performative quality, not just because of the openly self-conscious nature of the filming process but also because of their mode of representation. As Roger Odin suggests, in a pragmatic perspective on this type of filmmaking, a home movie is not really finished until it is projected for the family, at which point the images are completed by the commentary of the different family members. In this way, Odin explains, the events captured in home movies end up constructing an imaginary, a mythical recreation of a lived past that fulfills the social function of securing the family institution.[26] In this sense, although Yasui never met her grandfather physically, she did meet him vicariously through the home movies projected in her home, taking part in that final stage when the home movie is completed with the family commentary. For this reason, in the final scene, which shows the same home movies seen at the beginning of the film, the filmmaker repeats the "memory" she created based on her father's home movies, reinforcing the quality of mythical recreation of the family past identified by Odin: "Although my grandfather died before I had the chance to meet him, I always remember that one evening I stayed up late listening to him talking into the night" (49'–50').

Yasui in fact uses her family archive for a purpose that transcends the traditional view of it as a repository of the past, in order to highlight a more postmodern understanding of it as a site of knowledge production. Of particular relevance to this approach is Terry Cook's explanation, mentioned in chapter 2, of the record as "a cultural signifier, a mediated and ever-changing construction, not some empty template into which acts and facts are poured."[27] These home movies are understood in this way, with a meaning emerging not only from the original context in which they were created—their filming and family viewing—but from their subsequent reuse in *A Family Gathering*. In this process, these home movies acquire different layers of meaning that render them more complex: from an initial naturalizing function as evidential records of the filmed present, to their symbolic nature as a barrier blocking access to the past, to their status as a vehicle for postmemory, connecting intergenerational memories marked by traumatic historical experiences. Hence, in the end, Yasui's narration expresses a new perspective on this family archive: "Now I watch these movies and everything looks a little different. I'm aware of the history that lies behind these images; and the moments of togetherness recorded here I no longer take for granted. It's a past my family made for themselves. And it's a past they gave to me." The images illustrating this sequence (48'–49') offer an excellent encapsulation of these different dimensions: from scenes that exude innocence (her cousins as children smiling or playing, or her mother with her and her brother when they were small children) to a scene of her mother trying on kimonos with her mother-in-law, as another reminder of the family's multiethnic context. These are images of "togetherness" that Yasui is able to interpret with greater depth at a point when she has a better understanding of the family traumas caused by the years of incarceration.

A Family Gathering thus offers an original microhistorical approach, supported by the autobiographical voice of Lise Yasui, the memories of her relatives, and her family's home movies. At the same time, it clearly exhibits the features identified by Feng as characteristic of these types of films made by Asian American filmmakers, with their interplay between memory and history, fusing the family stories and the histories of ethnicity in order to explore personal and collective identity. The awareness of the constructed nature of the family story—the past that her family "made" for themselves and gave to her—adds a final note of reflexivity to her approach to history, which also highlights the value of home movies as visual documents and underscores the complexity underlying their apparent simplicity.

HISTORY AND MEMORY

The questions raised by A Family Gathering in its examination of memory and history are explored even more explicitly in the last case study of this chapter, History and Memory. This thirty-two-minute film made by Rea Tajiri, released in 1991, has captured the attention of academics both for its historiographical approach and for its more auteurial nature, straddling the boundaries between documentary, experimental, and essay film. As a microhistorical work, Tajiri's film tackles the history of the mass incarceration of Japanese Americans on a reduced scale of observation articulated around her own family. The film succinctly recounts the experiences of her family, who were transferred first to the Salinas Assembly Center and then to the Poston concentration camp. But Tajiri is not concerned with merely offering a chronological account of these events. Instead, she explores two threads that intersect repeatedly over the course of the film: one that is more personal, about the scars that these events left on her family and herself, and the other more speculative, related to the narratives constructed by history and the audiovisual representations that have supported or challenged them.

The sources that Tajiri works with are very diverse. They include oral sources, which the filmmaker uses very sparingly: the recollections of her father, uncles, and aunts; some of her own recollections of family stories; and the ambiguous testimony of her mother, who seems unable or unwilling to remember those years. She also uses a few family objects of special mnemonic significance: a wooden bird carved by her grandmother and a wooden heart carved by her grandfather in Poston, her grandparents' ID cards from 1942, and a handful of family photographs (her father as a soldier, her family before the war, a couple of photos at the Poston camp, and others that are undated). Tajiri fills in her story with other audiovisual sources: photographs of the internment camps, official propaganda films and newsreels, fiction films, the home movies of other families, some reenactments, and brief sections of footage shot specifically for the film. She makes no effort to conceal the fragmentary nature of her family's documentary sources, and in a manner in keeping with the work of microhistorians, she attempts to fill in the gaps with these other audiovisual sources, resulting in the kind of combination of erudition and imagination, proof and possibility, that Carlo Ginzburg praised in the work of Natalie Z. Davis, as mentioned in chapter 1.[28]

The autobiographical nature of the documentary again underscores the human agency of the microhistorical enterprise, doing so with a markedly postmnemonic approach. From the outset Tajiri makes it clear that the events of the 1940s have left a scar on her life that she needs to examine and to heal. This is conveyed in a scene with scrolling text over a black background, which tells the imaginary story of the spirit of her grandfather watching her parents "argue about the unexplained nightmares their daughter has been having on the 20th anniversary of the bombing of Pearl Harbor" (1'). Later, she will elaborate on this in a voiceover, while we see home movies by David Tatsuno at another camp

(Topaz), in a metonymic reference to the place where her family lived during the years of their incarceration:

> I began searching for a history, my own history, because I had known all along that the stories I had heard were not true and parts had been left out. I remember having this feeling growing up that I was haunted by something, that I was living within a family full of ghosts. There was this place that they knew about. I had never been there, yet I had a memory of it. I could remember a time of great sadness before I was born. We had been moved, uprooted. We had lived with a lot of pain. I had no idea where these memories came from, yet I knew the place. (12'–13')

In this way, Tajiri makes the postmnemonic nature of her autobiographical work explicit; she has a memory of that past, she can "remember a time of great sadness" as her own, despite the fact that it occurred before she was born. The filmmaker returns to this idea again when she decides to visit the place she already knew, even though she had never been there: the Poston concentration camp. In a scene of this visit to the camp, which shows images of buildings in ruins, she speaks again in a voice-over of the nature of her personal search for her family's traumatic past: "I began searching because I felt lost, ungrounded, somewhat like a ghost that floats over terrain, witnessing others living their lives, and yet not having one of its own" (22').

Tajiri does not base this postmnemonic experience, as might be expected, on stories told by her relatives or material objects like family photographs. The most significant exception to this occurs in the brief sequence that shows a close-up of a wooden bird over a black background (12'). In a voice-over, Tajiri tells us that it was a gift from her grandmother to her mother, who kept it in her jewelry box and would not let anyone touch it. Many years later, Tajiri would discover a photograph of a wood-carving class at the Poston camp in which her grandmother appears, and thus she came to understand the mnemonic value of the object for her mother. Apart from this reference to the wooden bird, her postmnemonic experience is articulated with a more experimental approach, based on a subjectivity that pervades the whole film through her voice-overs, which recall these moments of great sadness that occurred before she was born and her feeling haunted by traumatic events that she herself never experienced. The intergenerational links that give rise to this post-memory become ghostly here, but real, expressed most clearly in the image she recreates of her mother filling a canteen at Poston (see figure 4.5), with the filmmaker herself playing the role of her mother. This is an image that, as Glen M. Mimura suggests, represents "a symbolic reconciliation that imaginatively restores the history of the internment to the narrative structure of personal memory and family history."[29] Introduced very close to the beginning of the film, this image becomes a visual and narrative leitmotiv: an image linked to the only memory Tajiri has of her mother talking about the internment camps, which she now decides to reenact, vesting it with a performative quality that is key to her narrative. It is an image that reappears several times during the film, as her particular way of constructing a tunnel of memory that can lead her into that traumatic past and reconnect her with her mother. It is an image

FIGURE 4.5 *History and Memory.* Reenactment of the scene of Rea Tajiri's mother filling a canteen at Poston camp.

that she has placed in a specific physical location, the Poston camp that she goes to visit, at the barracks where her mother had lived. It is an image that she has given a story, which she has created with her film, and which she offers metaphorically as a gift to her mother, as she says in her final voice-over: "For years I've been living with this picture, without a story, feeling a lot of pain, not knowing how they fit together. But now I found I could connect the picture to the story, I could forgive my mother her loss of memory, and could make this image for her" (30').

Consistent with her more essayistic and experimental style, Tajiri relates her investigation of her family's past to the investigation conducted by a fictional character in *Bad Day at Black Rock*, the only postwar Hollywood film to deal with the anti-Japanese prejudices that existed before the war and, more incidentally, with the incarceration of Japanese Americans. Its protagonist, John J. Macreedy (Spencer Tracy), comes to a small town looking for a Japanese American named Kimoko, but instead of finding him he discovers that he was killed after the attack on Pearl Harbor, due to racist prejudices and envy because of his financial prosperity after he had brought water to a barren land. Tajiri establishes some interesting parallels between this Hollywood film and her own family history, from the prosperity of Japanese Americans—who even brought water to the land at the Poston camp—to her mother's train journey to Poston, illustrated with images of Macreedy's train trip (20'). But the filmmaker goes a step further, linking Kimoko's disappearance with the fate of Japanese Americans: "Kimoko's disappearance from Black Rock was like our disappearance from history. His absence is his presence. Somehow, I could identify with this search" (26'). Macreedy will never find even a picture of Kimoko, Tajiri tells us in a voice-over, while giving us a fleeting glimpse of a picture of her father in the army in 1942 and another of her mother from around the same time. She does have a picture, she seems to say, but it is a picture without a story, because her mother was unwilling or unable to remember. This is why she creates the image that her mother does remember—filling a canteen with water—an image that Tajiri inserts into a story as a gift for her, but also as a way for the filmmaker herself to make sense of the traumatic memory of her family, turned now into to a personal memory, into postmemory.

Into this microhistorical investigation focusing on her personal and family experience, Tajiri interweaves a more openly essayistic dimension, focusing on the way history is told and the way that the relationships between memory, history, and archive are understood. This brings the film close to a postmodern approach to history, as Robert Rosenstone suggests.[30] As discussed in chapter 1, Rosenstone argues that the most genuinely postmodern history is being done by filmmakers, specifically in films like *History and Memory*: works with a self-reflexive dimension, making sense of past events "in an open-ended, rather than totalized, manner," without a classical narrative structure, and very conscious of the fact that the present is the site of all past representation.[31] Tajiri's film effectively conveys this postmodern historiographical sensibility, as through a highly self-conscious autobiographical voice the filmmaker offers an exploration of the past interwoven with the present, eschewing a conventional narrative structure in favor of a rich, complex network of sources and relationships that open up different pathways for the viewer. However, it is also an approach that upholds the referentiality of history, avoiding a skeptical view often associated with postmodernism, even if it does use deconstructive strategies to question the ways in which that history is told.

To achieve this, Tajiri makes decisive use of collage as a means of exploring the complex relationships between personal memory and public history, constructing a film that in Bakhtinian terms could be described as polyphonic.[32] With an essay style that evokes Jean-Luc Godard's *Histoire(s) du cinéma* (1988), the filmmaker weaves together complex relationships between image, voice, and text. An example of this can be seen in the previously mentioned opening sequence, where text describing an imagined scene scrolls over a black background. The filmmaker's voice overlaps with the titles, forcing the viewer to relate two expressive verbal channels that appear simultaneously. This tactic, which is used again several times, is complicated further when layers of images with different origins are added. This is the case in another elaborate sequence, where excerpts from *Bad Day at Black Rock* are inserted for the first time (13'–15'). The filmmaker juxtaposes images from the Hollywood film with footage of a girl skating at an internment camp (taken from a home movie), while we hear dialogue from the Hollywood film and the testimony of Tajiri's niece. This is followed by the sound of Tajiri's mother's voice over a black background, while a caption indicates that she is not able to remember, that she can only remember why she has forgotten. After this we see text scrolling over a photo-negative image, and finally we return to *Bad Day at Black Rock*, which connects with the present of Tajiri's mother through a motif of flowers. In such a complexity of layers and time frames, viewers must find their own way of discerning the meaning of the sequences, which are not always explicit and lack a closed or chronologically linear narrative.

Despite this sometimes labyrinthine structure, there is a thread that does give a certain continuity to this historiographical endeavor: a criticism of the official history, which condemned Japanese Americans to silence for several decades. Indeed, it could be argued that the film offers an interesting cinematic expression of a Foucauldian counter-history. As José Medina explains, for Foucault, "a counter-history reflects and produces discontinuous moments in a people's past, gaps that are passed over in silence, interstices in the socio-historical fabric of a community that have received no attention."[33] In opposition to the unitary vision sought by the official history, Tajiri presents a piece of history that has been kept in the dark or in shadows, positing a counter-history, which Foucault himself describes as "the discourse of those who have no glory, or of those who have lost it and who now find themselves . . . in darkness and silence."[34] In *History and Memory* this counter-history translates into the exposure of the mass incarceration of Japanese Americans (through an autobiographical prism), but also into a critical revision of the official discourse on the events and the popular discourse on American national identity, carried out with the tools of the essay film, combining word, image, and editing.

The deconstruction of the official discourse—shown mainly through newsreels produced by the U.S. government to justify the incarceration—begins with its juxtaposition against the microhistorical narrative of the filmmaker and her family, which foregrounds her bewilderment and suffering over the inexplicable nature of the government's actions. Tajiri emphasizes this critical reading the first time she shows one of these newsreels—"Japanese Relocation"—by superimposing the question "Who Chose What Story to Tell?" over the images (8'; see figure 4.6). Immediately thereafter, the filmmaker takes a step further by including an excerpt from the patriotic Hollywood musical *Yankee Doodle Dandy* (1942). This film highlights the mainstream discourse that promoted a unitary vision of the nation in times of war, made explicit by the musical

FIGURE 4.6 *History and Memory.* An image from the U.S. government newsreel "Japanese Relocation," with Tajiri's superimposed title: "Who Chose What Story to Tell?"

number shown, with its refrain "we're one for all, all for one," a message that clashes drastically with the flagrant violation of the rights of U.S. citizens of Japanese ancestry that was taking place at the time. Tajiri inserts the testimonies of an aunt and an uncle and footage of the camps filmed by the army, while maintaining the patriotic tune from *Yankee Doodle Dandy* in the background, now openly undermined by its collision with this material.[35] The final part of *History and Memory* makes reference to a third Hollywood movie, the only high-budget film made about these events, much later in 1990: *Come See the Paradise.* Although it could be considered a laudable effort by Hollywood to raise public awareness about events that had been silenced for decades, Tajiri is highly critical of this new piece of mainstream cinema. The filmmaker now expresses her deconstructivist revision through a voice-over reading a film review written by her nephew after the film was released, full of irony toward its commercial and excessively sentimental approach. In addition, the filmmaker intersperses images from *Come See the Paradise* with footage from the internment process at the camps and pictures of Japanese American families posing in front of the U.S. flag. The clash of documentary photographic records with Hollywood fiction thus visually underscores the criticism expressed in the voice-over toward the superficial nature of the Alan Parker film.

But Rea Tajiri goes further in her historiographical reflection, as she makes use of an openly reflexive strategy to examine how history is told. This happens very clearly in a sequence early in the film (5'–7'), where she proposes four types of relationships between historical events and the images that represent them. The first refers to images of an evidential nature: "There are things which have happened in the world while there were cameras watching, things we have images for." This category is illustrated with footage of the bombing of Pearl Harbor taken on location and a caption that reads: HISTORY. The second category is associated with images that are restaged in fiction films: "There are other things which have happened while there were no cameras watching, which we restage in front of cameras to have images of." This category is illustrated with scenes of the bombing from fiction films: one Japanese film, *Hawai Mare Okino Senjo Eigwa* (1942); and two Hollywood movies, the docudrama *December 7th* (1943) and the classic *From Here to Eternity* (1953). What is interesting here is that Tajiri also labels these scenes with the same caption, HISTORY, calling to mind the approach of historians like Robert Rosenstone or Marc Ferro, with their argument that historical fiction films constitute another way of doing history (see figure 4.7).[36] Tajiri then adds two more categories: "There are things which have happened for which the only images that exist are in the minds of observers, present at the time, while there are things which have happened for which there have been no observers, except the spirits of the dead." Her voice-over is heard here over a black screen, on which scrolling text appears, telling how a crew of workers took away the family house, because it was the property of "enemy aliens." There are no images for this scene, but it is a scene witnessed by the spirit of her grandfather, according to the text. In this way, the filmmaker implicitly raises the question of the reliability of the different types of representation and the ways that history is told. Tajiri seems to support a narrativist approach to history, which is also suggested in the question the filmmaker asks (as already noted above) over the image of the government newsreel "Japanese

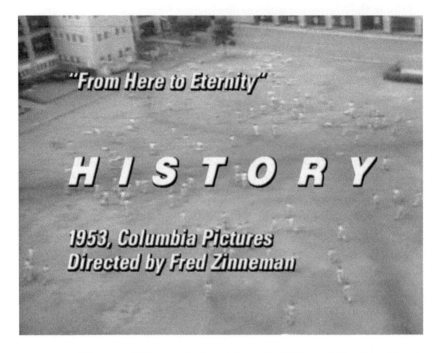

FIGURE 4.7 *History and Memory*. An image from the Hollywood film *From Here to Eternity*, labeled as HISTORY by the filmmaker.

Relocation": "Who Chose What Story to Tell?" However, as Janet Walker argues, the filmmaker recognizes the possibility—and indeed the necessity—of knowing the truth about what happened, as her "*insistence* on an irrevocable truth" is evident, although it is expressed through a "*refusal* of the realist mode," assigning a central role to memory, oblivion, and interpretation in historical processes.[37] In this sense, Walker identifies this film as a paradigmatic example of what she defines as "trauma films," a type of film that addresses traumatic events "in a nonrealist style that figures the traumatic past as meaningful, fragmentary, virtually unspeakable, and striated with fantasy constructions."[38]

The central role given to this traumatic experience makes memory a basic building block of the investigation in *History and Memory*. This constitutes a clear example of the assertion made in chapter 1, that the autobiographical perspective of these microhistorical documentaries makes personal memory the basis of the historiographical enterprise, establishing a specific link between the lived memory and public history. Tajiri insightfully articulates this personal memory through its different temporalities, with past and present dynamically intertwined, as suggested in the Greek concept of *kairos*. In this way, the film eschews a chronological structure to rely more on Deleuzian "crystal-images" that include this interweaving of temporalities and underscore the complexity of remembering.[39] It does this in ways so diverse that they are difficult to summarize here: by evading synchronous sounds and images; by overlapping expressive layers of text, voice, and image referring to different time frames; by including characters not anchored in chronological time, like the spirit of Tajiri's grandfather; or by constructing temporal relationships between fiction scenes and documentary records.

This personal/family memory is a memory that has been scarred by traumatic events. The filmmaker bares these family scars subtly, revealing them mainly through the frailty of her mother's memory.[40] The film could thus be understood as a kind of cure for her mother's amnesia, symbolized in the image of the canteen being filled up with water, which Tajiri offers to her as a gift, and at the same time as a remedy for the collective amnesia of American society, which had forgotten the trauma suffered by Japanese Americans. These traumatic scars also give the silences and gaps a special significance, returning to Feng's ideas about the nature of Asian American identity, and turns them into a driving force for the filmmaker's historical/creative work, as Marita Sturken argues: "Tajiri is compelled by the gaps in her mother's memory, by her own sense of incompleteness, and by the absent presence of the camps in national memory to counter the historical images of her parents' families' internment."[41] The filmmaker understands these gaps actually not as obstacles but as eloquent statements, in an approach that echoes the way microhistorians often deal with the scattered and fragmentary sources for their written works. This is made explicit in her voice-over comment about Kimoko's disappearance in *Bad Day at Black Rock*, which she compares to the disappearance of Japanese Americans from history. "His absence is his presence," says Tajiri, who considers the Hollywood movie in parallel with her own process, as a "search for an ever-absent image and the desire to create an image where there are so few." The movement between personal/family memory, trauma, microhistory, and public history is encapsulated in this reflection, which is paradoxically inspired by a Hollywood fiction film. It is yet another example of the formal and thematic complexity of Tajiri's film, which uses an experimental, essayistic approach to present a highly provocative variation on the microhistorical documentary.

The journey taken in this chapter from *Something Strong Within* to *History and Memory*, with *From a Silk Cocoon* and *A Family Gathering* as intermediate points, has revealed a diverse range of microhistorical approaches to the same historical event: the incarceration of Japanese Americans during World War II. It has also served once again to underscore the value of home movies as historical documents with a complexity not evident at first glance, by placing them in dialogue with other historical sources, especially the written or oral testimonies of people involved in the historical events. The filmmakers Ina, Yasui, and Tajiri have also undertaken intense explorations of intergenerational memory in the construction of their microhistorical narratives, offering thought-provoking variations on postmemory in their films. In doing so, they have enriched our understanding of history through microhistorical and autobiographical perspectives, where personal memory and family archives become a central focus.

5

RITHY PANH'S AUTOBIOGRAPHICAL NARRATIVE OF THE CAMBODIAN GENOCIDE

The Missing Picture

The Cambodian filmmaker Rithy Panh has garnered an international reputation for his films about the genocide perpetrated by the Khmer Rouge in Cambodia (1975–1979), which he witnessed personally in his teenage years, and which resulted in the deaths of roughly 1.7 million Cambodians (around a quarter of the country's population). Panh explores this event in depth in six films made over the course of more than twenty years: *Bophana: A Cambodian Tragedy* (1996); *S-21: The Khmer Rouge Killing Machine* (2003); *Duch: Master of the Forges of Hell* (2011); *The Missing Picture* (2013); *Exile* (2016); and *Graves Without a Name* (2018). In the first three documentaries, Panh takes something of a microhistorical approach to this historical period, which becomes rather more explicit in *The Missing Picture*. In this chapter, I offer an analysis of these films, beginning with a brief study of *Bophana*, *S-21*, and *Duch*, followed by a more detailed examination of *The Missing Picture* as an essayistic, microhistorical documentary.

A DOCUMENTARY INVESTIGATION OF THE CAMBODIAN GENOCIDE: FROM *BOPHANA* TO *DUCH*

It is very significant that the first documentary that Rithy Panh made about the Cambodian genocide, in 1996, centered on an unknown individual,

Bophana, who in a way represents a national tragedy, as reflected in the film's full title: *Bophana: A Cambodian Tragedy.*[1] Panh did not actually discover Bophana, as her case had already been made public by Elisabeth Beker, who dedicated a chapter to her in the book *When the War Was Over: Cambodia and the Khmer Rouge Revolution.*[2] Bophana was an educated woman who survived the horrors of the civil war only to become a victim of the repression of the Khmer Rouge that followed it. Married in 1975 to a former Buddhist monk turned Khmer guerrilla, Bophana and her husband were arrested the following year when the leader her husband served was purged from the regime. The couple were taken to Tuol Sleng—the infamous Security Prison-21 (or S-21) for disgraced party members—and executed a few months later. Years afterward a dossier on Bophana was found in the S-21 archives; this dossier was rather unusual, since in addition to the forced confession written and signed by all "suspects," it contained the letters Bophana had exchanged with her husband. With this material Rithy Panh decided to make a documentary exploring the painful history of his country through the specific story of this woman.

The background briefly outlined above suggests an approach that could potentially be classified as microhistorical. This is evident in the scale of observation, which examines the scars of those horrific years through the personal story of one woman, using a narrative structure that traces her life's journey. It thus reflects the kind of prosopography from below posited by Carlo Ginzburg and Carlo Poni, based on the investigation of a case study tracing an individual proper name not visible in public history.[3] The film also involves the filmmaker/historian working with archival sources that are quite limited but at the same time highly revealing—the letters exchanged between spouses—as they offer an original perspective that is antithetical to the prisoners' forced confessions. This documentation makes Bophana one of those cases that microhistorians label as the "normal exception," which function "as clues to or traces of a hidden reality, which is not usually apparent in the documentation."[4] Moreover, Bophana's story is framed within its macrohistorical context with the occasional support of archival footage of the Khmer Rouge regime and the explanatory narration of a voice-over, thereby transcending its individual nature and making her case historically representative. It is true that the voice-over adopts an omniscient perspective typical of expository documentaries, with a predominantly explanatory purpose, giving an impression of objectivity that is not normally a feature of microhistorical documentaries, where more room is usually given for questioning historiographical processes. This is probably because the documentary was made for television, which generally requires a more informative approach that is often supported by this type of omniscient narration.

Perhaps the most characteristic element of the documentary is the image of Bophana herself, taken from a mug shot, which becomes the visual leitmotif of the film (see figure 5.1). These images of prisoners are not mere descriptive photographs, because as Vicente Sánchez-Biosca explains, "they do not document a suspect, but produce a culprit," which makes them "performative photographs insofar as they transform reality."[5] Panh uses Bophana's mug shot to establish a particular filmic dialogue that infuses it with life, redeeming it from oblivion. Right from the

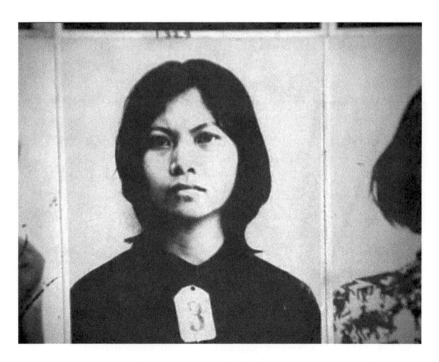

FIGURE 5.1 *Bophana: A Cambodian Tragedy.* Bophana's mug shot at the Tuol Sleng Genocide Museum (the former S-21 prison).

first few minutes, where we see the walls of the former S-21 prison (now the Tuol Sleng Genocide Museum) covered in mug shots of anonymous prisoners, the camera zooms in on this specific photograph of Bophana, with its frontal gaze, giving it greater depth as her story is revealed. This photograph ultimately acquires a symbolic quality that Panh maintains in his subsequent documentaries, becoming a visual icon of the Cambodian genocide in his films and in the collective imaginary of audiences familiar with these historical events.

However, in the last twenty minutes, the documentary shifts away from this microhistorical investigation of Bophana to broaden the focus to the history of the S-21 prison. We are shown the place where Bophana was interned and interrogated, although in fact this final part focuses mainly on explaining the history of this place of repression, through the testimonies of three people: two survivors (one being the painter Vann Nath) and one of the prison guards. After their testimonies, the scene shifts to the house of Bophana's mother-in-law, to conclude the film with her final testimony and with pictures of Bophana and her husband, along with an explanatory caption with the dates of their arrest and execution.

The change of focus in the final part of *Bophana* could be interpreted as a prologue to Panh's next documentary on the Cambodian genocide, *S-21: The Khmer Rouge Killing Machine*, released in 2003. In this film, which had a major impact in the documentary film community, Panh reconstructs the dynamics of the prison based on testimonies of a few prison guards and survivors. Particularly important among these witnesses are two who were already featured in *Bophana*: the painter Vann Nath and the guard Him Houy. The film could still be described as taking something of a microhistorical approach, although here Panh relies much more on the oral testimonies of the witnesses and on reenactments performed by the guards of their work in the same cells at S-21, without the presence this time of a voice-over narration. The archival documents from the prison—including Bophana's mug shot—again form part of the exploration, but more as catalysts for the testimonies than as objects of the investigation itself. The filmmaker also makes use, in the first part of the film, of propaganda films produced by the Khmer Rouge to provide the context necessary to explain what happened at S-21.

The power of *S-21: The Khmer Rouge Killing Machine* thus lies in the access it gives us to "everyday life" in the prison, through the dialogue and confrontation established between survivors and guards. In this way, Panh advocates an approach to history based on the testimony of its anonymous protagonists, who can provide alternative narratives to the official discourse, as Leshu Torchin explains: "Panh's *la parole filmée* is a form of speech that privileges the vernacular and the incomplete in order to counter the violent, artificial, and totalizing language (and language systems) of the Khmer Rouge. This speech is collective and polyphonic in opposition to the purity that characterized the cultural dictates of Angkar."[6] The account of the brutal treatment of the prisoners, of the torture methods, and—in the final part of the film—of the usual place and manner of execution, is approached with an almost naive attitude toward the people involved, both perpetrators and victims. To recover this past, Pahn's decision to have the former guards reenact their prison routines proves especially revealing. As Deirdre Boyle points out, these scenes, which are "neither scripted nor directed and only minimally staged," are central to the film because "we witness the past become present. . . . It is a moment of memory relived" that would never be effectively expressed in an ordinary interview due to its traumatic nature.[7] The documentary thus swings between the oral testimony of the protagonists and the performative dimension of the reenactments in order to rescue the victims from oblivion and to offer an ambivalent portrait of the executioners, providing a strange and awkward balance between empathy and condemnation.

Eight years later, in 2011, Panh released a new documentary, *Duch: Master of the Forges of Hell*, posited as a kind of sequel to *S-21*. In the earlier film, both the prison guards and the survivors make frequent references to Duch, the prison director, who was charged with ensuring the effectiveness of the machinery of death and the loyalty of the young prison guards under him. At that time, Panh was unable to interview Duch, who had been captured four years earlier. But a few years later Panh obtained permission and decided to interview Duch in prison in order to make a film about him. The result exhibits some microhistorical features, as it places the focus on this singular individual with a detailed exploration of his years as director of the S-21 prison under the repressive regime of the Khmer Rouge, a role that gives him a certain historical representativeness, immersing the spectator in the dark history of the Cambodian genocide.

The film is constructed using a strategy similar to that of *S-21*, as the central focus is on the interviews with Duch, presented in an austere mise-en-scène, with numerous frontal shots of the seated interviewee (usually behind a table). However, this interview is intertwined with the frequent insertion of three types of brief fragments: Khmer Rouge propaganda films (most of which were already used in earlier films); interviews with survivors and prison guards, some of them viewed by Duch himself on a computer; and reenactments of scenes from the lives of the guards at S-21. In this way, the film is constructed using overtly intertextual strategies, combining materials and references from Panh's two earlier documentaries on the subject, *Bophana* and *S-21*.

Despite the importance of the interviews, Panh also makes use of different archival materials for the construction of his film. In addition to the archival footage of the Khmer Rouge, the filmmaker gives a great deal of importance to written and photographic documents. The table in the interview with Duch is covered with reports and photographs that Duch examines and comments on, for example, checking over his handwriting as "proof" of the veracity of his story. Notable among these materials is Bophana's mug shot, which appears several times on the table. Panh expressly compels Duch to refer to the case of Bophana, which he comments on briefly, amplifying the microhistorical echo of Panh's documentary about her. In this way, *Bophana*, *S-21*, and *Duch* make up a trilogy, closely linked to the history of the former S-21 prison and the documentation found there, which gives us access to the history of the Cambodian genocide through characters who are not deemed important to the country's public history. However, in none of these films does Panh himself appear, either as the filmmaker or as a survivor of the genocide. This changes in his next film, *The Missing Picture*, which constitutes this chapter's main object of study.

THE MISSING PICTURE: THE AUTOBIOGRAPHICAL TURN

Rithy Panh's next exploration of the genocide perpetrated by the Khmer Rouge was not in the form of a film, but a book of memoirs recounting his experiences during the years of the regime: *L'elimination* (2012), which he wrote with the help of Christophe Bataille.[8] This autobiographical turn was expressed in cinematic form the following year with *The Missing Picture*, which received major international recognition.[9] The film was written and directed by Panh, but again with the assistance of Bataille, who was responsible for writing the voice-over narration. *The Missing Picture* is a film with a complex combination of formal and thematic layers, characterized by a hybridization of autobiographical and essayistic approaches: a historical chronicle of 1970s Cambodia and a deconstruction of the official narrative of the Khmer Rouge, a reflection on the filmic image as document and on the lack of images to tell a story. The focus here is on its status as a microhistorical documentary, with a study of its features as an autobiographical and mnemonic work, an examination of its critical revision of the Khmer Rouge's narrative, and, finally, an analysis of the archival materials used and their relationship to the "missing picture" that gives the film its title.

In *The Missing Picture*, the main element of continuity with Panh's previous documentaries is the reduced scale of observation, which again underlines its microhistorical character. The centrality of the proper name reflects a prosopography from below that clearly echoes *Bophana: A Cambodian Tragedy*, but with a more complex structure, based on an autobiographical premise that emphasizes individual agency as the means of exploring the past. Moreover, Panh offers a memoir with a clear essayistic dimension, interweaving his personal experiences with the official narrative of those years, and exposing the historiographical problems raised by this confrontation. In this way, the Cambodian filmmaker distances this film from a more typical "biography," a category that could be more easily ascribed to *Bophana*. Applying the distinction between biography and microhistory posited by Jill Lepore (mentioned in chapter 3), instead of a biographical perspective that highlights the unique nature of the individual and his contribution to history, *The Missing Picture* is more clearly microhistorical, as it gives the personal history narrated an exemplary character, in an effort to explain an era and a society through the individual story.[10]

Panh's autobiographical approach, while relying on a more essayistic treatment, is nevertheless constructed using a fairly classical narrative framework. The film begins in the present moment of his life, in 2013, when he is about to turn fifty. From a narrative point of view this opening sequence is best understood as a prologue (0'–4'), which is followed by the main part of the film, covering the period from 1975 to 1979, and a final section serving as a kind of epilogue (86'–93').[11] In this temporal framework, the diegetic time of the autobiographical journey follows an apparently linear chronology, interrupted by external flashbacks clearly signaled by the voice-over, which reconstruct or evoke moments prior to the Khmer Rouge regime. Over this narrative structure, Panh introduces different layers, with an essayistic approach that explores the relationships between his personal memory and the public history, combining scenes with a historical tone and others that have a more experimental or dreamlike quality.

Because of the autobiographical nature of the film, personal memory plays a central role in the remembrance of past events, giving rise to a creative proposal that can be described as a "memory film" in the most literal sense of the term.[12] The retrospective dimension inherent in all autobiography is conveyed here, as is common in this type of first-person film, through the autodiegetic narration of the voice-over, with the unique feature that it is a narration mediated on two levels, as it has been written by Panh's co-writer Bataille and is narrated by the actor Randal Duoc. Panh brings this first-person voice-over narration into dialogue with a rich and complex network of visual sources, thereby highlighting the most characteristic features of memory films, which, according to María del Rincón, Marta Torregrosa, and myself, can be summed up using three basic categories: subjectivity, temporal indiscernibility, and performativity.[13]

From the very beginning of the narration, these three features are hinted at, when the voice-over states: "I seek my childhood like a lost picture. Or rather it seeks me. Is it because I am fifty? Because I've seen troubled times when fear alternates with hope? The memory is there now, pounding at my temples" (2'). The subjectivity is foregrounded, with the "I" of the narrator, identified with the filmmaker, at the heart of the narration right from the beginning. The spectator is thus "submerged" (to echo the metaphor of the waves of the sea, which are shown at the start and end of the film) in the filmmaker's mnemonic journey, which is distanced from any objectivist pretension in its account of those years of suffering. Throughout the film the voice-over repeats the first person, this "I/we," often accompanying it with the verb "remember," emphasizing the work of memory again and again. The subjectivity is thus based on this autodiegetic declaration, in close dialogue with other film techniques, resulting in a narrative charged with intimacy. In the final part of the film Panh goes even further to highlight this subjective dimension, becoming even more detached from the chronological narration of the events, as reflected in the scene of a session with the psychoanalyst (85'–87') and the scene of a burial of a body, repeated in a loop (91'–93'), which ends the film. The voice-over in this last scene highlights the identification of the filmmaker/narrator with the invisible protagonist who throws dirt over the dead body: "Mourning is difficult. There's no end to the burial. . . . Every morning, I worked over that pit. My shovel hit bones and heads. As for dirt, there is never enough. It's me they will kill" (91'). In this way, Panh emphasizes the deep scar that those years have left on him, a traumatic memory that the filmmaker has transformed into a film narrative of unusual depth.

At the same time, *The Missing Picture* underscores the intrinsic relationship between past and present, both through the marked essayistic style and personal tone of the narration and through the work with visual materials. From the way Panh reuses the archival footage, which reverberates in the present with unexpected undertones, to the use of figurines and dioramas to reconstruct the past, everything points toward a conception of memory as an active process, in which the past is not "recovered" but updated in the present, saturating the narrative with a temporal indiscernibility, as the narrator suggests when he states that "the memory is there now." It is an approach that views memory and history as interconnected, through an understanding—as Geoffrey Cubitt describes it in a more general context—of "the past as it exists in its current awareness, a past constructed through the complex mixture of reflection and recollection, research and imaginative representation, that allows us the feeling of conscious retrospection . . . a past that makes sense for the present."[14] It is remarkable how fitting this quote seems to describe *The Missing Picture* in its articulation of memory and history. Indeed, Panh's past—his childhood—"seeks him out" in the present, and it is based on this premise that the filmmaker constructs his intricate story of the Khmer Rouge regime. It is a premise that effectively locates the narrative in a time that is more personal than linear, closer to the

Greek concept of *kairos* than to *chronos*. This intrinsic connection between past and present, the temporal indiscernibility that is such a characteristic feature of this memory film, is sustained on a labyrinthine structure with a Deleuzian flavor, where "memory-images" (to use Henri Bergson's expression) ultimately predominate, combining the actual and the virtual, and the present, the past, and the future.[15]

Panh never appears physically in the film and his voice is never heard in the narration (with the sole exception of a diorama in which his parents are watching television, which shows a real interview with Panh on the television). Nevertheless, he is present not only through the "I" of the voice-over but also through a figurine that represents him. Although the Khmer Rouge made the forced laborers wear black clothes, Panh presents his alter ego wearing a colorful shirt, an effective strategy to make his figurine recognizable, but also another way of visualizing the interweaving of memory in the revision of the past, which colors the past moments through their contemporary reconstruction (see figure 5.2). The figurines are also the most obvious way of giving the narrative a performative dimension—the third main feature posited for any memory film. Panh provides the first sign of this performative approach by including scenes where his and his father's figurines are being made,

FIGURE 5.2 *The Missing Picture*. Rithy Panh's figurine, with its colorful shirt, making him stand out against the black attire of his companions.

turning the clay into memory. His subsequent use of these figurines is not limited to placing them in the dioramas representing the more chronological narrative. He also superimposes them over different kinds of films, and places them in imaginary or dreamlike territories, thereby underscoring their performative nature as "producers" of memories in the mnemonic project posited by the film. This performative dimension is also evident in the use of photographs, which are discussed in more detail below. Panh includes only three photographs in his film: the mug shot of Bophana and two family snapshots with children. None of them are contextualized, as if they were being intentionally stripped of their referential function to emphasize their nature as traumatic memory triggers. It is a common approach in this context, as Frances Guerin and Robert Hallas point out in their study of the image as a witness to historical trauma: "The agency of the material image . . . is grounded in the performative (rather than constative) function of the act of bearing witness. Within the context of bearing witness, material images do not merely depict the historical world, they participate in its transformation."[16] In the case of the two snapshots, their inclusion exposes their nature as mnemonic objects that link the filmmaker to his traumatic past, as surviving remnants of the genocidal storm suffered by his family and his country in those years. The narration also reinforces this performative dimension more explicitly right at the end of the film. After stating that he has not found the missing picture, the narrator addresses the spectator directly: "And so I make this picture. . . . I hold it in my hand like a beloved face. This missing picture I now hand over to you, so that it never ceases to seek us out" (93'). The film, which nearly ends after this statement, is thus presented as a shared experience, as a shared traumatic memory that will haunt us always.[17]

DECONSTRUCTING THE OFFICIAL HISTORY OF THE KHMER ROUGE REGIME

The microhistorical character of *The Missing Picture* is the result of transcending an autobiographical narrative focusing on an individual, so that its memory work becomes a means of access to historical knowledge. To

this end, the change in the scale of observation inherent in the autobiographical perspective is complemented with an explicit reflection on the
historical past that seeks to present Panh's personal experience as representative of the hardships and suffering of the Cambodian people under
the Khmer Rouge regime. Panh approaches this investigation both
through the contrast between the macro- and microhistorical dimensions and through the revision of the ideological discourse of the Khmer
Rouge regime.

On a prima facie reading, *The Missing Picture* could be understood as
a film that continues Panh's investigation of the Cambodian genocide,
and in this sense numerous intertextual references to his previous films
can be found. But Panh also wants his film to be accessible to viewers
unfamiliar with what happened in Cambodia in the 1970s, which is why
he includes enough historical context to make his personal experience
understandable. Thus, at the beginning of the film (4'–7'), the filmmaker
provides some historical context, briefly mentioning his memory of the
outbreak of civil war, the victory of the Khmer Rouge, and the forced
deportation of two million people from the cities to the countryside,
beginning with the capital, Phnom Penh, where Panh lived. Throughout
the film other historical details are provided (if only briefly) about the
ruling Angkar party, about its leader Pol Pot, and so on, usually supported visually with newsreels produced by the regime. However, Panh
goes further than the mere historical contextualization characteristic of
a traditional expository documentary to delve into a more specifically
historiographical exploration, with a critical revision of the ideological
apparatus that sustained the Khmer Rouge regime, including both its
verbal discourse and its representations on film (analyzed below in the
discussion of the use of archival materials). This revision of the discursive practices of the Khmer Rouge contains an obvious deconstructive
intention, although distanced from a radical understanding of this
method as well as from a narrativist approach to history. With a stance
reminiscent of Carlo Ginzburg's dispute with the theories of Hayden
White, mentioned in chapter 1, Panh acknowledges the constructed
nature of historical representation, but with the cognitive confidence—in
his case, a confidence imbued with a personal urgency—in the ability to
gain access to the past and expose the lie that sustained the oppressive
regime and the genocide it perpetrated.[18]

Panh's revisionist perspective on the Khmer Rouge regime pervades the whole film. There are sections nonetheless where he addresses it specifically, to refer either to events that could be defined as the regime's "public history" or to what can be more strictly described as its ideological discourse. The first section where Panh revises the public history (18'–20') is a clear example of the complexity of layers of images and sounds that he brings into play, combining historical analysis, film essay, and autobiographical narrative. The section begins with the presentation of the leader Pol Pot and his closest supporters arriving at a party assembly. The images, which have an official and triumphalist tone, are undermined by jarring electronic music, which, however, gives way to the singing of the socialist anthem "The Internationale." The two pieces of music are ultimately blended together, and the image switches from the Khmer Rouge with their fists in the air to other, radically opposed images: a diorama of a school in ruins, followed by archive images of the S-21 prison, with its torture cells, filmed after the fall of the regime. Meanwhile, the filmmaker offers a rather cold account of how all that was left in the empty capital was the Central Committee and the S-21 prison, about which he explains: "Here they whip, they electrocute, they cut, they force-feed excrement, they get confessions. It all starts with purity and ends with hate" (20').

A second, similar sequence begins at minute 38. After describing how in his childhood he used to like going to film shoots and studios, Panh talks about how everyone in the film industry was murdered or deported. The new industry that replaced it only made propaganda—"A Khmer Rouge film is always a slogan," he says—and its only actor is Pol Pot: "He is the Revolution. His myth must be forged." Using footage from official newsreels, he explains how Pol Pot's myth was constructed, in a blend of orthodox communism and native Cambodian customs: "It's Marx and Rousseau, integral communism and the pure, original world. A perfect society." In this perfect society there is no private property and "the new people"—referring to the urban, educated population—must be re-educated in the rice fields or eliminated. This sequence has a less complex composition than the previous one, as it is sustained mainly by official newsreels with commentary by the voice-over, although there is a brief ironic digression with a reference to the rural workers who joined the Khmer Rouge, who are shown in a photograph that was subsequently used on the regime's new currency: "They look good on the new country's banknotes, which will never be used."

A third section, no longer quite so homogeneous, can be found from minutes 68 to 76. In this segment, there are three moments when Panh again explicitly revises the official narrative of the Khmer Rouge regime. It begins with a visit by Chinese leaders (68'), supported visually by the typical official newsreels, but with a voice-over that tinges the images with an unquestionably ironic hue: "The great leap forward [the slogan of the Khmer Rouge], is it not wonderful? Is not each day a celebration? Is not Kampuchea succeeding, through purity, through void, where the Chinese Revolution failed? Is not Kampuchea an extraordinary laboratory of ideology?" Shortly after this (72'), Panh describes his hard work at the hospital, and here he inserts a new reference to the communist paranoia of the regime, again deconstructing the official images shown in the scene: "The Khmer Rouge have banned capitalist medicine. They chop roots. They boil them. They experiment with traditional and therefore revolutionary remedies." And a little later (79'), he offers a reflection on the source of the conflict, in response to those who explained the Cambodian genocide in terms of a kind of social conformism that could be associated with a Buddhist mentality and its grim acceptance of fate. Panh critiques this explanation bitterly: "How do you revolt when all you've got are black clothes and a spoon, when you are lost, when you are hungry?" And he offers an unusually caustic reply: "Where were those fine minds then? In their books? In their lofty ideas? Here it is not karma, not religion that kills. It's ideology." Panh accompanies these words with dioramas of deported workers making their way through the jungle to their new workplace, as if to underscore the bluntness of his answer.

In this critical revision of the communist regime, Panh examines more explicitly the propagandistic rhetoric of the Khmer Rouge, which formed an inevitable part of his years of forced labor. Practically from the beginning of the film, the narrator cites slogans from those years, and quotes or paraphrases the Khmer Rouge's propaganda. The inclusion of these quotes serves an informative function (it is what they heard at the labor camps), but its main purpose is deconstructive, a purpose that clearly intensifies in certain sequences. The first such sequence begins in minute 7, after an account of the fall of Phnom Penh and the deportation of its inhabitants, when the narrator exclaims the official slogan: "Long live the glorious April 17th, a day overflowing with joy," while we see aerial images of the capital in those years, with its streets empty. This strategy is repeated in the subsequent account of their deportation. A paraphrase of the communist rhetoric of the new regime is occasionally mixed with more exact quotes of their slogans, such as when the narrator asserts, after describing how they were separated and dressed in uniforms: "We are the new people: bourgeois, intellectuals and capitalists, to be reeducated, to be destroyed. *You must embrace the proletarian condition!*" (10'). The sequence continues with a certain rhythmic structure, with further alternations between paraphrase and slogan: "*The Angkar takes care of you all, comrades! Brothers and sisters, fathers and mothers!* The Angkar is the organization. It is all. It is everyone. It is the young Khmer Rouge, the village chief, the head of the torture center, and Pol Pot" (11'). The paraphrase is only apparent, as can be seen, because it includes the deconstruction of this official discourse, through the juxtaposition of re-education and destruction, or the insertion of the torturer into an apparently fraternal and inclusive discourse. Meanwhile, the visuals show dioramas of the deportation process and scenes of forced labor, combined with newsreels showing multitudes of people marching around a collective work site, like human ants. The reality of poverty and hunger depicted in the dioramas repeatedly exposes the falseness of the slogans, such as the declaration "*Long live Democratic Kampuchea, a prodigious leap forward!*" over a diorama of forced labor. The voice-over continues delving into the ideological discourse until it becomes explicitly dark, underpinned once again by the same kind of jarring music: "Soon there will be no more faces, no more friends, no more love, no more father and mother. Soon there will be no more emotion, and even words will be transformed. Each being will be a revolutionary, or fertilizer for the rice fields" (12').

Another section of the film with an intense revision of the ideological discourse begins in minute 63, with a more frontal attack on its rhetorical construction. It begins with images from a newsreel of young people gathering rice, with serene, smiling expressions, leading the narrator to declare: "At last I see the Revolution they promised us. It exists only on film" (63'). The newsreel continues, showing the workers threshing the rice and loading it for shipment to an unknown destination, while the Cambodian population suffered famine, inciting the narrator's open complaint against the Khmer Rouge: "Did they not know? Did they not see? Could they not act? Does the truth lie in the glorious slogans? Or in these pictures that are not missing?" (65'). Once again, the contrast between the rhetoric of the regime and the ghastly reality is exposed. This contrast is even sharper in the next scene, which shows Pol Pot giving a speech—which is translated literally—on the wonders of the collectivist cooperatives, who enjoy "a perfect existence in terms of food, health, sanitation, culture, studies and education." Panh begins to question this description by juxtaposing it with images of the antlike workers at the public construction site, underscored by unsettling background music, before coming right out and contradicting it in the voice-over: "The reality is this: Straw huts. Drought. Exhaustion. Hunger. Neon lights to work by night. Speakers blaring slogans. Ideology was rampant in the fields" (66'–67'). This refutation is reinforced by the new footage that illustrates it, completely at odds with the official rhetoric, with workers in the foreground trudging along slowly as if in exhaustion.[19]

Later in the film, there is one more significant scene in the deconstruction of the regime's discourse. After describing more hardships and telling how it became harder to survive, Panh begins to remember what life had once been like around the central market in the city, with its abundance of food and goods, its hustle and bustle, and its laughter. The filmmaker illustrates this with archival footage from those years before the Khmer Rouge, showing a Phnom Penh full of life, into which once again he inserts his figurine as a visual mnemonic link. Then, in an abrupt leap, we cut to the same street, empty after the regime change. The contrast is underscored by the narrator: "It's the same street, lively, then empty." And over this graphic image of desolation and ruin, he concludes with a sentence that somehow sums up the scene: "I remember this world so imperfect and human. '2000 years of slavery,' said Pol Pot" (83'). It is a terse sentence that resounds like an anguished cry, despite being pronounced in the narrator's usual emotionally detached tone, making this scene to exude sadness in its gaze on the past while denouncing the ideological rhetoric of the communist regime.

As noted above, this deconstruction of the ideological framework of the Khmer Rouge is supported by the narrator's frequent use of irony. This strategy, which is often associated more with fiction film,[20] proves highly effective in Panh's hands, thanks in part to Bataille's carefully crafted narration. Irony is present in much of the juxtaposition of discourse and reality analyzed here, exposing the emptiness of the propaganda slogans, through both the verbal discourse and intonation of the voice-over and their contrast with the visuals. Sometimes, however, this ironic contrast is made especially obvious. One example can be found in a scene showing a diorama of an indoctrination session for the deportees, where the voice-over provides a detailed commentary on all the triumphalist rhetoric of the Khmer Rouge heralding a perfect world and a society without classes, and concludes: "Flying over this utopia is a red flag, and of course this truth: Comrade, you are so very free!" The contrast is immediate and openly ironic when he continues: "For now, you must obey, dig ceaselessly, move earth, move rock" (15'). Visually, an aerial pan shot from a diorama of well-cultivated fields, paved roads, and people on bicycles shifts to an adjacent one—separated by a wall that is more symbolic than real, separating the ideology from the reality—where we see the forced labor of the deportees, digging and transporting earth. Another scene with an unusual ironic contrast, which would even be comical if it were not still referring to the harsh reality of the deportees, shows the "re-education" of automobiles (42'–43'). It begins with a diorama showing a car being transported over rice paddies by eight workers and placed in the paddies to transport water; this is followed by archival footage showing an actual car being reused to channel water from a river up into the irrigation canals of the rice paddies. Meanwhile, the voice-over declares: "The Angkar never uses any object from imperialist or feudal society. Capitalist automobiles confess their crimes. They too are reeducated. These cars work toward edifying the new country" (43').

THE USE OF ARCHIVAL MATERIAL AND THE SEARCH FOR THE MISSING PICTURE

In *The Missing Picture*, Panh faces the inevitable problem of the absence of images of the genocide. In this sense, his work runs into the same obstacles faced by a microhistorian dealing with the investigation of cases that, by their very nature, lack the kind of archival support that the events examined in macrohistory normally have. There are no images of the mass deportations or of the systematic extermination carried out by the Khmer Rouge. Nor does Panh have a family archive to support his memories, apart from a few childhood snapshots. His main primary source therefore consists of his personal memories, which are expressed most directly in the voice-over narration. To compensate for the absence of more specific archival material, Panh makes use of footage from different sources. He often uses newsreels, most of them filmed by the communist regime as part of its propaganda machinery. He also uses footage filmed prior to the victory of the Khmer Rouge, showing the capital and its central market (and the Apollo 11 expedition), or taken after their victory, like the brief images of the S-21 prison. Occasionally, he inserts scenes from two fiction films: *Apsara* (1966) and *La joie de vivre* (1969).

Panh works with this archival footage to create a rich network of relationships, in an effort to give an account of the Cambodian genocide. In a certain sense, his approach falls within the parameters posited by Carlo Ginzburg for the work of the microhistorian, mentioned in previous chapters, when he argues for a combination of erudition and imagination to fill in the lacunae with documentation that is contiguous in space and time, in order to construct a better picture of what the era being studied would have been like.[21] The difference in this case lies in the fact that the protagonist of the story is the filmmaker, whose memories serve as its guiding thread. But this does not save the filmmaker/historian from facing a serious challenge in constructing a convincing and balanced story of those terrible years, evoking the pain of a whole nation through his microhistorical narrative.

Much of the archival material that appears in *The Missing Picture* had already been used by Panh in previous documentaries, thereby creating an audiovisual conversation that expands with each new film. Among these reused archival images, the most symbolic is, again, the mug shot of Bophana, an icon of his lifelong research on the Cambodian genocide. It is mentioned only briefly, as a visual response to the investigation into why the Khmer Rouge took pictures of the victims: "What would the picture of a dead man reveal? I prefer this anonymous young woman, who defies the camera, and the eye of her torturer, and still looks straight at us" (21'). It is an intertextual reference that is understood only by viewers familiar with his work; yet even without this context it is significant in itself, as it is one of only three photographs of victims of the genocide shown in the film, and the only one taken in an extermination camp. The filmmaker does not delve further into the exploration of the photographic archives of the regime's repressive machinery, not only because he has already done so in his previous films *S-21* and *Duch*, but because this film traces the narrative thread of his personal journey, and he himself never suffered incarceration in one of the regime's prisons.

To compensate for the lack of images available, Panh proposes a strategy that becomes a defining feature of his film, to the point that it even features on the film's poster: the use of figurines placed in dioramas. This approach places Panh's film in the tradition of animated documentaries, albeit far from the realist animation techniques that have made documentaries like Ari Folman's *Waltz with Bashir* (2008) so popular. These dioramas exhibit an apparent rigidity that gives them the aspect of *tableaux vivants*, theoretically quite distinct from an imitative realist aesthetic. However, Panh constructs an elaborate mise-en-scène around these dioramas, with a detailed shot-by-shot breakdown, supported by an evocative autobiographical voice-over, which gives these representations an authenticity of great persuasive force. In fact, the effect is so convincing that the footage from the films of the Khmer Rouge, despite the indexical quality of its images, seems artificial and lifeless compared to the powerful realist effect of the dioramas. There is a similar contrast when the dioramas are juxtaposed against other types of footage, as can be seen in one of the most curious scenes in the film, when Panh tells the story of the moon landing to the Khmer Rouge guards. What is surprising here is that the filmmaker illustrates this story with the iconic (television) images of the Apollo 11 mission, including Neil Armstrong's legendary first step on the surface of the moon. These images, which still have a strong impact today based on their indexical nature, acquire something more like an eerie, ghostlike quality here due to their paradoxical contrast with the "reality" of the suffering depicted in the dioramas, and to their connection to the dreams of the teenage Panh, who imagined himself stepping on the moon alongside Armstrong. The strategy of the figurines also gives the filmmaker considerable freedom to represent the past, as Panh moves fluidly between the past that functions as the frame story—1975 to 1979—and the past prior to the Khmer Rouge, shown in various external flashbacks. It also allows him to construct dreamlike scenes, like the scene of his brother or his cousins flying away, as well as more essayistic scenes, like the scene that sets up an imaginary dialogue with his parents, or the scene located in what looks like a psychoanalyst's office, where he is surrounded by all his loved ones.

Panh quite often combines the figurines visually with archival footage, constructing complex images that allow him to explore the relationships between memory, history, and archives. The filmmaker inserts the figurines into the filmic image through an obvious superimposition, creating a collage in which the photographic status of the image is fused with the artisanal dimension of the figurine in a hybrid expressive regime that highlights the constructed nature of the image.[22] Panh develops a range of variations of these hybrid images, with superimposed languages and time frames, through the visual fusion of dioramas, snapshots, and newsreels, with extraordinary expressive complexity in some sequences. One of these scenes that stands out for its tragic conclusion is the one recounting the death of three children—Panh's cousins—at the labor camp (47'–48'). In a particularly moving scene, we learn about their deaths through the voice-over, while the images show their figurines covered in a white cloth, like a kind of shroud, over which a snapshot of the three children appears (see figure 5.3), followed by a shot of their

FIGURE 5.3 *The Missing Picture*. A snapshot of the three children whose death has just been narrated, superimposed over the cloth covering their figurines.

figurines flying freely in an open sky. As Sánchez-Biosca explains, the photographic image of Panh's cousins acquires a redemptive value, as a kind of "redemption through the image," whereby "a recovered childhood emerges as a sort of resurrection not only of the little girl, but of a vanished world."[23] Panh uses a similar strategy in one of the external flashbacks, introduced explicitly by the voice-over: "I return to the past. To all those who died. My sisters, my brothers, my cousins, my parents" (58'). Over the dioramas of the family house with all its inhabitants appears the picture of the three children shown in the scene described above, followed by another snapshot with five children, and archival footage of soldiers and people in the street projected over the facade of the house (see figure 5.4). This blend of expressive languages might be considered reminiscent of the ending to the animated documentary *Waltz with Bashir* or Art Spiegelman's graphic novel *Maus*, both of which conclude with indexical images. Here, however, the two registers are not used consecutively, but are hybridized through the visual superimposition and blending of temporalities, creating genuine Deleuzian crystal-images in a highly effective filmic representation of personal memory. This can also be seen in two other scenes including hybrid images, both located in the final part of the film. In these scenes, Panh uses previously

FIGURE 5.4 *The Missing Picture.* Images of Khmer Rouge soldiers projected on the facade of the diorama of the family house.

shown archival footage of the deportees working at a public construction site, now projected onto two different dioramas: the psychoanalyst's office with Panh lying on a couch (91') and another scene of childhood memories (74'–75'). This last scene, in its brevity, exhibits a remarkable semantic complexity. Without a voice-over introduction, the story moves again to the family home, the music turns joyful, and the dioramas are filled with adults and children. But night comes, and projected onto the facade of the house we see the footage of the deportees working. Meanwhile, the narrator's voice takes on an especially evocative tone: "In the middle of life, childhood returns, sweet and bitter, with its pictures. Childhood as drowning. Childhood as a question: How is it that I am here? Why couldn't I have helped my loved ones more? Already in childhood, death is present" (75'). The present of the narrator meditates on the childhood evoked by the house, cut short by the rise of the Khmer Rouge and by the years of forced labor: three time frames fused in another display of the effective temporal indiscernibility that characterizes the exploration of personal memory, contained in this brief sequence that synthesizes the core issues of *The Missing Picture* with poetic mastery.

There is still one more scene in which Panh briefly makes use of the hybridization of dioramas and indexical images. This one shows his parents in a diorama, watching Panh himself being interviewed on television, talking about *Duch* (83'). It is a unique moment, with a certain air of *mise-en-abyme*; the first scene in which the filmmaker appears, in an intertextual reference to his filmography, which is also commented on self-consciously by his parents (as figurines):

> THE FATHER: Our son sure jabbers now. On and on he rambles. At least he's good with words.
> THE MOTHER: You'd rather he be a teacher, like you. But it's our story he's filming. That's us.

The father then goes on to criticize the lack of reference to the context of poverty before the war that partly justified the rise of the Khmer Rouge, which is then explained by the son/narrator to briefly contextualize this earlier stage of history. Nevertheless, it is still curious that the only appearance of the filmmaker's image should occur in such a self-referential way as this, once again working with the hybridization of temporalities and expressive registers.

The alternative or hybrid strategies used to make up for the absence of images ultimately point to the core of this film, which is effectively expressed in its title. Panh poses numerous questions and reflections in relation to this missing picture, which is in fact open to various interpretations, as suggested by Stéphane Bou, who proposes six possible meanings.[24] Without delving here into a detailed breakdown of those meanings, the question is worth further consideration, as in a certain way it encompasses all the other issues touched on in *The Missing Picture*. It is no accident that the film begins by showing piles of tangled film rolls. These give the impression of being abandoned images, among which perhaps the picture sought by the filmmaker can be found. A similar situation reappears later in the film (76'), when a pair of anonymous hands takes some rolls of old, rusted film out of some canisters, their images literally lost.[25] Panh thus starts with this direct reference to the materiality of film, which can fall into oblivion without the necessary preservation and cataloging, with the consequent loss of the images.

The next level of interpretation given the most attention in the film is that of the absence of images of the genocide. This is expressed tersely by the narrator near the beginning of the film, while we are shown a diorama with the transportation of the deportees: "Phnom Penh's deportation is a missing picture" (9'). In fact, this is one of the film's main threads of continuity, the one that compels Panh to make use of dioramas and to work with the supplementary materials analyzed above (propaganda newsreels, etc.). Yet Panh also gives specific attention to this absence of images of the genocide in several scenes in the film. One of the most explicit occurs when the narrator refers to the fact that the Khmer Rouge used to photograph the executions, after which he says: "I look for this picture. If at last I should find it I could not show it, of course" (21'). On other occasions, his references acquire a tone of complaint, like a mute cry against the silence imposed about the genocide. One example of this is when he describes the hardships, the hunger, and the disease they suffered, and finally asks: "Who filmed the sick people? Who filmed the pagodas turned hospices? The maggot-eaten knee of my bunk neighbor? Or the young woman who can't deliver, who screams all night, alone, hitting her belly, to death?" (70'). The images that accompany these questions echo them in a way, as we see the craftsman carving one of the figurines, which will make up for what nobody actually filmed.[26] His complaints take on a broader dimension on two other occasions. In the first, he recalls the moments when a plane passed overhead and he asked whether they might see them and help them: "Will it parachute a camera to me? So the world will know at last?" Then he concludes with resignation: "The missing picture: that's us" (46'). His lament becomes more embittered when he addresses the intellectuals of the West, some of whom very publicly supported the Khmer Rouge: "In Paris or elsewhere, those who loved our slogans, those who read books, have they seen these pictures? Or were they missing?" (57').

The absence of images of the genocide is presented as a denunciation, but also as a framework for another key level of interpretation: the autobiographical level. The missing picture is also the one of a lost childhood, which, as the voice-over stated earlier, comes back as a haunting image that pervades the traumatic memory of those years. Panh asserts this simply at the beginning of the film: "In the middle of life, childhood returns. . . . I seek my childhood like a lost picture" (2'). This opening reference is echoed explicitly in a scene mentioned previously that appears in the final part of the film, where the narrator repeats it in part, adding new nuances—"childhood as drowning, childhood as a question" (75')—while we see archival footage of the deportees working, projected on the family house. It is therefore no longer a question of the desire to recover a material image that could show what they suffered, but the longing for a biographical period that the war and the Khmer Rouge cut short—marked, furthermore, by the pain over the death of loved ones, parents, brothers, sisters, and other relatives who died during the years of the genocidal regime. This is expressed a little later in the film: "It's not a picture of loved ones I seek. I want to touch them. Their voice is missing, so I won't tell. I want to leave it all, leave my language, my country, in vain, and my childhood returns" (86'). The poetic tone points to a complex blend of temporalities that are also reinforced by the image, with that same temporal indiscernibility that characterizes earlier moments of the film. The narrator's reflection is now visually associated with the figurine of the grown-up Panh lying on the couch in the psychoanalyst's office, which is replaced in a dissolve by his figurine as a teenager with his colorful shirt. From there we go on to contemporary images of a child and an adult—who might function as his own alter ego in his childhood and adulthood—walking over arid terrain, while the narrator adds: "Now it's the boy who seeks me out. I see him. He wants to speak to me. But words are hard to find" (87').

Searching is a constant throughout the film: for the missing picture of the genocide, for the lost childhood, for the dead loved ones. It is thus hardly surprising that Panh should end his narration by referring to this search: "Of course I haven't found the missing picture. I looked for it, in vain. . . . And so I make this picture. I look at it. I cherish it. I hold it in my hand like a beloved face. This missing picture, I now hand over to you, so that it never ceases to seek us out" (92'). The film is a search that he shares with the viewers, in a thought-provoking echo of *History and Memory*, when Rea Tajiri gives the film to her mother as a gift to heal the gaps in her memory. Rithy Panh ends *The Missing Picture* in a similar way, but with an appeal to the spectator. In this way, the filmmaker fore-grounds the performative nature of his mnemonic enterprise, construct-ing his film as a personal process of understanding a past era, which he then shares with viewers so that they can understand the suffering of the Cambodian people and the senselessness of the evil perpetrated by the blind ideology of the Khmer Rouge regime.

6

IDENTITIES AND CONFLICTS IN
ISRAEL AND PALESTINE

Israel: A Home Movie, For My Children, My Terrorist,
My Land Zion, and *A World Not Ours*

The history of Israel and Palestine is characterized by a complex network of conflicting relationships, wars, and peace efforts that continue today with no sign of a conclusion. This troubled history has been reflected in numerous documentaries made mainly by Israeli filmmakers, but also by Palestinians. Some of these films focus on the current situation, others seek to explain the public history of the region (its "macrohistory"), and still others offer approaches from a microhistorical perspective. In this chapter, I analyze films that fall into this last category, exploring the microhistorical approaches they take to the history of these peoples and the conflicts they continue to face.

In the diverse context of Israeli and Palestinian documentary production, it is not always easy to discern which films reflect a microhistorical approach, as there are many that deal with contemporary history that seem to fit into this category, since their perspectives bear little relation to public history. Two such possibilities are the well-known films *Happy Birthday, Mr. Mograbi* (Avi Mograbi, 1999) and *Waltz with Bashir* (Ari Folman, 2008), although on closer analysis neither of these films seems to qualify as microhistorical. With *Happy Birthday, Mr. Mograbi*, Avi Mograbi has made a very personal film about Israel that is rather hard to classify. Taking as its premise the country's fiftieth anniversary, the film adopts an essay style that ultimately dominates the narrative and pushes the historiographical perspective into the background. In *Waltz with Bashir*, Ari Folman presents a more explicit exploration of the past, focusing on the Lebanon War of 1982. Based on interviews conducted by the filmmaker, mostly with soldiers like him who took part in the war, the film is more about memory and trauma than about history, made with the visual freedom offered by animation, with its versatility for changing from a realist to a dreamlike register, and from present to memory. Although the film is based on the testimonies of anonymous soldiers recalling the war, Folman puts the focus less on the task of recounting the past than on the inner wounds caused by the war, on its protagonists' traumas, repressed memories, and processes of mnemonic recovery.[1]

Falling more clearly into the category of microhistory are the films that are analyzed in detail in this chapter: *Israel: A Home Movie, For My Children, My Terrorist, My Land Zion*, and *A World Not Ours*. Although they differ in various ways from the most paradigmatic cases of a microhistorical approach, all certainly offer a meaningful historiographical reflection articulated chiefly around the tension between macro- and microhistorical scales of observation. In a manner similar to the films on Japanese American incarceration analyzed in chapter 4, these five films show how different microhistorical approaches can examine the same historical events, although the historical period in this case is much broader, running from the 1930s through to the start of the twenty-first century. The chapter begins with an analysis of *Israel: A Home Movie*, a collective portrait created using different collections of home movies. It then turns the focus to microhistorical explorations conducted from autobiographical perspectives, beginning with an examination of the diaristic approaches of some films dealing with similar issues, followed by a close analysis of the documentaries of two filmmakers with some significant parallels: Michal Aviad's *For My Children* and Yulie Cohen's *My Terrorist* and *My Land Zion*. The chapter concludes by considering the Palestinian context, with an analysis of *A World Not Ours*, a chronicle by Mahdi Fleifel that introduces the spectator to the microhistory of a Palestinian refugee camp.

ISRAEL: A HOME MOVIE

Israeli documentary productions dealing with the country's contemporary history do not generally make use of home movies as an archival source. The most notable exception to this can be found in the film *Israel: A Home Movie* (2012).[2] Directed by Eliav Lilti and Arik Bernstein, this film offers an overview of the contemporary history of Israel from the 1930s through to the late 1970s—the historical period when home movies were filmed using small-gauge cameras. Apart from a nonhistorical prologue and epilogue, the film follows a chronological order, with onscreen captions indicating different years. The visuals are comprised mainly of home movies and, more occasionally, amateur films.[3] The soundtrack consists of voice-over testimonies by the people featured in the footage, often accompanied by extradiegetic music. With these elements, the film might be expected to constitute a typical case of a microhistorical documentary constructed as a collective story, in the style of *Something Strong Within*. Indeed, this is what Bernstein seems to suggest: "What we're showing is an alternative way of storytelling, an alternative historiography."[4] However, Lilti and Bernstein's film seems more ambiguous, as revealed by an analysis of the scale of observation adopted and the role given to the home movies in the film.

The scale of observation seems more clearly microhistorical at the beginning of the film, as the first years (up to 1938) focus on family stories, especially those of the Zaltzmans and the Moussaieffs. But, after 1938, this focus begins to blur somewhat, taken over by scenes related more to Israel's public history, referring to the wars of those years (the War of Independence, the Six-Day War, the Yom Kippur War), but also to other events, such as Independence Day parades (of which three are shown: 1948, 1967, and 1968). This results in an abundance of images of soldiers, tanks, transit camps, Palestinians leaving their homes, and so on, which are often included without any specific connection to the narration of the testimonies, although all were supposedly filmed by home moviemakers. This is why a sequence like the one showing the snowfall of 1951 (38'), which of course caught the interest of the home moviemakers, stands out as something of an exception to the general structure of a film that seems otherwise much more concerned with following the country's political events. The end result is somewhat ambiguous in terms of its historiographical intention, due to the hybrid quality resulting from the conflation of the microhistorical perspective derived from the use of home movies and amateur films (and the voice-over commentary by the people featured in it) and the macrohistorical character of many of the events shown in the film. This hybridization is more visible in certain sequences that reflect a singular mixture of scales of observation, which warrants a more detailed analysis here.

The most interesting instances of this hybridization of scales occur when macrohistory interferes in the home moviemakers' "domestic" scenes. One example can be found in a sequence referring to the *Altalena* Affair, when the Irgun paramilitary group brought a ship filled with fighters and weapons to Israel in 1948, leading to a brief armed conflict between Irgun's forces and the newly created Israel Defense Forces, and ending with the ship running aground on the shores of Tel Aviv. The documentary includes some home movies of the Zaltzman family (25') showing the mother and a young daughter bathing at the beach with the grounded ship, the *Altalena*, looming in the background, in a striking visual contrast between scales of observation within the same frame. Meanwhile, two daughters explain the episode and argue about whether they went there merely to swim at the beach or because their father wanted to give them a history lesson, while the home movie seems to support the first opinion.

Later in the film, there is a section dedicated to showing the immigration of Diaspora Jews to the new State of Israel, presented mainly through the stories of three different families: one from Yemen, one from Iraq, and one from South Africa. The home movies and the voice-overs by people featured in them recounting their memories give this section a clear microhistorical tone, although its brevity prevents a more in-depth development of this historiographical approach based on these family stories. The story of the Iraqi family (35'–36') is the most powerful, as, despite its brevity, we hear the testimonies of four family members, conveying an ambiguous message, as the images in Iraq show them happy and with a very comfortable lifestyle, while the testimonies reflect different perspectives on the immigration experience. While one family member asserts that "we had a good life, until we decided to go to Israel; then things got bad," another explains that "I wanted to come to Israel, and I had no choice."

In the section covering the period after Israel's seizure of additional Palestinian territories in the Six-Day War, the documentary includes two sequences that also reflect this hybridization of scales very effectively. The first is Miriam Lulu's wedding, shown through the traditional images of bride and groom before and after the ceremony (54'–56'). What made this wedding unique was that it was the first to be held in the Cave of Machpelah, which had just been reclaimed by the Jews after two thousand years, generating so much excitement that the wedding turned into something of a national event. The sequence that follows, about Jews visiting the newly occupied territories, is even more interesting and unsettling (56'–57'). Here the travelogue tone typical of many home movies is mixed with the frequent appearance of military images: a tank, projectiles, a cemetery for Syrian soldiers, and so on. The voice-over commentary underscores the singular nature of the situation: "We went to the territories, but it wasn't comfortable. People weren't friendly."

In two other segments, this blending of scales appears even more explicitly. The first is in the section about the Yom Kippur War, which begins with a group of friends on a trip to Ras Muhammad (on the southern tip of the Sinai Peninsula), who happen to see (and film) an Egyptian MiG flying overhead, shot down moments later by an Israeli Phantom (71'). This is how the group discovers that war has just broken out, prompting them to leave the campsite quickly to get back home and enlist in the army, as the home moviemaker recounts in the voice-over. The other segment consists of home movies filmed by Udi Dayan, son of the well-known military and political leader Moshe Dayan. Here the hybridization is even more obvious, with a case that is also relatively typical: the portrayal of a public person, Moshe Dayan, through home movies, with the novelty that they are also commented on by his son Udi in a voice-over. Of the assortment of scenes included here, the most interesting in this context is the one where Udi shows a busy market where photographs of his father are displayed (hanging up on stalls, stuck to weighing scales, etc.) after the Six-Day War, when he was at the height of his popularity (63'; see figure 6.1).

The combination of the home movies and the voice-over commentary amplifies the hybridization of historiographical scales in diverse ways. A primary marker of the home movies is provided by deictic expressions—like the typical "that's me"—which anchor the images in a specific time and space, linking them explicitly to the person speaking in the voice-over. This enhances their air of authenticity by eliminating their anonymity, often serving to introduce the home moviemaker. A new layer of meaning is added when the commentary provides the historical context

UDI DAYAN

This was after the Six-Day War.

FIGURE 6.1 *Israel: A Home Movie.* An image from Udi Dayan's home movies, when his father, Moshe Dayan, was at the peak of his popularity after the Six-Day War.

necessary to better understand the home movies. In this sense, it is highly significant that this commentary often reflects the dreams of the speaker at the time the footage was taken, sometimes with a connotation of disappointment resulting from the passage of time and the realization that the conflict is still ongoing. This is evident in various comments about the years before independence, when Arabs and Jews lived together in relative harmony; and in the remarks made in relation to different wars, especially the Six-Day War: "We were sure it would be the last war," or "I thought we were starting a new life." One of the most self-conscious of such comments is made by the journalist Benya Binnun, in the sequence on the three-day march through the occupied territories, masterfully put together by Lilti and Bernstein and their editors Roni Klimowski, Avigail Avshalom-Dahan, and Tania Schwartz. Binnun highlights the sense of celebration and recalls the friendly, smiling attitude of the Arabs—about which he muses "Could it have been different?"—but then shows the shock that the occupation represented for the Arabs, expressed by one Palestinian interviewed as "a knife put in our heart" (62'). It is not just this statement but images like the one of a Palestinian tilling his land while Israeli soldiers march past along an adjacent road that deconstruct the ingenuousness of the "Could it have been different?," giving the whole sequence a strong ambivalence (see figure 6.2).

Despite this interesting hybridization of scales of observation, *Israel: A Home Movie* blurs another of the basic features of the microhistorical approach, that is, the centrality of human agency, which, together with the microscale of observation, generally entails that the historical investigation focuses on an individual or a family. While it is true that this feature is also absent from the film *Something Strong Within*, analyzed in chapter 4, which offers a collective portrait of Japanese Americans incarcerated during World War II based on various collections of home movies, the absence of focus on a single individual or family in that film was compensated for by the portrait of a highly unique historical event, with similar

FIGURE 6.2 *Israel: A Home Movie*. Israeli soldiers marching in the newly occupied territories after the Six-Day War, while a Palestinian works on his land.

characteristics for all the people incarcerated, and restricted to a limited time period of three to four years. In *Israel: A Home Movie*, there is also an emphasis on the personal and familial perspective of the home moviemakers, who are also for the most part unknown individuals outside the public sphere. But the fact that the documentary covers a historical period of several decades and makes use of such a large number of witnesses has the effect of blurring the centrality of human agency. As many as forty-two different people are mentioned by name in the captions accompanying the voice-over testimonies, leaving no time to explore any of them in depth, resulting in a kaleidoscopic view that makes the film quite distinct from a typical microhistorical investigation. There are certainly a few participants who receive a little more attention, such as Tzfira Eyal (Zaltzman), whose name appears in the titles on seven occasions, making her the dominant narrator for the 1930s and 1940s. In the three decades after that, Benya Binnun's name also appears on five occasions, giving him a relatively prominent position. But none of the individuals featured are given sufficient continuity to develop their history with the depth necessary to make them the focus of a microhistorical study.

Moreover, as the documentary progresses, the macrohistorical approach seems to become increasingly predominant, so that by the end, the spectator is left with the impression that this is a film about the public history of the country, with an emphasis more on the "Israel" than on the "home movie" of the title. This is not only because there are a lot of sequences with home movies that are not explicitly associated with a specific home moviemaker, so that they might be confused with amateur or professional footage if they did not often reveal their "imperfect" nature, with excessive camera movements, extremely brief shots, or gazes to camera by the people filmed. It is also due to the increasing attention given to political and public events, as noted above, that has the effect of blurring the microhistorical approach. Already by the halfway point of the documentary, in the year 1967, an eight-minute sequence (46'–54') is dedicated to the Independence Day parade, the Six-Day War, and the subsequent forced displacement of Palestinians. Later, a fourteen-minute sequence is dedicated to the Yom Kippur War (71'–85'). And, apart from the nonhistorical epilogue, the documentary effectively ends with the presentation of two macrohistorical events: the 1977 electoral victory of the Likud Party and Anwar Sadat's visit to Israel (89'–90').

In the epilogue, Lilti and Bernstein highlight the importance of home movies in a context unrelated to historical research, a rather paradoxical and even contradictory conclusion, given their use in the film as visual archive materials to support its historical chronicle. They begin this section with the words of TV host Meni Peer, who argues for the truth value of home movies compared to the massive impact of television, which "didn't film the truth, it filmed a staged truth" (91'). Immediately thereafter begins the epilogue proper, articulated around a poem by Raquel Chalfi about the passage of time, which make a series of comparisons of two different stages of life in a rhythmic manner. These lines are illustrated with home movies of couples, of children and adults, smiling to the camera or kissing, in black and white and in color, but all imbued with a marked sense of the passage of time. This foregrounds the value of the film image as a medium that freezes the moment and embalms time, in a clear echo of the Bazinian understanding of cinema. It is a conclusion with an undeniable poetic charge that pays a heartfelt tribute to home movies, but it is a tribute that seems slightly at odds with the historicized value they have been given throughout the film. It is in this tension between family document and historical document, between microhistorical and macrohistorical perspective, between the truth value of home movies and their amplification through oral testimony, that *Israel: A Home Movie* is articulated as a documentary whose very title carries a tension that its filmmakers handle with uneven success, with a result that is, in any case, an innovative contribution to Israeli historical documentary cinema.

THE DIARY/AUTOBIOGRAPHICAL PERSPECTIVE ON THE PALESTINIAN-ISRAELI CONFLICT

As indicated above, the other documentaries that are studied here all take an autobiographical perspective: *For My Children, My Terrorist, My Land Zion*, and *A World Not Ours*. These films give more attention to the present moment than the autobiographical documentaries analyzed in previous chapters do, because the key questions they explore are contemporary. But to answer those questions, the filmmakers need to examine and understand a recent past that is intimately intertwined with the conflicts that currently afflict the region. They are questions that are always posed from personal perspectives, although in direct relation to macrohistorical contexts: the ongoing Palestinian-Israeli conflict, the identity of the new State of Israel, or the precarious future of a possible Palestinian state. In this way, as Linda Dittmar points out, invoking a well-known principle that emerged out of the feminist movement but has had broader repercussions, these films situate "the personal within the political, and the political within the personal quite deliberately."[5]

The present is usually explored in these films through diaristic approaches. This is an approach that can also be found in other Israeli documentaries with similar themes and structures, but that are not strictly classifiable as microhistorical documentaries because of the absence of a significant examination of the historical past. Examples include David Perlov's diary films and documentaries like *Out of Love . . . Be Back Shortly, Another Land*, and *5 Broken Cameras*. Although these films all contain an interesting combination of macro- and microscales of observation, they are marked by a focus on the present, on the account of a witness, rather than on the perspective of a historian conducting an analysis of a past period. Nevertheless, it is worth offering a brief overview of these documentaries here to identify elements in each that come close to a microhistorical approach.

The film diary format is rather unusual in nonfiction cinema and bears a number of features that distinguish it from standard autobiographical practices. These particularities are analyzed in more detail in chapter 7, which is dedicated to the films of Jonas Mekas, but for the discussion here it is useful to distinguish between two approaches visible in the films mentioned above: diary films and documentaries with a "journal entry approach," a term proposed by Jim Lane.[6] Diary films reflect a style closer to written diaries, as they consist of footage filmed at regular intervals, which is subsequently edited while maintaining the character of the images as a visual diary, generally supported by autobiographical voice-over commentary. Documentaries made using a journal entry approach have a diaristic temporal and formal structure, but their time frame is more restricted, with a beginning and an end related to the specific project, which is usually established before filming begins. This distinguishes them clearly from diary films because, as Philippe Lejeune explains, diaries have no ending because there is always an expectation that they will continue; they look to the future, in contrast to autobiographies, which are written from the perspective of the end with a gaze toward the past.[7]

The diary films of David Perlov are a clear example of the first approach. They consist of two different series: *Diary* (from 1973 to 1983, divided into six parts) and *Updated Diary* (from 1990 to 1999, in three parts). In these two series, the Brazilian Israeli filmmaker has put together a film diary of his life, focusing mainly on everyday situations with his family, friends, his native Brazil, and so on. However, in his diary entries on life in Israel, Perlov also includes important political events. For example, in his first chapter he includes the Yom Kippur War and Egyptian president Anwar Sadat's visit to Israel. The end of part 3 and much of part 4 are dedicated to the Lebanon War and to various protest demonstrations. And much of part 2 of *Updated Diaries* is taken up with public history, such as Perlov's recollections of Yitzhak Rabin's assassination and the electoral victories of Bibi Netanyahu in 1996 and of Ehud Barak in 1999. The distinctive aspect of Perlov's films is the personal perspective he offers on macrohistorical events, through both the footage filmed and his reflections in the autobiographical voice-over. Yet these sections are firmly anchored in the present of his diary entries, with more of an emphasis on his role as an eyewitness of public history (either as a participant or as a television viewer), at the expense of the more analytical, retrospective view normally associated with the work of the historian.

In the case of films structured according to a journal entry approach, similar dynamics can be found in the documentary *Out of Love . . . Be Back Shortly* (1997) by Dan Katzir (a former student of Perlov's at Tel Aviv University). This documentary offers an autobiographical account of his life in Tel Aviv from 1994 to 1997, interweaving his everyday experiences (focusing on his romance with Iris) with political events of the 1990s, such as the terrorist attacks of those years, the peace treaty with Jordan, and the assassination of Rabin. Like Perlov's, Katzir's perspective is closely linked to the present of his life, although its interesting combination of the private/family and public spheres gives it a clearer association with a microhistorical approach. The film effectively captures the hopeful perspective of a young filmmaker (this was his first feature film) who has found love, and who at the same time is optimistic about his country after the Oslo Accords, an optimism undermined by frustration when Rabin is assassinated. The assassination is established as the key event in dialogue with the personal love story (forming the central pillar of its narrative structure), not only for the impact it had on his generation but also because it ends up slipping indirectly into his autobiography when his girlfriend joins the army and meets one of Rabin's granddaughters there. The filmmaker actually highlights this public episode as the axis around which his autobiographical narrative turns: "I think that everyone remembers the hope that we had then. My film is trapped between these two poles of sadness and this desire for something. For me it's love. I think this film belongs to Yitzhak Rabin because his time in office will be remembered as a time of hope and my film is filled with this hope."[8]

One year later, Amit Goren released the documentary *Another Land* (1998), a film similar to Katzir's in its combination of personal/family elements and public history. The Israeli filmmaker structures his film as a diary of his life from 1992 to 1996, with a few brief final entries from 1997 and 1998. With a style reminiscent of Ross McElwee's *Sherman's March*, Goren narrates the ups and downs of his family life: his romantic relationships (his separation from his wife, Tal, and two subsequent partners) and his relationships with his two children, his siblings, and his parents (who travel from New York to Tel Aviv every summer). But this family chronicle is interwoven with key episodes in public history: the First Intifada, the Oslo Accords, Rabin's assassination, and so on. The images of these events sometimes look like the product of his work as a journalist (although this is never made explicit), adding new dimensions to this personal chronicle. His autobiographical voice-over also articulates a reflection on the relationship between these different scales, leading to an interrogation of the meaning of "home," a concept that is literally associated with moving house (his own moves, his brother's, and his parents' between the United States and Israel) and, more symbolically, with his connection to the land and the nation. This last dimension echoes a specific theme of his previous documentary, *'66 Was a Good Year for Tourism* (1992), which tells of his family's immigration from Egypt to Israel and then to the United States. In this life journey, their status as Mizrahi Jews plays a very important role, an element also present in *Another Land*, although more in the background.[9]

Another film with a journal entry approach, but this time from the Palestinian perspective, is *5 Broken Cameras* (2011). Directed by Palestinian Emad Burnat, with co-direction by Israeli activist and filmmaker Guy Davidi, this film documents events that occurred a decade later from the 1990s films we've been discussing, from 2005 to 2010. Burnat is a farmer living in Bil'in, a West Bank village, who began using a camera on the occasion of the birth of his fourth son, Gibreel. At that time, the Israeli government decided to build a barrier to separate his village from a nearby settlement. Outraged by a measure that cut them off from their farmland, the villagers begin weekly protest demonstrations that gradually turn into a symbol of the struggle against Israeli occupation. At this point, Burnat extends his home moviemaking to filming the protests and the Israeli repression and its consequences for him, his family, and his neighbors (ranging from prison to death, as in the case of his friend Phil). The documentary thus becomes a film diary combining everyday life (school, birthdays, etc.) with the fight for land and subsistence in this small village. There is a kind of evolution in the images and the scenes filmed, from a more naive perspective at the beginning toward a growing self-awareness of the filmmaker's duty as a privileged witness to this struggle, probably underscored thanks to the involvement of the Israeli filmmaker Davidi in the project. However, the film never completely loses the intimate, ingenuous tone it has in the beginning, moving the spectator with its portrait of the lopsided confrontation between the villagers of Bil'in and the Israeli soldiers. The scale of observation is definitely micro, but the story as a whole has more the quality of a chronicle of events as they are happening than a historical account, even though the film covers a five-year period. In any case, the filmmakers have managed to create a portrait that transcends the trials of this small village to convey the Palestinian-Israeli conflict from the perspective of its weakest victims, the ones who suffer the consequences of the occupation and who try to respond without resorting to violence. In this sense, Gibreel, whom we watch grow and celebrate his first five birthdays, becomes the best symbol of this village, without hardly uttering a word, simply inhabiting the film that his father had never imagined making when he filmed him as a newborn in his crib.

MICHAL AVIAD'S *FOR MY CHILDREN*

Notable among autobiographical films with a more significant microhistorical approach are the works of two female Israeli filmmakers, Michal Aviad and Yulie Cohen, whose filmographies present some striking parallels. The similarities between them begin with their biographies: Aviad was born in 1955 and Cohen in 1956, both spent time in the United States at the beginning of their careers, and both returned to Israel when they started their respective families. Both also made personal documentaries about Israel that were released in 2002, Aviad's *For My Children* and Cohen's *My Terrorist*, although Cohen would end up making a trilogy, with the subsequent films *My Land Zion* (2004) and *My Brother* (2007). These parallels have prompted authors like Yael Munk and Linda Dittmar to study the two filmmakers together. Munk considers them in the broader context of the emergence of female filmmakers who, since the early 1990s, have been contributing a feminine gaze to Israeli cinema, focusing on "the Other in order to create visibility for those ignored by the hegemony—women, children, the elderly and those defined by the hegemony as enemies."[10] Dittmar, meanwhile, situates them in the context of the autobiographical production of those years, along with filmmakers mentioned above such as Folman, Mograbi, Goren, and Katzir, pointing out how these films "position themselves critically in relation to Israel's foundational myths."[11] Dittmar argues that they show a dialectic of repression and recognition that is expressed in contradictory vectors: "a belief in a Jewish birthright to that country (by heritage, birth and daily practice), and a recoil from the brutal consequence of that belief," making it impossible for them to ignore "the realities of conquest and ethnic cleansing that underlie the heroic narratives of a land 'redeemed' by Jewish sacrifice."[12]

This interpretive context is definitely where Michal Aviad's historical documentaries belong, especially *For My Children*, but also to some extent *The Women Pioneers* and *Dimona Twist*. Neither of these last two films adopts an autobiographical perspective, but they do reflect some of the tensions described above, while also incorporating something of a microhistorical approach. *The Women Pioneers*, released in 2013, tells the story of five Jewish women from the moment of their immigration to Palestine in the early 1920s through to 1948. This story is based on their diaries, which are read in a voice-over, and illustrated by public archival footage and photographs of these women in the 1920s and 1930s (complemented in the final part of the film by recent pictures of them, now older). The fact that these are not people of public importance and that their diaries serve as the main archival source gives the film a certain microhistorical quality, even though the visuals are made up mostly of footage that is not strictly biographical, although it is thematically and historically related as it shows life on the kibbutzim (communal farms) in those years. In *Dimona Twist* (2016), Aviad explores the history of the small town of Dimona, founded in 1955, through the stories of seven Jewish women who immigrated there in the 1950s and 1960s from North Africa. The film is structured in chronological chapters (immigration, childhood, adolescence, adulthood) and ends with a shorter chapter ("the time that went by") as a kind of recapitulation, illustrated with images of Dimona today. The main source of information is a series of interviews conducted with the women, visually supported by old family photographs of theirs and especially by public footage of Dimona in those years. It is thus an approach to the history of a small town with a microhistorical tone, told by seven women who arrived there when it was still an inhospitable place, in stark contrast (as the family photographs of their homelands show) to the lives they had come from, especially the ones from cosmopolitan Casablanca, the cultural and economic center of French Morocco at that time.

However, *For My Children* (2002) is the film by Aviad that most clearly reflects a microhistorical approach. From the perspective of the turbulent present of the outbreak of the Second Intifada in September and October 2000, the filmmaker offers a portrait of contemporary Israeli history directly connected to her personal and family experience. The title of the film itself, *For My Children*, makes this explicit, as the question of what country Israelis are leaving to their children effectively constitutes the premise of the whole narrative. This question finds visual expression in a recurring scene in the documentary, which also serves as its opening and closing scene: her two children leaving the house to go to school, their mother filming them from the terrace while they make their way down the street (see figure 6.3).

Aviad starts her film in the uncertain present of the Second Intifada, but her aim is to look over the State of Israel's past in search of clues that

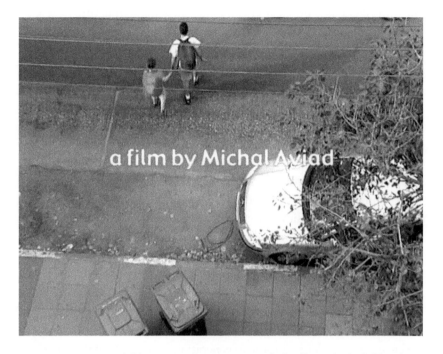

FIGURE 6.3 *For My Children.* Opening sequence, with the filmmaker's children leaving home for school.

might shed some light on what the future holds for her children. In this sense, *For My Children* offers a thought-provoking exploration of a past in which the micro- and macrohistorical dimensions are intimately intertwined. This mixing of scales also happens in the present of the film, as can be seen in the numerous sequences located in the home, where she and her husband (and sometimes her children) watch the intensifying conflict on the television news and discuss it. Her investigation into the past follows a similar pattern, as the country's history is explored through her own personal stories and those of her husband, her parents, and her in-laws. This serves to underscore two of the main features of microhistory: the human agency of the historiographical investigation, and the choice of a reduced scale of observation.

To give shape to this interweaving of scales, *For My Children* elaborates an intricate palimpsest of materials and time frames, giving it a complexity that reflects different conflicts, eras, and mentalities. Throughout the film Aviad uses public archival material, generic in nature or related to specific historical periods, a few times even with her own family members taking part in the events shown in the footage (her husband and her brother-in-law at the protest marches of the 1960s, her father-in-law at the Vatican, and her father working on a kibbutz). There are also home movies from her time in California in the 1980s, and later at her house in Tel Aviv. And she also includes contemporary footage, in the form of interviews with her parents and in-laws, conversations with her husband, and everyday family scenes, where the domestic nature of the images acquires a certain ambiguity given that they were filmed by a professional filmmaker who perhaps already had them in mind for this specific project. In addition, as mentioned above, numerous scenes showing television news are included, sometimes accompanied by conversation, others focusing more on the news itself. All these materials are combined in a way that blurs temporal frames, with a kind of diaristic chronological sequencing applied only to the scenes in the present, where they are shown at home watching the news on the Second Intifada. The rest of the film fluctuates between the older generation's memories of the 1930s and 1940s, both older and younger generations' memories of the 1960s and 1970s, Aviad's memories of the 1980s with her husband in California, and memories of the 1990s that include the third generation (the children/grandchildren).

It is not Aviad's intention to offer a conventional historical chronicle of the Zionist movement or the State of Israel. Indeed, she barely contextualizes the historical events, taking it as a given that the spectator is already familiar with the macrohistorical context. Only the dates of the immediate present are signaled on the screen, although it is not even indicated that we are in the first days of the Second Intifada. Her chronicle centers instead on the life journey of her parents, Gabi and Nora (and more briefly on that of Gabi's second wife, Mitka); her in-laws, Geoffrey and Deborah; and her husband's and her own experiences. What makes it interesting is that the very different life paths of these seven people help convey a sense of the complexity of contemporary Israel. Nora speaks of her Italian background, the rise of Mussolini, and the enactment of anti-Semitic laws in Italy. Gabi, who is of Hungarian origin, talks about the rise of Nazism, his arrival in Israel in 1947, his work on the kibbutzim in those years, and his participation in the war of 1948.

Geoffrey has passed away, but we are told about how he immigrated to Israel on the insistence of his wife, and how he became increasingly involved in interreligious dialogue. Deborah has quite an unusual background, as she is an American of Irish Catholic origin who converted to Judaism. Shimshon, the filmmaker's husband, got involved when he was young in the leftist Matzpen movement and in the protests against the occupation of the Palestinian territories and discrimination against Mizrahi Jews. With all these stories, Aviad weaves together a narrative filled with tensions. On the one hand, the life journeys and memories of the first generation (Gabi, Nora, Mitka, and Deborah) all uphold the national project of the State of Israel, with different nuances. Geoffrey's life, however, points in another direction, expressed clearly by his son Shimshon, when he suggests that in his years in Israel, he became progressively more Jewish and less Israeli. It is Shimshon who has most openly questioned the official historical narrative ever since his youth. His wife is not quite so explicit, combining an affectionate attitude toward the previous generation with a critical perspective that she effectively conveys through the focus she places on her husband in the film. Overall, the historical overview presented in *For My Children* follows more along the lines of the revisionist historians, also referred to as New Historians, who since the 1980s have questioned the official historical narrative, opening up an avenue for more critical readings that give the question of the Palestinian-Israeli conflict a central focus.[13] While it is true that the revisionist tone that seems to pervade the film does not go so far as giving a voice to the Palestinians (a fact that Lisa Polland remarks on with surprise in her lengthy review of the film),[14] this omission is consistent with a microhistorical perspective, which does not seek to give a voice to all sides, but to engage in an intensive study of a historical period through one family—in this case the family of the filmmaker herself.

As can be seen, the different threads used by Aviad to weave together this rich microhistorical tapestry are highly diverse: stories of migrations (forced or voluntary), tumultuous personal and historical periods, and questions about the uncertain future of the country. The filmmaker moves deftly between these stories and time frames, combining materials and sources to achieve resonances that offer a deeper understanding of the complex history of contemporary Israel and its conflict with the

Palestinian world. Her style, in any case, is not opaque, as she works with the standard elements of a documentary narrative, such as interviews, archival material, and contemporary footage taken with a journal entry approach. The interviews sometimes seem to become the main resource, thereby bringing the film closer to an oral history approach. But Aviad places these interviews in close connection with the archival materials to amplify their implicit and explicit meanings. Although this archival material is sometimes used in a naturalized way to illustrate what the interviewees are saying, even in such cases a certain amplification of their meaning can be discerned. This is evident, for example, when Nora talks about her fascination with Mussolini and the sensation of betrayal she felt when he promulgated the anti-Semitic laws, while we are shown public footage of Mussolini's visit to Trieste, which visually translates and contextualizes Nora's initial fascination with the dictator (10'). On other occasions, the connection is more metaphorical, opening the footage up to interesting associations. An example of this is the sequence where the family goes to the countryside to celebrate Gabi's eighty-first birthday (17'–23'). Aviad establishes a dialogue here between three time frames: the present of the celebration, another near present moment of an interview with Gabi at his home, and a black-and-white newsreel from 1947 about the establishment of the HaOgen kibbutz. Gabi's off-screen gaze in the countryside leads into alternating cuts between that day of celebration and the foundation of the kibbutz in Wadi Qabbani in 1947, as if this archival footage were bringing his memories to life. This temporal indiscernibility so typical of personal memory is accentuated by his voice-over narration taken from the interview, which moves between the nostalgia of his memories of those years on the HaOgen kibbutz and his resigned acceptance of the failure of a hoped-for peaceful coexistence between Jews and Palestinians. This resignation is made even more obvious by his silence in response to his son-in-law's question about what remains of those values: an eloquent silence that somehow pervades the rest of the film as well.

The home movies that appear in *For My Children* also add different values and new layers of meaning to the microhistorical tapestry. The oldest, from the 1930s, belong to the Wigoder family and show Geoffrey's bar mitzvah in 1935, and other scenes from 1939. The temporal distance underscores the nature of this footage as a historical record, a repository for the family memory reused in a naturalized way, without altering its original meaning. The next home movies we see were filmed by Aviad and her husband in California in the 1980s and conform to the usual celebratory mode of such footage: the birth of their first son, a festive parade in the street, their parents' visit, and so on. But now they acquire a new dimension, since their insertion here in contrast to the uncertain present serves to underscore the anxiety and fear and to underline the question of whether it was the right decision to return to Israel. Aviad also includes everyday scenes at the house in Tel Aviv, with her mother, Nora, or with the children, occasionally related to Italian cuisine, which serve to connect history to everyday life. The final layer of this domestic palimpsest is composed of the scenes filmed at home after the outbreak of the Second Intifada—where the married couple's fears and uncertainties become much more explicit—and the ones showing Aviad's children going to school, with an eloquent silence in which those uncertainties reverberate. Aviad's use of these home movies is versatile, as can be seen in one of the most effective sequences in this sense (40'–43'), which once again highlights the temporal indiscernibility resulting from personal recollection. A contemporary domestic scene between father and son, Shimshon and Itamar, playing at home, cuts to another similar scene ten years earlier, where father and son are play-acting a military march, with the boy carrying a toy machine gun (see figure 6.4). The playful tone of the old home movies contrasts openly with the subsequent conversation in the present, when Aviad expresses her anxiety at the thought that in four years Itamar will have to do his military service, while the television set continues to show the news of the current conflict.

The film displays these approaches and themes further in other scenes not commented on here, since they do not add relevant variations to the sequences already analyzed. These clearly show how *For My Children* offers a different approach to the history of Israel and its conflict with Palestine. Aviad has created a powerful film positioned between the personal and the historical, with a complex combination of time frames and filmic strategies, to offer a highly interesting microhistorical perspective based on the rich tapestry of testimonies and archival materials it contains.

FIGURE 6.4 *For My Children*. The filmmaker's husband and son play-acting as marching soldiers in a home movie.

YULIE COHEN'S *MY TERRORIST* AND *MY LAND ZION*

The filmmaker Yulie Cohen has made a trilogy on Israel, its national identity, and its relationship with the Palestinian people, with obvious parallels with Aviad's work, but also with noticeable differences.[15] While both filmmakers take an autobiographical perspective, Cohen's films give the present more weight than it has in *For My Children*, as the context from which she engages in a decisive examination of the past. This gives her films a significant microhistorical perspective, with different degrees of intensity throughout her trilogy: more explicit in *My Terrorist* (2002), more essayistic in *My Land Zion* (2004), and more tenuous in *My Brother* (2007). This last film focuses on the filmmaker's quest to recover her relationship with her brother, who separated from his family twenty-five years earlier when he became an Orthodox Jew. Cohen uses this premise to examine the contrast between contemporary secular and Orthodox Israel, with her exploration of the past centered mainly on family relationships. Given its less historiographical orientation and its main focus on contemporary issues, this film is not included in the close analysis that follows. The other two films, *My Terrorist* and *My Land Zion*, have more in common, as they both adopt a revisionist approach to the hegemonic narrative of the State of Israel, in a manner even more explicit than *For My Children*. The first film does this mainly through the narration of a personal story, while the second engages in a closer examination of the foundational myths of Zionism.

My Terrorist tells the story of a terrorist attack in which Yulie Cohen was a victim in 1978 in London, and her reconciliation, twenty-three years later, with the Palestinian responsible for it, Fahad Mihyi. The film traces Cohen's evolution away from her stance as an Israeli nationalist, who grew up in a neighborhood of army officers and later served as an officer in the military, toward a questioning of this vision and of the causes of the Palestinian-Israeli conflict. The Lebanon War and the Sabra and Shatila massacre deepened this personal crisis and prompted her to leave the army. Years later, while working as a coordinator on a film shoot in the occupied territories, she came to realize that both Israelis and Palestinians played a role in perpetuating the conflict. This led her to seek out the person responsible for the 1978 attack, who was still in a British prison. Discovering that he had completely changed his attitude, she met with him in the prison, forgave him, and eventually even endorsed his parole application. Cohen does not ignore the extraordinary nature of her decision in the tumultuous context of those years; on the contrary, she highlights it through the inclusion of a subplot about her relationship with a woman whose daughter was killed in another terrorist attack. The documentary includes two long sequences, one showing both women interviewed on television (2'–7'), and the other showing a subsequent meeting between the two in a hotel (33'–39'), which present their antithetical and seemingly irreconcilable positions, despite their mutual efforts to understand one another.

The documentary has a structure that swings between contemporary scenes with the filmmaker and scenes recounting the past. In the present, we see scenes in Cohen's house of her talking to her two daughters and worrying about their safety and scenes of the meetings with the woman who lost her daughter, her correspondence with Mihyi and her trip to London to visit him (which does not include the meeting itself, as she was not allowed to film inside the prison), her crisis after the Twin Tower attacks in 2001, a meeting with an Israeli friend sympathetic to the Palestinian cause, and so on. Into this contemporary narrative Cohen inserts elements of her own background as a sixth-generation Israeli, and an overview of her personal experience of Israel's contemporary history: from the Six-Day War in 1967, when she was eleven, to the Yom Kippur War, the peace with Egypt, the war with Lebanon, the Oslo Accords, all the way up to the Second Intifada, a conflict ongoing at the time she made the documentary.

Cohen's position is one of actively searching for an alternative to the ongoing conflict, and it is this that leads to her decision to forgive Mihyi, as a public example to show that such an alternative is possible. Underlying this is her theory, controversial for many Israelis, that Fahad is also a victim and that Israel actively contributes to the perpetuation of the conflict with its expansionist and repressive policies. She openly expresses this view when the Second Intifada breaks out, criticizing both Ariel Sharon's visit to the Temple Mount (as the catalyst that served to provoke it) and the Israeli government's response to the uprising. Cohen sees this response as a war of expansion to create a "greater Israel," without the moral justification of the previous wars (1948, 1967 and 1973), which were always defined as defensive wars in the official narrative. "This is not my war," she asserts in a voice-over, "this is not for my country, this is not a war of survival. This is the fight for greater Israel. And in this war, hundreds more Israelis, Jews, Muslims, Christians, will die, especially civilians, many of whom are children, and some soldiers" (26').

My Terrorist is thus a documentary that cleverly combines an intense examination of the present with a personal retrospection on recent decades. It is therefore not strictly a historical documentary, but its exploration of the recent past certainly offers a chronicle imbued with a microhistorical perspective, visible in its reduced scale of observation and in the central role of human agency that typifies autobiographical stories with a historiographical intention. However, the film does not rely on an investigation into the past as detailed as that found in *For My Children*, making its historiographical scope more limited. This is recognizable, for example, in the reduced use of archival materials, which also generally fulfill a primarily illustrative function; these include both public archival footage covering major historical events and footage from her family archive, basically family snapshots, as well as newspaper cuttings related to the 1978 terrorist attack. It is also evident in the filming, which sometimes seems to be closer to a reality television style, due to the professional standard of filming of many confessional scenes in which Cohen shares her thoughts and frustrations. The title credits and some extratextual research reveal that the person filming her is usually her husband, Moshe Gertel, which would explain the intimacy evident in the more confessional scenes, although this detail is never made explicit in the film and therefore would not affect the ordinary spectator's reception of these scenes.

The questions raised in *My Terrorist* are taken up again two years later in *My Land Zion* (2004), combining a microhistorical perspective on Cohen's family history with an analysis of the foundational myths of the State of Israel. This time, Cohen explores the past and present contradictions of her country more openly, tackling the challenge of finding a balance between her Israeli identity and her critical view of the prevailing nationalist narrative. Her analysis results in a thought-provoking interaction between present and past, and between macro- and microhistory, with a clearer effort to draw conclusions that could shed light on the complexity of the questions raised. She pursues this goal with a style similar to *My Terrorist*, with professional standards of filming that in this case do not strike a discordant note, as there are hardly any domestic scenes or confessional moments. Instead, there is an abundance of interviews, usually conducted in a fairly informal, conversational manner, as most of the people interviewed are relatives or friends.

Much of the film's first twenty minutes is dedicated to reviewing key points of the nationalist creed, which Cohen sums up concisely in her voice-over: "The State of Israel was the God and Zionism was the way, our secular religion" (6'). Two main sequences connect past and present, family story and national history, in a combination of scales of observation that gives this film its microhistorical perspective. In the first sequence (3'–6'), the filmmaker goes to Palmach Museum with her parents, and later on, she accompanies them to a Memorial Day commemoration at this museum, while she explains in voice-over that her parents had been members of the Palmach (an elite fighting force of the Haganah, the underground army of the Jewish community during the British Mandate for Palestine). In the second sequence (13'–20'), together with her friend, the historian Motti Golani, Cohen climbs up to the site of Masada, a fortification built in the first century BCE whose defenders committed mass suicide rather than give themselves up when the Romans laid siege to the site in 74 CE. Masada is a *lieu du memoire* with considerable symbolic power for the new State of Israel, and this is reflected in the archival footage and in the explanation offered by the filmmaker, who used to make the climb to this site every year with her parents.

At the same time, Cohen reveals the darker side of this nationalist narrative. On her visit to Masada, she makes it clear to Golani that she has never taken her daughters there because she no longer believes in the idea that places nation above life, one of the foundational myths of the State of Israel of which Masada is an unambiguous expression. Indeed, this is one of the leitmotifs of her film, which begins and ends with her questioning whether it was a good idea to return to Israel when she started her family, whether it is the right place for her daughters to grow up, in an obvious echo of Michal Aviad's premise in *For My Children.* Cohen also points out that the dark side of Israeli Independence Day is Nakba Day, the Day of the Catastrophe for Palestinian Arabs, the date that marks their displacement from the occupied territory by the Israelis in the war of 1948. An interview with Cohen's parents (8'–12') delves into this question, deconstructing the official narrative describing the departure of the Arabs as voluntary; this version is refuted by her father, who remembers the military campaign and acknowledges that they had the express objective of expelling the Palestinians from their villages. Her mother seems uncomfortable with the question, as now she works as a volunteer for an NGO that helps Palestinians at checkpoints, but she argues that those times of war cannot be judged by today's standards. She also refuses to answer the question about whether or not her granddaughter should do her military service, a refusal highly symbolic in someone of the generation that helped to build the State of Israel.

The connection between past and present, between micro- and macrohistorical narrative, is also made clear in another of the recurring elements of the film: the houses. This is evident in the contrast between the house belonging to Shula, Golani's mother, and a nearby house in ruins, which belonged to a Palestinian family expelled in 1948, who come back to visit it every year. Golani has never told his daughter who owned that house that they had seen so many times on their way to her grandmother's place (see figure 6.5). Shula, meanwhile, admits that she has always preferred to ignore it, as when they arrived their priority was security, although now that she is an old woman she understands that things could have been done differently. The filmmaker discovers that in this place there was once an Arab town called Daniyal, with 2,728 inhabitants, which has now disappeared; she finds this information in a book that is not available for sale in Israel, on the disappearance of Arab villages in 1948. This is one more example of the parallel stories that form the foundations of Israel's and Palestine's opposing visions, which reveal, in the words of the analyst Yossi K. Halevi, how both are caught in a "cycle of denial" that perpetuates the conflict.[16]

My Land Zion reflects this cycle of denial in various ways, so that in a certain sense it ends up becoming its main theme. Since Cohen bases the film on her autobiographical experience, she focuses on the problem posed on the Jewish side, delving further into the central question of *My*

FIGURE 6.5 *My Land Zion.* Yulie Cohen, her friend Motti Golani, and his daughter looking at a house, now in ruins, which belonged to a Palestinian family expelled in 1948, near Golani's mother's home.

Terrorist. This question is perhaps dealt with most clearly in the sequence beginning with the news of the murder of a Jewish settler who had been a casual acquaintance of Cohen's (19'–24'). On hearing the news, the filmmaker goes to visit the settler's family, leading to a sequence that allows the murdered man's widow to frankly express her point of view that there is enough space for Jews and Palestinians to live together in peace. But then Cohen revises this thesis, and while we are shown archival footage of the construction of a kibbutz and contemporary footage of new settlements, she states in a voice-over that the past decades have shown her that there are no limits to the Zionist dream, concluding with the statistic that "since 1967, 380,000 Jewish settlers have moved into the occupied territories." These tensions sometimes lead Cohen to verbalize her inner conflict, to the point of asserting that "we Israeli Jews must stop being an oppressive colonial state," convinced, as she had already acknowledged in *My Terrorist*, that Israel is also guilty of perpetuating the conflict. Golani makes a similar assertion when he suggests that the problem is in the present, in continuing to deny that "our right to exist is based upon the destruction of another people," as exemplified by the destruction of Palestinian neighborhoods to build the separation wall in Jerusalem in those years.

My Land Zion also addresses another of the central pillars of the State of Israel's foundational narrative: its relationship with the Shoah, a question that is also present in *For My Children*, but which in *My Land Zion* becomes a much more explicit theme, again through the combination of micro- and macrohistorical scales. The personal connection is established through Shula, Golani's mother, a Hungarian-born Holocaust survivor. The film does not attempt to analyze such a complex issue,[17] but the different conversations on the subject make it clear that the Shoah continues to serve as a justification for the defense of the State of Israel, including its repression of Palestinians. This is evident when Cohen herself seems to nuance her view of Israel as an "oppressive colonial state" by following this statement with her recalling a comment made by Golani's father that, after being released from the concentration camps and arriving in Israel, they "didn't care about the Arabs" (54'). Shula expresses a similar idea on one occasion when she remarks: "I believe that without the State of Israel our chances of surviving are much slimmer" (44'). The trip that Motti Golani and Yulie Cohen make with their respective daughters to Shula's childhood home in Hungary (34'-40') aims to explore this connection between the Shoah and the present, although the filmmaker seems to struggle here with the difficult balance between the need to investigate this link and a fear of delving into the complexity of the issue.

In the final part of the film, the filmmaker, supported by Golani's testimony, looks to a future with a single democratic state for both Jews and Arabs. To reinforce her idea, Cohen goes back to the past, once again through the microhistorical perspective of her family story (50'-54'). Accompanied by her father, Cohen visits the home of her great-grandfather, born in 1870 in Jaffa. Here, she reconstructs that era when Jews and Arabs lived together in peace, supported by archival material and the testimony of her father, who remembers how his family hoped for the establishment of an Israeli state, but never at the expense of the Arab population. The film ends with a long reflection by Cohen, finishing her documentary on an ambiguous note, with a defense of her Israeli identity associated with the land where she was born: "When I decided to come back to Israel to give birth to Stav, I believed that belonging was one of men's basic necessities, and that here I was giving her a profound sense of belonging. . . . I look and love the Israeli landscape, the senses, the sea, the land, the roots and the light. My love for this is what keeps me here" (57'). In this way, she exposes the root of the conflict, the assertion of the "native" status of the Jews (which in the Zionist ideology gives them the right to expel the Palestinian Arabs), but now without the counterweight of the arguments critical of Zionism unpacked throughout the film. It is for this reason that Yosefa Loshitzky criticizes Cohen's position, precisely because this ending seems to contradict her "newly gained understanding of the Palestinian conflict," shifting to a stance that Loshitzky describes as "soft Zionism, a political stance typical of the positioning of the Israeli left."[18] In the end, the film reflects its autobiographical character as a personal journey toward an understanding of "my land Zion," revealing tensions and contradictions closely related to the filmmaker's life journey. In this sense, it could be argued that the solution proffered by Cohen, with its assumption that Jewish nativism is compatible with Palestinian aspirations, is excessively naive or utopian. Nevertheless, it is clear that her perspective is articulated upon an openness to the plight of the Palestinians, facilitating a critical revision of the foundational myths of Zionism, an approach that sheds light on the issue, but that also leaves some paradoxical questions unresolved.

DOCUMENTING PALESTINIAN REFUGEE CAMPS: MAHDI FLEIFEL'S *A WORLD NOT OURS*

Finding microhistorical narratives in Palestinian documentary cinema is somewhat more difficult. One of the reasons for this is the smaller number of films made, due largely to the difficulties associated with film production within the Palestinian territories, as well as these films' limited distribution and visibility.[19] Some of the documentaries made by Mohammed Bakri—better known in Palestinian cinema for his work as an actor—might come close to a microhistorical approach. One of these, *1948* (1999), looks back to the Nakba fifty years earlier, remembering it through a collage of interviews with a wide variety of people: singers, poets, actors, residents, historians, and so on, including Bakri himself. Ten years later he released *Zahra* (2009), which tells the story of his aunt from 1948 through to the present day. Through her story, Bakri is able to reconstruct the history of a portion of the Palestinian population that fled during the war of 1948 but then returned shortly afterward to Galilee (in the case of his aunt's family, only to see their land confiscated to build the new Jewish town of Karmiel). However, Bakri focuses mainly on the family story, which he recounts through interviews with his aunt and her ten children, and the film falls short of pursuing a significantly historiographical goal. Moreover, it only occasionally mentions the macrohistorical context, with the support of material from public archives to illustrate the references to the wars of 1948 and 1967. Overall, the documentary stands out more as what Michael Renov classifies as "domestic ethnography" than as a microhistorical documentary.[20]

However, notable in the film production of the Palestinian diaspora is one documentary that portrays the lives of Palestinian refugees with an interesting microhistorical approach: *A World Not Ours*, released in 2012, which met with considerable success at international festivals.[21] Its director, Mahdi Fleifel, offers an autobiographical story about the Ain el-Helweh refugee camp (established in southern Lebanon in 1948, and with a population of 70,000 in 2011), which becomes somewhat representative of one of the most severe effects of the Israeli-Palestinian conflict: the refugee camps, whose collective population has grown from around 700,000 after the war of 1948 to more than 5 million as of 2021.[22] Fleifel's parents were born and grew up in Ain el-Helweh, and, after getting married, they moved to Dubai. They returned to the camp when Fleifel was seven years old, but three years later they immigrated permanently to Denmark, although they continued to spend many summers at the refugee camp. Years later, after studying film in London, Fleifel dedicated his first feature-length documentary to a portrait of life at Ain el-Helweh, based mainly on his stays there in 2009 and 2010. The importance given to this recent present would at first seem to distance this film from what a historical documentary is understood to be. But *A World Not Ours* goes further than chronicling life in a Palestinian refugee camp today, creating a narrative that explores the past through the (auto)biographical trials and tribulations of the filmmaker and his relatives living there. It is thus a historical narrative that exhibits some of the main features of microhistory, that is, the reduction in the scale of observation, the central role given to human agency, and the limited number of archival materials that Fleifel explores intensively.

The filmmaker offers a succinct macrohistorical context to frame his family story, although he takes as given that the spectator is already familiar with the basic points of the Palestinian-Israeli conflict. Near the beginning of the film (10'), he includes the only scene with an explicitly contextualizing objective: over footage from public archives, he offers a one-minute summary of the origins of the refugee camps, followed by a presentation of basic information on Ain el-Helweh. Later, he presents another important event in public history: the handshake between Arafat and Rabin at the Oslo Peace Accords (44'), but this time linked to a memory of his father, who recorded it and would play it over and over, as if unable to believe what he was seeing. A more original element is the periodic references to the World Cup soccer tournaments, where the two historiographical scales converge in a unique combination of everyday life and popular culture. The different editions of the tournament over the years mark both the evolution of life in the refugee camp and the filmmaker's biographical relationship with his origins: the 1994 World Cup, which Fleifel recalls as the best summer of his life, when the camp came to a standstill to watch the competition, and Brazilian, Italian, and German flags filled the streets for the whole month of the competition; the 2006 edition, when he met his friend Abu Eyad (see figure 6.6); and the most recent one, in 2010, overshadowed by Aby Eyad's weariness and desperation, and without even the incentive of having any of their teams in the final, which was won by Spain, as indicated fleetingly by a shot of a Spanish flag flapping on a rooftop at the camp at the end of the sequence (81').

What Fleifel is most interested in, as can be seen in the scenes related to the World Cup, is portraying the everyday life of people living in a refugee camp. The filmmaker thus does not attempt to explain the political and social conflicts at Ain el-Helweh, the fights between the different Palestinian factions, the complex relationships with the Lebanese authorities, or the confrontations with the Israeli army. Instead, he seeks out the human dramas of the people living there, through a portrait of three different generations: his grandfather, his uncle Said, and his friend Abu Eyad. With these three personal stories as guiding threads, he weaves past and present together, giving the film greater depth as we get to know their stories and the impact that the Palestinian-Israeli conflict has had on their lives. In keeping with the premise of focusing on life at

FIGURE 6.6 *A World Not Ours.* Watching the 2006 World Cup in the Ain el-Helweh camp.

the camp, he does not include his parents in the present, nor does he himself appear on-screen. His presence is nevertheless felt clearly, not only through his voice-over narration, but also through his interaction from behind the camera with the people filmed.

From a temporal point of view, the film presents an initial frame of reference linked to the filmmaker himself. From a present located geographically in Europe, Fleifel traces the main family milestones: his parents' wedding, Dubai, Ain el-Helweh again, and, finally, Denmark, all illustrated with snapshots and home videos filmed mainly by his father. The perspective of exile pervades this autobiographical thread as it does throughout the rest of the film, as the filmmaker acknowledges clearly in the sequence narrating their move to Denmark. In this sense, *A World Not Ours* could be characterized as "accented cinema," to use a category proposed by Hamid Naficy in his 2001 book, as it offers an autobiographical narrative from the perspective of exile. Paradoxically, however, the film lacks an "accent," both in the voice-over, narrated by the filmmaker in perfectly standard English, and in the music used, which consists mostly of American tunes with a jazz flavor, in a deliberate decision by Fleifel "to move away from what I felt had become a cliché in Palestinian docs—the use of *oud* music, which is very melancholic and sets a depressing mood."[23] In a way, this apparent paradox was already acknowledged by Naficy when he explained, in relation mainly to fiction films, that "the accent emanates not so much from the accented speech of the diegetic characters as from the displacement of the filmmakers and their artisanal production modes."[24]

Through this exilic voice, Fleifel also offers a kind of portrait of a transnational family, along the lines of other documentaries that rely on family archives to tell transnational stories marked by exile, such as *Exile Family Movie* (Arash T. Riahi, 2013) or *I for India* (Sandhya Suri, 2005).[25] Fleifel addresses the transnational dimension of his family more implicitly, as a frame of reference, as the members living in Europe (his nuclear family) only appear in the past, although the centrality of his own autobiographical position makes up for the absence of the rest of his immediate family in the present of the narrative. The tensions inherent in the transnational nature of his family are reflected in the contrast between his privileged situation as a European resident and the precarious conditions of life in Ain el-Helweh. This contrast results in an uncomfortable ambiguity, as Fleifel acknowledges, through the confrontation of his emotional connection and genuine personal commitment to this place and its people with the security that his current Danish citizenship gives him. This inner tension is reflected in his own understanding of the refugee camp as his home, which evolves from the his more idealized adolescent conception of the camp toward a progressive recognition of the harsh reality of the refugee camp and the personal conflict that this represents for his self-image as an outsider/insider. This struggle is also visible in an eloquent sequence showing his trip to Israel in 1997 with a group of Jewish schoolmates from his high school in Denmark (69'–71'). Fleifel records the trip with his handheld camera and provides a voiceover of his impressions on his first visit to his homeland—the villages of his grandparents—where he could also meet his cousins, in contrast with the sensation of being an outsider during the rest of the trip. This contrast is especially acute when he visits the Yad Vashem Holocaust Museum, another moment strongly symbolic of the clash of historiographical scales, as Fleifel cannot connect with this place because it brings to his mind the Israeli army's repression of the Palestinian people (illustrated briefly with archival images), in an inverse reflection of the argument presented in *My Land Zion* about the influence of the Holocaust on the Palestinian-Israeli conflict.

While the autobiographical perspective serves as a framework, the main focus of *A World Not Ours* is on the residents of Ain el-Helweh. Fleifel provides a collective portrait covering around ten years, from his first visit alone in the year 2000 (when he was twenty), to 2010, which is depicted as the present in the documentary, with other footage of his from 2006 and 2009, and a few other home movies of the family from earlier years. The older the images are, the more obvious their nature as home videos recorded for family viewing is. This domestic quality begins to give way to a more professional style in the footage filmed in 2009 and 2010—by which time Fleifel had graduated from a film school and had a documentary project in mind—without losing its intimate, familial tone, similar to that of other autobiographical documentaries made with a journal entry approach. Overall, *A World Not Ours* offers a portrait remarkable for its effort to capture the passage of time in the people and places filmed, resembling the style of longitudinal documentaries with their periodic returns to examine the signs of the passage of time in their protagonists.[26] While it is true that the time period that Fleifel covers is not very long (ten years), the home videos filmed by his family at the camp date back to 1985, providing a more marked impression of the passage of time during those intense decades in the evolution of the Palestinian-Israeli conflict.

This temporal arc expands even further if we include the biography of the oldest protagonist, the filmmaker's grandfather (see figure 6.7). Although no images of him are shown dating back earlier than the year 2000, it is stated that he has been at Ain el-Helweh since it was established, sixty-four years earlier, in 1948. He refuses to leave, because this for him would mean giving up his right of return, despite the fact that his wife, now deceased, often insisted that they should move to Europe with their children. But the character who reflects the history of Ain el-Helweh most poignantly is Fleifel's uncle Said. Using home movies from the 1990s and even images from a comic book made about them, the filmmaker tells the story of how Said and (especially) his brother, Jamal, became semi-legendary characters at the refugee camp. At the age of just thirteen, Jamal defended the camp against an Israeli invasion, and both brothers then helped to rebuild it. Years later, however, Jamal was injured by the Lebanese army and died at the age of twenty-three. Since then,

FIGURE 6.7 *A World Not Ours.* The filmmaker's grandfather in front of his house in the Ain el-Helweh camp.

Said has become an irrelevant and almost laughable character who lives alone, earning a living recycling soft drink cans, and putting all his energy into looking after his pigeons. The film offers an affectionate portrait of this character, a genuine loser in a seemingly doomed world. Curiously, his caring for pigeons, which appear on several occasions soaring through the sky, serves as a metaphor for the longing for freedom of a people trapped in a nation that is not their own, crowded together on a square kilometer of land, waiting for a return that never comes. The contemporary character in this drama is Abu Eyad, who is featured in much of the most recent footage. A member of Fatah, the largest faction of the Palestine Liberation Organization (PLO), he works in a security role at the camp. His growing frustration and disillusionment with life at the camp seem somehow to reflect the general weariness of the population with the stagnation of history for the Palestinian refugees. Abu Eyad decides to migrate illegally to Europe, but he is detained and eventually returned to Lebanon. *A World Not Ours* ends there, with a visit by the filmmaker to his friend in Greece, followed by a final caption informing us of his deportation. This final sad note contrasts with the tone of everyday resistance reflected in many scenes of the film. It is a resistance in a way different from that observed in other films analyzed in this book, as although it reflects the ideas of Michel de Certeau about the micro-resistances inscribed in everyday life, it also includes another, more collective kind of resistance, embodied in the whole population of Ain el-Helweh and their defense of a return to a land that seems to be slipping further and further out of reach.

Yet, just before this bleaker ending, there is another, more inclusive one (88'–89'), in which Fleifel condenses the different temporal layers and archival materials used, united by the music and the voice-over narration, to offer an autobiographical recapitulation that brings the macro- and microhistorical dimensions into dialogue with each other. While the filmmaker is leaving Ain el-Helweh for the last time (at least in the film's narrative), the images from old home movies from the 1980s and 1990s—with his grandparents and the people from the refugee camp—are mixed together with old footage of Palestine and Israel that he discovers on his return to London, including a scene with David Ben-Gurion, the former Israeli prime minister, then retired from politics, working on his farm. Fleifel remarks that when he found this footage, he began to wonder what things would have been like if his grandfather had stayed in his native land, how he might have spent his summers with him in Palestine instead of at the refugee camp. Once again, the autobiographical dimension shapes the complex portrait constructed in *A World Not Ours*, as the filmmaker makes explicit when he suggests that perhaps "the reason I've been so obsessed with filming Ain el-Helweh was more than just to keep a record of my family history; it was a faint hope that I can protect the sense of belonging to somewhere" (89'). The need to have roots, to belong, to recognize a place as one's home thus becomes the dominant trope of the whole documentary: that home the refugees lost when they were forced out of Palestine and which they continue to hope to return to (the grandfather), the home they try to maintain in Ain el-Helweh despite the fragility of their situation (Uncle Said), the home the filmmaker himself looks for by coming to a better understanding of his exilic condition. *A World Not Ours* could be understood this way as a kind of answer to the question posed in *My Land Zion* about the history and fate of the owners of the vacant Palestinian house next to the home of Motti Golani's mother.

From *Israel: A Home Movie*, to *For My Children*, *My Terrorist*, and *My Land Zion*, and to *A World Not Ours*, diverse microhistorical approaches have explored the recent history of Palestine and Israel and the ongoing conflict that has shaped their difficult co-existence. Like the chronicling of the incarceration of Japanese Americans analyzed in chapter 4, this variety of approaches to the same historical reality reflects a depth and complexity characteristic of documentary film to explain the complicated past and present of these territories. While it is true that most of these films take a critical view of the official Zionist discourse, it is also certain that the nuances they offer can contribute to a better understanding of the different sides of the conflict. This is thanks to the distinctive microhistorical approach offered by the film medium, imbued with a powerful emotional charge, often supported by the use of archival materials not only as historical sources but also as mnemonic catalysts—something absent from traditional historiographical approaches.

7

THE IMMIGRANT EXPERIENCE IN JONAS MEKAS'S *LOST, LOST, LOST*

he films of Jonas Mekas undoubtedly constitute the best-known filmography based on a diaristic approach. Chapter 6, on Israeli and Palestinian documentaries, offers an initial overview of films with a diaristic structure. In that chapter, I distinguish between "diary films" in the strict sense, exemplified by the work of David Perlov, and other films that exhibit a "journal entry approach," restricted to the time period of a specific film project. This chapter again explores diary films—in this case, Jonas Mekas's—with a focus on an aspect that has not been widely studied and that may at first seem somewhat unorthodox: their microhistorical dimension. To this end, after offering a very basic outline of Mekas's biography, I turn to a discussion of his diary film practice. This is followed by a brief consideration of *Reminiscences of a Journey to Lithuania*, and, finally, a close analysis of the film that presents the most interesting microhistorical dimension of all his work, *Lost, Lost, Lost*. This analysis examines the narrative of Mekas's experience as an American immigrant, supported by the chronotopic approach proposed by Mikhail Bakhtin for literary analysis, which offers a uniquely valuable framework for studying immigrant autobiographies.[1]

Jonas Mekas's life was marked by one of the many migration waves of the twentieth century: specifically, the immigration of Lithuanians to the United States after World War II. Lithuania was invaded by the Soviet Union in 1940, occupied by Nazi Germany in 1941, and then occupied again by the Soviets in 1944. These invasions resulted in the exile of members of the communities persecuted by these regimes, as well as mass deportations both to Germany and to the USSR. When World War II ended, many forcibly displaced Lithuanians chose to immigrate to other countries in Europe or the Americas, since their homeland remained under Soviet control. This was the case for Jonas Mekas, who had fled Lithuania in 1944 and decided to immigrate with his brother Adolfas to New York in 1949. By that time there was already a large Lithuanian population in the United States, concentrated mainly on the East Coast, having arrived in various waves since the nineteenth century.[2]

Jonas Mekas began diary keeping as early as 1944, when he started a written diary (which appears in *Lost, Lost, Lost* in parts of Reel 1 and portions of which he reads in the voice-over).[3] Five years later, just after arriving in New York, the Mekas brothers bought a Bolex 16 mm camera (with borrowed money), which Jonas started using to film his everyday life and events in the Lithuanian community in New York. Then, in the late 1960s, he decided to make films for public exhibition using the footage he had been taking for years. After *Walden* (1969), Mekas released *Reminiscences of a Journey to Lithuania* (1972), and *Lost, Lost, Lost* (1976). In the first part of *Reminiscences*, but especially in *Lost, Lost, Lost*, Mekas reflects on his experience as an immigrant, connecting it to the experience of the Lithuanian community in the United States, offering a perspective that could effectively be described as microhistorical. However, *Lost, Lost, Lost* evolves from a style closer to historical chronicle in the first part of the film toward an autobiographical reflection later in the film, when Mekas becomes more concerned with the process of integration in the new country, which in his case was channeled through the artistic and film world of New York City. Beginning in the 1950s and especially during the 1960s, Mekas gradually became one of the main promoters of independent and avant-garde film in New York, backing initiatives like the magazine *Film Culture*, the Film-Makers' Cooperative, and the Film-Makers' Cinematheque (which eventually grew into the well-known Anthology Film Archives). These initiatives and the filmmakers associated with them also appear in the second part of *Lost, Lost, Lost*, so that in a looser sense it also contains a kind of microhistorical chronicle of that artistic milieu.

Including *Lost, Lost, Lost* in a study of microhistorical documentaries may seem somewhat controversial. For one thing, it might be argued that the recognition achieved by Mekas means that his diary films no longer fit into the category of "history from below" normally advocated by microhistorians, where the focus is on individuals who are not figures in public history. However, as with Rithy Pahn and *The Missing Picture*, the film analyzed here covers a period of time (from 1949 to 1964) when Mekas was largely unknown, especially in his first years as a Lithuanian immigrant. It could also be suggested that a film that evolves toward an autobiographical perspective that is so authorial does not really fit the apparently more restrictive definition of historical documentary. Indeed, as is analyzed below, it is obvious that Mekas's work does not fit into the typical definitions of either historical or microhistorical documentary. But my intention in this last chapter is to explore new ways of understanding history, in line with the theories of Robert Rosenstone discussed in previous chapters, through the analysis of a borderline, historiographically unorthodox case.

It is also worth questioning whether film diaries constitute an appropriate source for the construction of a microhistorical chronicle. The more traditional format of written diaries has increasingly become a historiographical source, often used by historians with no personal connection to the materials, as Penny Summerfield discusses in her book *Histories of the Self*.[4] Some studies based on these sources have a clearly microhistorical orientation, as is the case, for example, with Vahé Tachjian's *Daily Life in the Abyss: Genocide Diaries, 1915–1918*, which draws on the diaries of two survivors of the Armenian genocide to offer a microhistorical chronicle of that episode in history.[5] The same can be said for Katherine Pickering Antonova's *An Ordinary Marriage: The World of a Gentry Family in Provincial Russia*, which constructs a portrait of provincial life in nineteenth-century Russia based on the diaries and other household documents of the Chikhachev family.[6] However, it is quite unusual to find filmmakers who make use of other people's film diaries, and even films made using a filmmaker's own film diaries are far from common. Such cases could be compared to diaries of writers or artists, as often such diaries are kept with the relatively explicit intention of being made public at some point in the future. In any case, like written diaries, diary films do not always contain a significant historical or historiographical dimension, although those that do often take a microhistorical view of the past. By their very nature, diary films involve a reduction in the scale of observation and give centrality to human agency. But in this case the filmmakers are working with materials that have been gathered over the course of several years and are related to their personal experience, which distinguishes their work with these film diaries from the conjectural approaches—adopted due to a lack of historical sources—of much microhistorical research. This does not necessarily reduce the value of the interesting microhistorical perspectives they can offer, supported by a double temporality that facilitates a more specifically autobiographical retrospection, which is not an inherent feature of written diaries. This retrospective dimension, introduced in the editing stage, is what gives these films a more characteristically historiographical approach of a microhistorical nature, as a distinctive way of constructing a history of the present. This inherent complexity of the diary film, as it is manifested in Mekas's work, is worthy of further consideration before moving on to an analysis of his films.

MEKAS'S DIARISTIC PRACTICE: FROM FILM DIARIES TO DIARY FILMS

Mekas's diary films seem to resist definitive labels. As diaries, they could be considered autobiographical films, although his work may fit better into the approach proposed by Paul John Eakin, who places autobiography within the broader practice of self-narration, with "narrative identity" as the key concept unifying the two practices. Eakin stresses that "narrative is not merely a literary form but a mode of phenomenological and cognitive self-experience." This is why he goes on to argue that "to speak of narrative identity is to conceptualize narrative as not merely about identity but rather in some profound way a constituent part of identity, specifically of the extended self that is expressed in self-narrations."[7] From this point of view, the diary films of Jonas Mekas, and particularly *Lost, Lost, Lost*, can be understood as a case of self-narration, an exploration of personal identity in narrative terms.

Mekas's films pose another problem in terms of labeling since they are usually considered to fall somewhere between experimental and documentary cinema. The unequivocally indexical character of the images is counterbalanced by the strong subjectivity of his films, placing them in a

middle ground between these two film modes, once considered antago-
nistic but now increasingly viewed as related.[8] This is due to the evolution in recent decades of documentary practice, which has amplified its
conventional focus to include more personal approaches. Mekas's work is
a good example of this type of personal approach, since almost all of his
films are based on the diaries he filmed and edited over more than fifty
years, documenting his daily activities. As such, Mekas's work offers a
remarkable perspective on the strengths and weaknesses of the diary
format in cinema.

Diary films and written diaries are both similar and different in various ways. Both possess the two basic features identified by Jean Rousset
for this genre: secrecy (in the sense of privacy) and regularity.[9] However,
audiovisual diaries have specific features that distinguish them from
written diaries; notable among these is their double temporality, as
David E. James indicates when he proposes two categories to better
describe this diary process.[10] The first category, "film diary," refers to the
daily footage filmed over the years. This stage has a close connection to
the standard written diary, although with no temporal distance between
the event and its diary entry. When filmmakers decide to make a "film"
out of these film diaries, they create a "diary film," transforming private
records into public discourse and expanding their original meaning. At
this point, as James points out, the film diary's reach is "extended into a
mode of greater discursivity, one capable of social extension and of dealing with the past."[11]

This double temporality points toward other peculiarities that become
evident when studying the process of making diary films. One of these is
the eternal "present" time of the filmed image, which has an immediacy
not achievable in written texts. The camera captures the instant of people
performing their daily routines. At the same time, both the characters
and the filmmaker openly acknowledge the process of filmmaking as
part of their lives, introducing a complex interplay between the factual-
ity of the recordings and their performative dimension. The film diarist
explicitly acknowledges the process of construction, engaging in practices inspired by the home movie approach, which is especially evident in
Mekas's films. But here the supposed defects of home movies become a
mark of style, a rejection of the standardized practices of industrial cinema. Mekas's work—and that of other diarists—thus acquires added

meanings, since it is presented as an act of vindication of a new kind of filmmaking, taken out of the private domain to be turned into a public statement.[12] The subjective dimension of this work is also reflected in the highly self-conscious molding of the film, making it function, as Susana Egan suggests, "as an extension of the body, as a source of experience rather than design."[13] For Mekas, the main challenge when filming a diary becomes "how to react with the camera right now, as it's happening; how to react to it in such a way that the footage would reflect what I feel that very moment."[14] To achieve this, Mekas needs to transcend standard styles, appropriating modes of the avant-garde: "I had to liberate the camera from the tripod, and to embrace all the subjective filmmaking techniques and procedures," in order "to merge myself with the reality I was filming, to put myself into it indirectly, by means of pacing, lighting, exposures and movement."[15]

The second stage in the construction of the diaries—the editing—actually takes place in two phases. The first happens in the present time of filming, when the filmmaker is editing during the shooting—"structuring the work," as Mekas describes it, as it is being filmed.[16] The second is the standard editing phase, when the different scenes are put together. In Mekas's diary films the cuts made in this stage are related mainly to reducing the span of time covered, while keeping the chronological and fragmented structure also characteristic of a written diary and respecting the in-camera editing so crucial to his films. In fact, he refers to this "second" stage of editing as simply "elimination, cutting out the parts that didn't work, the badly 'written' parts."[17]

In this final phase of editing, Mekas adds several layers of sound and texts, which enhance the subjectivity and creativity of the work. He introduces descriptive, symbolic, or poetic titles to punctuate the general structure of the film and adds asynchronous sounds—from street noise to music to human voices—for effect. His voice-over commentary is the most important later addition, explicitly foregrounding the double temporality of these diaries, transforming the present of shooting into the past of remembering. As Maureen Turim explains, "the cinematographic rendering of moments considered present at the instants of their recording *become* memoirs when recollected through montage, a montage that includes a voice situating the emotions of the time. The voice carries the weight of pastness. It turns the phenomenology of experience into that of reminiscence."[18] This voice-over brings in a highly reflexive dimension to the film, moving it away from an explicit diary format toward a more standard autobiographical work, since it introduces the retrospective perspective of the narrative that is absent in diaries. As Philippe Lejeune explains, "the autobiography is above all a retrospective and global narrative, tending toward synthesis, while the diary is a quasi-contemporary and fragmented form of writing."[19] The final outcome offers a singular balance between diary and autobiography: the visuals are strongly suggestive of the diary format, with the daily footage resembling the entries typical of a diary; but the final editing and the voice-over structure these visual entries into a particular narrative, giving closure to the images, or, as Turim suggests, converting them into memoirs.

Both James and Turim point out the historical perspective inserted into Mekas's diaries in the final editing stage, when they acquire "a mode of greater discursivity" capable of "dealing with the past," thanks to the intertitles added and to the voice-over that conveys "the weight of pastness," turning "the phenomenology of experience into that of reminiscence." Although it is true that this dimension is not present to the same degree in all of Mekas's films, it is especially noticeable in *Reminiscences* and *Lost, Lost, Lost*. In these two films, he offers a particular portrait of his immigration and exile experience, linked to the experiences of the Lithuanian community in the United States, by giving his film diaries of the 1940s and 1950s a historical perspective. In this way, Mekas's films offer a microhistorical view of this major phenomenon of migration in the twentieth century, constituting a paradigmatic example of what Hamid Naficy refers to as "exilic filmmaking."[20] Taking this framework into account, the next section briefly examines *Reminiscences*, before moving to a more detailed analysis of *Lost, Lost, Lost* in the section after that.

REMINISCENCES OF A JOURNEY TO LITHUANIA

Reminiscences of a Journey to Lithuania stands on its own as a reflection on the past, since it is composed of images of Mekas's first years in the United States and of his first trip back to Lithuania in 1971, after twenty-five years in exile. As Turim observes, "the artist creates a portrait of himself as a displaced person whose mother and past form the center to which he journeys as part of a quest for what is true of experience."[21] The film is divided into three parts. The first, in black and white, is dedicated to Mekas's first years in New York. The second, titled "100 GLIMPSES OF LITHUANIA,"[22] is the longest, documenting the trip taken by Mekas and his brother Adolfas to Semeniškiai, their hometown in Lithuania, in brief numbered scenes, with footage in color, and his characteristic impressionist style of filming, which he began using in the 1960s. The third, which is the shortest, shows two short stops made after the Lithuania trip: first to visit Elmshorn, a suburb of Hamburg where they spent almost a year in a forced labor camp during the war; and then Vienna, to meet their friends Peter Kubelka, Hermann Nitsch, Annette Michelson, and Ken Jacobs.

The chronicle of his trip to Lithuania is the main part of the film, not only by virtue of its duration but also because of its importance to Mekas's autobiographical narrative. These *"glimpses* of Lithuania" carry a powerful emotional charge, due to the reunion with the Mekas brothers' mother, family, and friends, and their return to the places where they grew up. Mekas offers a chronicle focused closely on the present of the trip, the emotions associated with the reunion, the materiality of the places (and even of the tastes: the fresh water from the family well or fresh cow's milk), conveyed not only by the images filmed—by Mekas or by his brother Adolfas and his wife—and his voice-over commentary, but also by the numerous sound recordings of conversations or songs, all inserted asynchronously. This present is intimately tied to the past, to the memory of the happy times of their childhood and youth, but with an autobiographical perspective focusing on a personal and family context, with hardly any microhistorical resonances or any macrohistorical contextualization. Only on two occasions does Mekas refer to the historical context in this section. The first time, he recalls the reason why he fled Lithuania—he was editing an underground anti-Nazi newspaper when the country was invaded by the German army—although he explains this in a section specifically titled "parentheses." The other reference—which is brief and indirect—appears when he visits the old school he attended as a child, and in his voice-over he wonders: "Where are you now my old childhood friends? How many of you are alive? Where are you scattered through the graveyards, through the torture rooms, through the prisons, through the labor camps of Western civilization?" (50'–51'). Later on, he makes his intention not to focus on social or historical issues explicit when he considers a hypothetical question about why he doesn't deal with the situation in Lithuania under the Soviet regime, explaining in the voice-over that he does not feel he has the authority to discuss it because of his exilic condition: "I am a displaced person on my way home, in search of my home, retracing bits of the past, looking for some recognizable traces of my past. The time in Semeniškiai remains suspended for me" (30'–31').

This status of "displaced person" is contextualized in the shorter first section (twelve minutes), which functions as a necessary prologue for understanding the scenes in the "present" of the trip taken in 1971. This first section can also be understood as a summary of the questions that Mekas addresses more extensively in the first two reels of his next film, *Lost, Lost, Lost*. In this first part of *Reminiscences*, he sums up ten years of his life, as he says at the beginning, marked by his immigration to Germany and then to the United States. Mekas does not follow a specifically chronological order, as he begins his film with images of a trip to the woods, while his voice-over talks of how on a trip he took around 1957 or 1958, for the first time, he forgot his homeland and didn't feel alone in America: "I was slowly becoming a part of it. There was a moment when I forgot my home. This was the beginning of my new home" (2'). He then presents a flashback to 1950, offering a ten-minute chronicle of his life as a displaced person, as a member of the Lithuanian community in Brooklyn. The sense of rootlessness dominates these scenes, not so much because of the images but because of his voice-over commentaries. While it is true that occasionally he shows solitary Lithuanians in the streets, or newly arrived immigrants with hopeless expressions, as if weary of life, most of the scenes are in a style typical of home movies: gatherings, celebrations, happy faces (see figure 7.1). Nevertheless, his commentary reveals his suffering in those years, filled with memories of his homeland, and a feeling of rootlessness that he shared with the rest of the Lithuanian community. He drives this point home in his commentary on one of the festive gatherings, introduced by the intertitle "A GATHERING OF DP'S IN STONY BROOK" (1950), underscored by the elegiac tone of his voice: "Somewhere at the end of Atlantic Avenue, somewhere there they used to have their picnics. I used to watch them, the old immigrants and the new ones, and they looked to me like

FIGURE 7.1 *Reminiscences of a Journey to Lithuania.* A Lithuanian community picnic in Brooklyn.

some sad dying animals in a place they didn't exactly belong to, in a place they didn't recognize. They were there on Atlantic Avenue, but they were completely somewhere else" (5'–6'). The use of third person to refer to the Lithuanian community is an early signal of Mekas's progressive distancing from his roots, which found full expression in the early 1950s in his move from Brooklyn (where most Lithuanian refugees lived) to Manhattan. However, his feeling of exile never seems to leave him altogether, judging by another reflection that he includes shortly afterward: "We still are displaced persons, even today. . . . The minute we left, we started going home, and we are still going home. I am still on my journey home" (8').

This first section of *Reminiscences* thus presents a brief narrative with a microhistorical tone of the Lithuanian community's immigration experience after the end of World War II. This would also be the main theme of the first two reels of *Lost, Lost, Lost.* The parallels between the first parts of these two films are very clear, as is shown below; so much so that in at least two specific moments Mekas even uses the same footage.

LOST, LOST, LOST: MEKAS'S IMMIGRANT EXPERIENCE

Lost, Lost, Lost is the film where Mekas explores his immigrant experience and his particular process of Americanization more thoroughly. He uses the footage he shot from the time just after his arrival in the United States in 1949 through to 1964, which he edited in the mid-1970s and released as a film in 1976. The film constitutes a unique blend of microhistorical chronicle and film autobiography, because the filmmaker is a first-generation immigrant sharing his own immigration experience through a diary format. Its singularity lies in the fact that autobiographical films related to the immigrant experience are usually made by filmmakers with immigrant backgrounds who feel a desire to dig into their family's past in order to gain a better understanding of their own identities. But these filmmakers are second- or third-generation immigrants trying to connect the life narratives of their parents or grandparents to their own life experience. In such cases, as Sau-Ling Cynthia Wong suggests, a different paradigm emerges, since they are not dealing with the opposition between Old and New World, but with a set of three systems: the "ideal" Old World values of their relatives, their "real" Old World values as actually mediated by those relatives, and the "real" New World values of the writers/filmmakers themselves.[23] This paradigm is absent from the films of Mekas, a first-generation immigrant with no relationship to other generations and with the sole company of his brother Adolfas, who immigrated with him.

A second feature that gives Mekas's autobiographical approach a quality of its own, this time in contrast to written autobiographies with a similar theme, is the absence of the homeland. As mentioned above, *Lost, Lost, Lost* begins in 1949, with Lithuania as its primary absent protagonist. James highlights this same idea with reference to Mekas's previous film, *Walden*, when he describes the film diaries as *"negative home movies, movies that begin from the fact of the absence of home."*[24]

Mekas's reflection therefore centers on the process of American accul-
turation, a feature common to most autobiographical films made by
immigrants, who are usually assumed to have faced a precarious economic situation in their countries of origin that would place home moviemaking out of their reach, especially in the 1930s and 1940s, before the
popularization of the Super 8 format. This material constraint results in
a specific approach to immigrant autobiography films that bypasses or
quickly skims the first two stages pointed out by William Boelhower as
characteristic of immigrant autobiography—the dream anticipation and
the journey[25]—to focus instead on the process of integration into the
new country.

Lost, Lost, Lost's microhistorical chronicle is analyzed here with the
help of a chronotopic approach drawing on Bakhtinian theory. Mikhail
Bakhtin proposed his chronotopic analysis for literature, and it has been
adapted to cinema by authors such as Michael V. Montgomery, Vivian
Sobchack, and Hamid Naficy.[26] Bakhtin's chronotopes are singular combinations of time and space in each work of art where narrative events
become specific: "It is precisely the chronotope that provides the ground
essential for the showing-forth, the representability of events. And this is
so thanks precisely to the special increase in density and concreteness of
time markers—the time of human life, of historical time—that occurs
within well-delineated spatial areas."[27] The chronotopic approach can be
applied to various kinds of narratives, but it seems especially valuable for
the analysis of immigrant autobiography films because the film medium
is so tied to the experience of time and space, both so crucial to the configuration of the immigrant's identity in the adopted country.[28] This is
even more visible when focusing specifically on the spatial experience,
contrasting the places left behind with their new locations. Boelhower
illustrates this when he explains that "*habitare* . . . is an essential property of existence and as such is also the foundational dynamic behind the
montage conventions of autobiography."[29] Boelhower is actually talking
about the crisis of *habitare* visible in the work of modernist autobiogra-
phers, who turn their focus from the temporal structure typical of autobiographies to a spatial understanding, a quest for dwelling where the
modern city is anathematized and the historic city mythologized. However, his idea can also be applied to the autobiographies of immigrants,
since their experiences can be explained as a quest for dwelling, a

struggle to fit into the modern city of an alien country, in sharp contrast with the idealized places left behind.

The centrality of space is expressed in Mekas's *Lost, Lost, Lost* through the interplay between the diary format and the immigrant experience. On the one hand, Mekas's experience of his new country is clearly marked by the places where he lives, first in the neighborhood of Williamsburg, Brooklyn, and later on in Manhattan. On the other hand, the structure of his film shifts the focus away from the temporal dimension, since the chain of events represented is not tied to a closed causal structure but rather is based on his daily filming of the ordinary events going on around him. The film's temporality thus comes quite close to the "cyclical everyday time" described by Bakhtin, where "there are no events, only 'doings' that constantly repeat themselves,"[30] which is precisely what happens in standard home movies.

The prominence of the spatial experience does not mean that the temporal dimension is irrelevant in Mekas's films. The double temporality of his work—the gap between the filming and the final editing—produces a discourse that links the spatial experience to the temporal axis, mainly through the voice-over commentaries. At the same time, this interplay between voice-over and images helps to foreground the different roles that Mekas takes on during *Lost, Lost, Lost*, as narrator and protagonist. His position as narrator is made dominant through the use of the voice-over, although it is evident too in his authorship of the titles. At the same time, he is the protagonist of the events, a presence felt through his elaborate and self-conscious shooting and editing, calling attention to himself as the filmmaker watching, recording, and reacting to events. This presence goes further, to the point of becoming literally visible when he is filmed by other people, like his brother Adolfas, but also Ken Jacobs, in the final part of the film. These two roles of narrator and protagonist acquire new meanings when Mekas brings them into dialogue and into relation with the places and times that define the main chronotopes. Through this interplay, Mekas appears variously as a wanderer, a watcher, or a guardian of the new cinema, depending on the place and time where he locates himself.

Having thus defined the specific nature of *Lost, Lost, Lost* as an immigrant autobiography and contextualized the Bakhtinian approach, I now offer a close analysis based on the film's structure in reels. The film is divided into six 30-minute reels, signaled explicitly by intertitles.[31] The first two reels cover the years 1949–1952 and focus on Mekas's exilic status and his relationship with the Lithuanian community in New York. The third and fourth reels trace his process of integration into American society outside the Lithuanian community, through his relationship with New York's independent and alternative film circles. The fifth and sixth reels conclude this integration process and show Mekas now firmly established in his adopted country. Although *Lost, Lost, Lost* evolves from a microhistorical chronicle toward a more autobiographical narrative, taken as a whole the film can be understood as the narrative of an individual experience representative of a process experienced by millions of people who immigrate to a new country, in this case anchored in the Lithuanian community in the United States, from which Mekas evolves toward a position connected to New York's cultural and film world.

THE MICROHISTORICAL NARRATIVE OF MEKAS'S IMMIGRANT EXPERIENCE: REELS 1 AND 2

As noted above, the first part of *Lost, Lost, Lost*, comprising its first two reels, offers a narrative of the immigration experience from the autobiographical perspective of a first-generation immigrant. This first section presents a clearer microhistorical perspective, observable in the reduced scale of observation and the centrality of human agency, at the service of an account of a personal experience intended to represent a wider historical community, that is, Lithuanians who immigrated to the United States after World War II. However, as also discussed above, this is not a typical microhistorical film, but a variation that combines visuals drawing from the filmmaker's film diaries and a soundtrack with a characteristic retrospective voice-over. Although the film diaries have a style very similar to home moviemaking, their focus is not on a particular family but on the Lithuanian immigrant community, understood here as a kind of extended family, although reflected not only in their celebratory routines but also in their political activities in support of their homeland. Through his voice-over narration, Mekas highlights his role as a chronicler of this community, as on several occasions he explicitly identifies himself as such, presenting himself as "the recording eye . . . the camera historian of the exile" (31'). In a way, the images included in this first part of the film are reminiscent of the collective chronicle composed by Robert Nakamura and Karen Ishizuka with the home movies of Japanese Americans in *Something Strong Within* (analyzed in chapter 4), despite the obvious differences in terms of origin, filming, and final structure, as both films offer a collective portrait of an ethnic community in a situation of rootlessness, based on images that reflect their collective routines from a microhistorical perspective.

In this particular microhistorical chronicle, three parallel stories can be identified: the community life of Lithuanian exiles, appearing mostly in the first reel; the more specifically political side of these exiles, which takes up much of the second reel; and the personal experience of Mekas himself, conveyed mainly through the voice-over narration. The first two narrative threads are not always clearly divided, as some of the gatherings shown include moments of celebration (greetings, meals, entertainment) and more formal meetings with an apparently political purpose. But, in general, Mekas exhibits a clear intention to focus first on the everyday experience of exile in his life and the lives of other Lithuanian immigrants, and then, second, on the political dimension.

The portrait of Lithuanian community life has many aspects in common with the tradition of home moviemaking. This is primarily because in his first years of filming Mekas uses a very transparent, less personal style, very similar to that usually found in home movies. Moreover, many of the scenes filmed also fit perfectly into the typical repertoire of home movies: a day relaxing in a park, a dinner at home with friends, a picnic, conversations on the way out of church after the Sunday service, dancing, playing soccer, a celebration in a restaurant, a wedding, and so on. On several occasions Mekas also uses footage in color, giving the scene a chromatic range that underscores its celebratory or ludic dimension, like the gathering in Prospect Park on a spring day or another similar gathering in Connecticut. Mekas provides minimal contextual information, beyond occasionally informing us in the intertitles of the location or the names of the people shown. In this sense, these scenes also function like home movies, as spectators outside the community lack the context to enjoy the familiarity that every home movie provides when it is screened for the family in question. This limitation extends here to the use of Lithuanian popular music, used by Mekas quite frequently for the soundtrack, which would not form part of the collective imaginary of most viewers.

Alongside this thread showing the life of the Lithuanian community, Mekas's voice-over narration introduces a melancholic tone that contrasts openly with the images of leisure and celebration. This brings into play the second way of appropriating home movies explained in chapter 2, when the most obvious interpretation of the original home movies is contested, adding supplementary meanings, in this case underscoring the rootlessness of immigrant life. In fact, the film begins with an explicit lament by Mekas, asking Ulysses to sing the story of "a man who never wanted to leave his home, who was happy and lived among the people he knew and spoke their language. Sing, how then he was thrown out into the world." Ulysses can be understood as a kind of alter ego for Mekas, as a symbol of the displaced person coming from a country rich in tradition and culture. This metaphorical identification is actually reinforced in his written work: first, in his written diary from these years, *I Had Nowhere to Go*, which ends with a letter to an imaginary Penelope; and, later on, in the English edition of his collection of poems, which were written originally in Lithuanian from 1947 to 1951, which is titled *There Is No Ithaca*.[32] Mekas reminds us of his exilic status at least one other time in the voice-over in Reel 1, when he seems to address his artistic community in the 1970s, associated more with the avant-garde world: "I know I'm sentimental. You would like these images to be more abstract. It's ok, call me sentimental. You sit in your own homes but I speak with an accent and you don't even know where I come from. These are some images and some sounds recorded by someone in exile" (14').

This experience of displacement resulting from his exilic status is expressed in these first reels in the chronotope of the street, which functions, paraphrasing Bakhtin's formulation, as the essential space for the representability of Mekas's struggle during his first years in America. The street's role here is similar to that of the chronotope of the road described by Bakhtin in his work, since it shares some of the same qualities as a place of random encounters, of collision and interweaving for different groups and social classes.[33] But the street of these first reels lacks direction, becoming more a place where people can stop awhile or pass through, but where no one establishes a home. It is a place with no owner, where no roots can grow, where one is surrounded by crowds but can in fact be alone. The street also serves here as representative of other open urban spaces with a similar meaning in these first reels: the park, the square, and so on. This use of public open spaces can be explained partially by the routines of home moviemaking, associated with the fact of filming special occasions, usually related to "going out." But in *Lost, Lost, Lost* the street acquires a deeper meaning, as the place where Mekas feels more attuned to his feelings as a displaced person. He roams the streets of New York as a wanderer, aimlessly, feeling the loneliness of his displacement as an immigrant deep inside.

This idea is very clear from Reel 1, where Mekas is briefly seen walking alone in the streets, while a title reads: "THRU THE STREETS OF BROOKLYN I WALKED," followed by "I WALKED MY HEART CRY-ING FROM LONELINESS" (6'). Just after these titles, over images of dif-ferent public spaces in New York, his voice-over underlines the same idea: "Those were long, lonely evenings, long, lonely nights. There was a lot of walking, walking, through the nights of Manhattan. I don't think I have ever been as lonely." This figure of the wanderer is also echoed in the image of people sitting in the streets with no apparent purpose, the old Lithuanians that he shows in Reel 1, "WITH NO MEMORIES," as he comments in the title (4'). Mekas resorts to the streets as a way to avoid the loneliness, as he explains when he comments on the images of Ginkus in front of his candy store: "We couldn't sit home. It was too lonely. The streets were empty. We stopped at Ginkus's candy store" (13'). Mekas is creating a representation of loneliness, mixing literal and symbolic fig-ures through the images and soundtrack. In the voice-over, he mixes the denotative descriptions of some of the images with the poetic strains of other sentences. The image also becomes symbolic when he is shown on screen, since the loneliness is no longer literal, because someone— probably his brother Adolfas—was filming him (see figure 7.2). Mekas's feeling of displacement, of having been "thrown out" of his country, is intensified by the contrast between the Lithuania recreated by the immi-grants and his growing perception of the impossibility of recovering his country and his home, as he expresses in his voice-over: "I look at you now from a distance, crowds, early Sunday afternoon. I look at you. Then you thought it was all so temporary. . . . We thought it will be all so

FIGURE 7.2 *Lost, Lost, Lost.* Jonas Mekas walking alone in the streets of New York.

temporary, we will be all home, soon. And then we all went to different directions" (25').

This displacement is also explored by Mekas in more explicit political terms in Reel 2. In the first minutes of this reel, the figure of Ulysses reappears, as Mekas twice calls upon him in the voice-over, but this time to protect Lithuania: "Sing Ulysses, sing the desperation of the exile, sing the desperation of the small countries" (34'). Nevertheless, Reel 2 introduces a slight change of mood in Mekas's narration of his experience, as he becomes a chronicler of the political and social life of the Lithuanian community in New York. The street as chronotope acquires a more overtly political quality, with Mekas as the reporter on the Lithuanian refugees. As he says in the voice-over, he is there as "the chronicler, the diarist," or "the camera eye . . . the witness." In this sense, in Reel 2 Mekas steers between the microhistory of the Lithuanian community and its public history, with its exiled leaders engaged in the struggle to recover Lithuania's independence. Mekas makes no effort to provide a detailed macrohistorical context, assuming that the basic issue—the Soviet annexation of Lithuania—is widely known. In his portrait of this more public history, he shows street protests against the USSR on a couple of occasions (see figure 7.3). He also films meetings of politicians and activists, although he does not identify them, or only does so in a generic way, such as when he introduces one of these meetings as the "Committee for Independent Lithuania." On a few other occasions he does single out individuals, usually in the intertitles: Professor Kazys Pakštas, who lives in Philadelphia; the Futurist poet and orator Juozas Tysliava; Stepas Kairys, one of the signatories of the Lithuanian Act of Independence in 1918; and Povilas Žadeikis, the ambassador of independent Lithuania in Washington. Mekas films these scenes as a member of this community, which gives them a certain hybrid quality, as they reflect a historical reality but are viewed from an intimate perspective, maintaining the familial air that pervades his microhistorical chronicle in these first two reels. Nevertheless, when he returns to these images nearly twenty years later, Mekas feels himself to be a "historian" of those times, as he recalls

FIGURE 7.3 *Lost, Lost, Lost.* Anti-Soviet protest by Lithuanian immigrants in New York.

in his voice-over: "I was there with my camera. I recorded it. This was the seventh year, for some of you the eighth year in exile. There they were. The only thing that mattered to you was the independence of your country. All those meetings, all those talks, what to do, what will happen, how long, what can we do. Yes, I was there, and I recorded it for others, for history, for those who do not know the pain of the exile" (47'–48').

Exile thus continues to be the dominant theme of these two reels, experienced in both personal and community terms, resulting in a histo riographically effective tension between different scales of observation that is highly characteristic of microhistory. Mekas inserts his own exile experience into a specific historical community whose hopes and dreams he shared for four years, and to which he dedicated much of his film diaries in those years. In this way, the filmmaker constructs a particular history of the present related to the Lithuanian exile community in the United States, conveyed through two complementary mnemonic channels: the footage contemporaneous with the events, and his personal memory looking back retrospectively on those years. As noted in chapter 1 of this book, the film thus contributes a historical dimension to the time of the personal experience by bringing the personal journey into dialogue with a basic macrohistorical context. It is a history of the present that acquires a more literal sense here, as the diary record adheres closely to the temporal flow of the events, in a quasi-literal replication of Henry Rousso's explanation of the way historians of the present "act 'as if' they could seize hold of time as it passes . . . slow down the process of time's retreat and the oblivion that lies in wait for any human experience."[34] It is in the postproduction stage, with the editing and especially the addition of the retrospective voice-over narration, that this present acquires "a substantiality, a perspective, a time frame, as all historians engaged in periodization do."[35]

MEKAS'S PROCESS OF INTEGRATION IN AMERICA: REELS 3 AND 4

At the end of Reel 2, Mekas recounts his decision to break ties with the Lithuanian community. The celebration of New Year's Eve in 1952, which ends the reel, is the last event he shares with them, as he explains in a voice-over. Mekas recognizes that their shared dream of returning to their homeland is unreal, and he decides to start his life over again in the new country: "I began to feel that if anything can be done for Lithuania, it can be done only by the people who lived there. The only way I can be useful to Lithuania is by building myself from scratch, from the beginning, and then giving myself back to it" (53'). Because of this perception, Mekas resolves to leave his life in Brooklyn behind and move to Manhattan, together with his brother Adolfas. Once again, the spatial understanding of the self is foregrounded. Mekas understands that there is no point in trying to live off past memories. Since that life was embodied by the neighborhood of Williamsburg, to begin from scratch meant moving away, into a new exile, however painful that decision might be ("I felt I was falling to one thousand pieces," he says). The new home was not very far away, but the distance was more symbolic than physical, because it meant acknowledging the impossibility of recovering his homeland.

The change to his new place is clearly marked in the film by the change of reel. Reel 3 begins with Jonas and Adolfas living in Manhattan, with new friends and activities. This reel, which covers the period from 1953 to 1960, therefore portrays a second stage in the process of Mekas's integration into his adopted country. This reel is also dominated by the domestic tone of the images, with his brother Adolfas as the other frequent protagonist (who also often takes the camera to film Jonas). The domestic is highlighted by the attention given to their homes, even indicating the changes of address in the intertitles (109th St., Avenue B, 13th St.). Moments of leisure are also included, such as strolls through Central Park, various outings, or a snowfall in the city. New friends also appear, in several cases named in the intertitles: Susan, Gideon, Dorothy, Storm and Louis, Fennis, Tina, Arlene and Edouard, Frances. All of this gives these years a tone of normality; the rootlessness of exile does not disappear completely but shifts progressively into the background.

This process of integration has some characteristic features, as once they move to Manhattan, Mekas and his brother very quickly become involved in the world of independent and avant-garde cinema. Reel 3 includes the launch of the magazine *Film Culture* (in 1954), some scenes from an unfinished film, the film shoot for a movie by Robert Frank, and a gathering of poets at the Living Theater. Mekas's process of

Americanization is thus quite atypical, since his point of view always remains rather critical of the mainstream values of American life. His diaries therefore move away from the standard pattern of autobiographies written by immigrants, which tend to legitimize, as Betty Bergland explains, the "dominant cultural images of the transformed American while containing the Other in pre-adult, childlike states."[36] Mekas transcends that pattern because he adopts New York as his home, but in its more cosmopolitan and cultural sense, becoming part of the alternative cultural life where the dominant values of Americanization do not exclude the Other, but rather welcome diversity. In this context, Mekas's camera work can be understood as a metaphor for the role played by culture in the construction of his new life, since the mediation of the camera leads him to a more conscious and detached gaze, creating a distance that helps him to open up his point of view, to search for new roots through a culture that is both "American"—cinematic, visual, industrialized—and cosmopolitan.

Mekas's involvement in New York's cultural life has its filmic correlative in his growing consciousness as a diarist and filmmaker. In the first two reels, his visual style is restrained and unobtrusive. From Reel 3 on, the marks of his presence are more explicit, through his visual style and his commentaries in the voice-over. In these reels we begin to see the first signs of the kind of loose camera work and rapid in-camera editing so frequent in his subsequent diaries. Mekas also reflects on his role as a diarist, remarking that "it's my nature to record everything" (85'). This is an idea that comes up again in Reel 4, where he points to the reason why he tries to record everything: "I have lost too much, so now I have these bits that I have passed through" (109'). This statement links his filmmaking to the home movie approach, because what he saves from oblivion are only "bits" that he has "passed through." The sense of loss acquires a deeper meaning because it is related to his experience as a displaced person, as someone who has left his home, his family, and much of his life far behind. Mekas feels a need to stress this point, beginning with the title of the film repeating the word "lost" three times. His statement is also an acknowledgment of the therapeutic nature of filming, as a healer of the hurts created by the loss of important things; he thus places his work within the broader tradition of autobiographical practices understood as "narrative recovery."[37]

Visually, urban public spaces are less dominant in Reel 3, but Mekas's voice-over continues to invoke the street as the dominant chronotope, reflecting a mood that wavers between loneliness or nostalgia and his efforts to build a new life. His recollections shift between a sense of newness expressed early in this reel ("The city, the people, everything was new. We walked through the city, we submerged in it." [65']) and his earlier feelings of loneliness, now expressed in the third person: "He was very shy and very lonely during this period. He used to take long, long walks. He felt very close to the park, to the streets, to the city" (67'). The urban settings compete now with new scenes of the countryside, but New York City is still the main space: not only its streets, but also its parks, especially Central Park. Nevertheless, the meaning of these public spaces gradually changes. Mekas needs time to make himself at home in this new land, and he spends time getting to know these places, "submerging" himself in them. The space thus becomes almost a co-protagonist, a companion that Mekas needs to get to know better if he is to begin again. He even establishes a dialogue with it at the end of Reel 3: "We were driving back to New York that day, with Bellamy. I was looking at the landscape. I knew I was in America. What am I doing here, I asked myself. There was no answer. The landscape didn't answer me" (88'). We have to wait until Reel 5 to find that answer.

Following a structure that in a sense mirrors the first two reels, Mekas devotes most of Reel 4 to footage of different political activities in New York. He joins demonstrators against air raid tests, picketers at the women's prison on Eighth Street, and various activities of a strike for peace held in 1962. The street remains the main chronotope, but this time Mekas moves away from the more domestic approach of Reels 1 and 3, making room for the public life that engulfs him in his new milieu. Mekas is again the "watcher" of Reel 2, going out into the streets of New York to record it all. He reflects on this in the voice-over, expressing a kind of impulsive, unrationalized need: "I do not know if I've understood you. . . . I was just a passer-by, from somewhere else, from completely somewhere else, seeing it all, with my camera, and I recorded it, I recorded it all. I don't know why" (91'). He needs to get to know his new place and its people—and the camera is his tool to approach them. He does not feel completely at home there, but he keeps coming back because, as he explains later, "I wanted to feel its pulse, to feel its excitement" (97'). Mekas as autobiographical subject is struggling between the centripetal and centrifugal forces that Bergland identifies as distinctive trends in ethnic autobiographies, borrowing Bakhtin's well-known metaphor.[38] He needs to feel part of New York life, but his attention turns to the alternative social and political struggles of that time.

One of those struggles, the night march of the strike for peace that Mekas shows toward the end of Reel 4, becomes a kind of metaphor for the changes that are taking place in his own life. Mekas makes this explicit when he comments on the images of the people marching: "So let me continue. I don't want to look back. Not yet, or not anymore. Ahead, ahead" (104'). Through the images and the voice-over, the street seems to incorporate a goal, a destination, fusing the spatial and temporal dimensions. In this way, the street is more like a road, a symbol of the course of a life, as Bakhtin explains in his description of the road as a key chronotope of the novel form: "Time, as it were, fuses together with space and flows in it (forming the road); this is the source of the rich metaphorical expansion on the image of the road as a course."[39] The incorporation of a direction (the people marching), of a goal (literally a political one), thus changes the axiological implications of the street, which until now was the place of the lonely wanderer, to make it more like a road, symbolizing a direction in life, pointing to a new meaning in Mekas's struggle. This street/road here becomes, as Bakhtin also describes it, the space of sociohistorical heterogeneity, of the collapse of social distances, helping Mekas fully embrace his new country and share its goals.[40]

MEKAS IN THE NEW YORK ART AND FILM COMMUNITY: REELS 5 AND 6

The change experienced by Mekas finds its full expression in Reels 5 and 6, which portray a kind of rebirth that gives him a sense of stronger self-confidence in his future. This change of mood is translated gradually into a new daring and experimental style that explores camera speed, lighting, focus, and movement, in a jazz-like fashion. The structure of these two reels is also less dependent on chronological time, moving away from a strictly historiographical (and therefore microhistorical) approach toward an exploration of personal identity through a more poetic and experimental approach. This is revealed very clearly in the two most distinctive sequences of Reel 5: the twelve-minute sequence titled "RABBIT SHIT HAIKUS," and the shorter, four-minute "FOOL'S HAIKUS" sequence. In the first one (115'–127'), Mekas adopts a nonchronological structure using very short scenes of visual motifs related to nature, separated by numbers, and with the voice-over stating the same word three times, evoking the three-verse format of the haiku. Some of the images are not very different from others used in previous reels, but their organization and the voice-over give these haiku sequences a nonnarrative, nonchronological quality that liberates the film from its home movie look and links it more clearly to the modes of avant-garde cinema. The "FOOL'S HAIKUS" sequence (132'–136') has a similar tone and the same structure, with brief numbered scenes, although this time the pattern of stating the same word three times is absent and most of the sections feature Mekas himself and various female friends of his, walking or joking around in different parts of Central Park.

Mekas's new confidence is reflected in a different chronotope in these last two reels. Now "nature"—understood spatially, associated with the countryside, with the rural space—becomes the dominant chronotope. The temporal dimension of the events portrayed in these final reels has less relevance than in previous reels. This makes sense since the chronotope of nature is associated now with "paradise," a place where there is no time but eternity. This idea also echoes the idyllic chronotope proposed by Bakhtin in literature.[41] For Bakhtin, in a narrative of this type, space is the main axis, articulated around familiar sites, full of details of everyday life. Time acquires a cyclical rhythm associated with folk tradition. And human life is linked to the life of nature, connected by "the unity of their rhythm, the common language used to describe phenomena of nature and the events of human life."[42] Mekas's approach in Reel 5 mirrors this idyllic chronotope clearly, with nature becoming a visual metaphor for his newfound harmony.

Different strategies mark this change of chronotope in Reel 5. In the voice-over, Mekas talks metaphorically about the uselessness of a road through a poetic tale that evokes his own struggle. The story, told twice, is about a man who wanted to know what was at the end of the road, and "when later, many years later, after many years of journey he came to the end of the road, there was nothing, nothing but a pile of rabbit shit"

(127'). The conclusion—that "the road leads nowhere"—is not experienced as a failure, but rather as a deconstruction of a temporal understanding of personal identity in favor of a spatial understanding. Because Mekas *does* find a new identity, although it is one associated with a paradise regained, that place of happiness that he lost after his departure from Lithuania. This paradise is defined visually through his communion with nature, inextricably linked to childhood and playing. The beginning of Reel 5, with his stay at Stein's house in Vermont, introduces this change. But it is most evident in the two haiku sequences of this reel. Mekas uses a clear nonnarrative structure to underline the experience of paradise, a space not marked by temporality, since the goal is already reached. The reconstruction of paradise is underlined in the "RABBIT SHIT HAIKUS" sequence with the repetition of the word "childhood" in four of the haiku entries, illustrated by different visual motifs, among them Mekas's childlike behavior playing the accordion and running through snowfields (see figure 7.4). In the "FOOL'S HAIKUS" sequence, despite a change of location (Central Park), again we can see the playfulness of the

FIGURE 7.4 *Lost, Lost, Lost.* Mekas playing the accordion in the snow (section 20 of "RABBIT SHIT HAIKUS").

characters, "making fools" of themselves, as Mekas says, celebrating a new happiness through the attitudes of childhood.

These themes point to what David E. James considers to be the basic narrative of Mekas's diary films: "the attempt to regain Lithuania, a mission that has several components whose isomorphism and fungibility supply the massive energy of Mekas' myth."[43] According to James, this myth is constructed on various complementary levels: the recovery of the mother, of the organic village community, of the rural scene, and of a cultural practice appropriate to it. These ideas are recognizable in Mekas's first diary film, *Walden*, which James is referring to, but they are also noticeable throughout *Reminiscences* and *Lost, Lost, Lost*. In *Reminiscences*, Mekas is reunited with his mother and revisits the childhood and youth he left behind when he had to flee in 1948, albeit with the bittersweet taste of someone who is aware of the fleeting nature of the family reunion and the impossibility of returning permanently to his birth country. In *Lost, Lost, Lost*, they are evident again, with the same framework of a narrative told by a displaced person, marked by exile, but who now overcomes his exilic condition through the integration of the values of nature and countryside associated with his birthplace into his new home.

This integration is closely related to Mekas's understanding of filmmaking, linked to the "folk art" that he saw reflected in the filmmakers who work with small-gauge formats (8 mm, 16 mm).[44] As James rightly points out, Mekas distanced himself both from the industrial mode of film production and from the modernist avant-garde, and embraced a type of filmmaking inspired by folk art, which he appropriated from the home movie mode to articulate a personal perspective.[45] This unique symbiosis of a folk art at the service of such a personal style was already conveyed masterfully in the main section of *Reminiscences*, with its visual and narrative experimentation fusing with the nature and the people of Semeniškiai, its direct gazes to the camera, its scenes and landscapes unchanged with the passage of time, and its traditional songs sung to the tune of an accordion. Now, *Lost, Lost, Lost* achieves a fusion that evokes this same symbiosis, but that has a more direct relationship with the process of Mekas's integration into his new country, which transcends a conventional sociopolitical explanation to engage more directly with cultural and artistic parameters.

This process is expressed in Reel 6 through its emphasis on Mekas's role as a filmmaker, stressing his understanding of paradise as being regained through culture, mainly through cinema. The main parts of this reel—a trip to the Flaherty Film Seminar and a visit to Stony Brook, New York, on Long Island—reflect an intense fusion of his filmmaking practice with the playful engagement with nature already shown in Reel 5. His trip to the Flaherty Seminar in Vermont, together with some friends (including avant-garde filmmakers Ken and Florence Jacobs), becomes an act of vindication of Mekas's work as a filmmaker, while also introducing an ironic commentary on the documentary film industry. Rejected by the Flaherty Seminar, Mekas and his friends stand outside as the true guardians of filmmaking, "the monks of the order of cinema," wrapped up in their sleeping blankets as if they were religious habits, with a soundtrack of chiming bells and Gregorian music reinforcing the metaphor (146'–148'). Meanwhile, we see Mekas (filmed by Ken Jacobs) moving around freely with his camera, filming the flowers in the grass as a visual celebration of this new order of cinema. Paradise has been regained, and Mekas celebrates it in his interplay with nature as seen through the lens of his Bolex camera.

The presence of Ken Jacobs and other people of New York's independent and avant-garde film community gives the film a new dimension (which is also present in other diary films by Mekas), as a chronicle of this artistic world that emerged in New York City in the 1950s and 1960s. As noted at the beginning of this chapter, Mekas (along with his brother Adolfas) played an active role in the promotion of this filmmaking community, founding the magazine *Film Culture* (1954), and then leading or forming part of the group that established the Film-Makers' Cooperative (1962), published the manifesto of the New American Cinema movement (1960), and created the Film-Makers' Cinematheque (1964), which in 1970 became the Anthology Film Archives. In those years, Mekas created a network of relationships with filmmakers and artists who pursued careers in this more alternative environment, including some figures who had a huge media impact, such as Andy Warhol, John Lennon, and Yoko Ono. In parallel with the promotion of these initiatives, Mekas continued making his film diaries, in which many of these filmmakers, artists, and writers would appear, because they formed part of the filmmaker's everyday interactions. As a result, when these film diaries were subsequently turned into diary films, they constituted a unique chronicle of the New York film community.

This chronicle was completed in other diary films by Mekas, which also frequently combine everyday scenes of his family with others showing people and activities in the film community, often blurring the boundary between the two worlds. Jeffrey Rouf highlights this blurry boundary when he describes Mekas's films as "the home movies of the avant-garde," arguing that his diaries are constructed as genuine home movies "produced by, for, and about the avant-garde community."[46] This may perhaps be an overstatement, because Mekas's diary films do not have such an exclusive focus on the avant-garde community and because, as noted above, they transcend a typically home movie approach to construct an autobiographical narrative articulated in films with an artistic personality of their own. The French scholar Laurence Allard takes a more nuanced view of this relationship when she describes Mekas's films—which she links to the work of Stan Brakhage—as a personal oeuvre that brings home moviemaking and experimental filmmaking together.[47] The similar way that these two filmmakers have of making and understanding films reveals a close kinship between these two apparently opposed cinematic modes, as Allard explains: both home moviemaking and experimental film have a family air that makes outsiders uncomfortable watching them, as they contain a biographical connection between "author," "actors," and audience; moreover, these audiences meet at private exhibition venues, thereby creating "communities of communication" and restricted interpretation, which in the case of Mekas (or Brakhage) are communities by virtue of an artistic affinity.[48]

This particular chronicle of New York's artistic community that Mekas offers in *Lost, Lost, Lost* can be understood in microhistorical terms, along the lines posited for the analysis of the first part of the film, although now applied much more loosely. The film maintains a reduced scale of observation, with an especially fragmentary structure in keeping with its diaristic nature, which does not provide significant historical contextualization but instead assumes a basic knowledge of the general context. In this sense, as Allard suggests, it offers an experience similar to that of home movies, as only those who belong to this "family" of the New York film community or who know it well can really appreciate the appearance of its members, even when they are not named by Mekas in the film. Nevertheless, with the elements provided fairly explicitly in the film, it is possible to put together a kind of microhistorical chronicle of New York's independent and avant-garde film community. The first member of this community to be featured in the film first appears in Reel 2: the Lithuanian painter George Maciunas, who also immigrated to the United States at the end of the 1940s. Mekas filmed a gathering of friends in Maciunas's house in the early 1950s, years before he became famous as the founder of the Fluxus movement.[19] The poet and film-maker Storm de Hirsch and her husband, Louis Brigante, also a film-maker, already appeared in Reel 3, but they appear again in this last reel. De Hirsch was one of the founding members of the Film-Makers' Cooperative, along with the Mekas brothers and Ken Jacobs and his wife, Florence. Mekas actually dedicates an important sequence in Reel 5 and another in Reel 6 to the Film-Makers' Cooperative. In the first appears P. Adam Sitney, the most influential scholar of the American avant-garde, who is also identified by name in the intertitles (see figure 7.5). In Reel 6,

FIGURE 7.5 *Lost, Lost, Lost.* P. Adam Sitney, a well-known scholar of the American avant-garde and experimental film, at the Film-Makers' Cooperative.

the experimental filmmaker Ed Emshwiller appears, along with images from the premiere of *Twice a Man*, a film by George Markopoulos released in 1963. Ken and Florence Jacobs also have an important presence, both in the long sequence of the trip to the Flaherty Seminar and in the Stony Brook sequence (described below), not only as participants in the trip but also through the images taken by them and included by Mekas in the film, in the only two scenes where he uses footage not filmed by himself or his brother.[50] As all this makes clear, over the course of the film Mekas develops a portrait of the New York film community that is attuned to a microhistorical perspective, as he seeks to offer an alternative to conventional historical chronicles through fragments provided by the available archival sources, which in this case are his own film diaries.

Lost, Lost, Lost ends with a section (157'–165') introduced with its own intertitle—"A VISIT TO STONY BROOK"—which in a way confirms the conclusion of the process of Mekas's integration into his adopted country. Supported for the second time by the dialogue between Mekas's and Ken Jacobs's footage (which allows us to see Mekas filming and then to see the result of his work), this sequence underscores Mekas's autobiographical perspective, with nature as the dominant chronotope. On the beach in Long Island, surrounded by his friends, with the Gregorian chant playing again, Mekas remembers the experience as "good"—as "like being in a church." Playfulness is the overriding mode in this new harmony with nature. And once again, nature and cinema merge, in a very self-conscious sequence where filming parallels enjoying nature and friendship. The possible contradiction between the harmonic world of nature and the mechanical mediation of the film apparatus is blurred by the home movie style of the filming, fusing them into a unique blend, challenging both the industrial and the avant-garde modes of filmmaking, as James points out.[51] Mekas distances himself from industrial narrative cinema with his personal, autobiographical film; however, although he makes use of some avant-garde film techniques, with a jazz-like, self-conscious style, he also steers clear of the structural and political variations of avant-garde cinema that were prominent in the 1960s by foregrounding home moviemaking as his dominant stylistic approach.

The last sentences of Mekas's voice-over in this sequence close the film with a new reworking of the spatial understanding of his personal quest.

An echo of his exilic condition reappears briefly when he remarks: "Since no place was really his, no place was really his home, he had this habit of attaching himself immediately to any place" (162'). But the final note is positive, since now he is able to create memories of his new life in the United States: "He remembered another day. Ten years ago, he sat on this beach." In this way, Mekas posits a temporal tension in his inner reconstruction, although always linked to a place: "Again I have memories. I have a memory of this place. I have been here before. I have really been here before. I have seen this water before. Yes, I have walked upon this beach, these pebbles" (164'). These new memories are ultimately not a sign of his paradise lost in Lithuania, but of his new identity in America, now embraced with a sense of recovery and hope. Mekas no longer presents himself as the lonely displaced person of the first reels. He has regained a home through culture, and from that moment his film diaries deal with that home and the friends who inhabit it. The final proof of this change, as Scott MacDonald points out, can be found outside of the narrative, in the completion of the film *Lost, Lost, Lost*,[52] because it reveals how, some twenty years after shooting this footage, Mekas feels confident enough to face his work from those early years, editing it to give shape to this powerful and personal chronicle of exile and rebirth.

This close analysis of *Lost, Lost, Lost* has shown how the film effectively provides an insightful portrait of the immigrant experience, which can be read productively from a microhistorical perspective, understood in a broader but nevertheless truly revealing sense. Mekas constructs a microhistorical narrative about the community of Lithuanians who immigrated to the United States after World War II, with a reduced scale of observation that offers a multifaceted portrait, combining the celebratory routines of this community shown in the visuals with the pain caused by their uprooting from their native land, expressed mainly in the voice-over. To this end, the film fuses the hardships suffered by Mekas and his compatriots as first-generation immigrants with the specific challenges Mekas faces when he decides first to make film diaries of that experience and later on to turn those diaries into a decisive testimony of his process of integration into a new country. After deciding to separate himself from the Lithuanian community, Mekas dedicates the rest of the film to that process of integration, which is somewhat unique because it is closely tied to his involvement in the activities of the independent and avant-garde film world. Mekas covers this artistic community in his film diaries too, offering, in the second part of the film, a certain chronicle of its people and activities that can also be understood in a loose sense as microhistorical. In this way, *Lost, Lost, Lost* contains an alternative historiographical approach to two different worlds through the prism of Jonas Mekas's personal experience, testing the limits of the microhistorical approach in the film medium.

EPILOGUE

Looking to the Future

The different case studies presented in this book have shown how documentary films taking microhistorical approaches can help us to better understand past eras and societies, ranging from more canonical examples like the work of Péter Forgács (*The Maelstrom, Free Fall,* and *Class Lot*) to more hybrid proposals like Rea Tajiri's *History and Memory*. These films all share the main constituent features of written microhistory, while adding elements specific to the film medium. Especially notable among the former is the reduction of the scale of observation to offer a deeper or complementary understanding of the past. This change to the scale of observation is adopted with the intention of being historically representative, connecting the microhistory in various ways to its macrohistorical contexts. At the same time, the documentaries analyzed here are usually supported by narrative structures articulated through personal or family histories. This underscores another common feature of microhistory: the centrality of human agency. To this end, the films analyzed generally draw from family archives, with an emphasis—as may be expected given their audio/visual nature—on snapshots and home movies, but also using other types of more personal archives, such as letters or diaries. Family archives tend to be somewhat limited, and when working with them filmmakers have to adopt something like the conjectural approach taken for written microhistory, considering both the information the archives provide and the lacunae evident in them.

Microhistorical documentaries also have some specific features of their own. Notable among these is the frequent use of autobiographical approaches as a means of access to the microhistorical past, reinforcing the role of the protagonists' personal memory in the reconstruction of the past and, consequently, their consideration as "histories of the present." In addition, whether or not they include an autobiographical perspective, these documentaries often highlight an affective dimension in their reconstruction of the past, a feature rarely found in professional history but central to films like *The Missing Picture* or *A Family Gathering*. In some cases, they also adopt an essayistic approach that may help to highlight the temporal indiscernibility and performative nature of personal memory, in line with a postmodern historiographical approach that can also be found in certain features of some written microhistory.

Taking into account this framework developed throughout the book, this epilogue offers some reflections on how the microhistorical documentary might evolve in the future. The considerable breadth and pace of current technological changes is having a big impact on professional history and archival practices as well as on documentary filmmaking. Indeed, the progressive digitalization of archival sources and the rise of the Internet—both as a means of access and as a source of information— have reshaped the concept of archives and even the work methods of professional historians, sparking intense debate in contemporary historiography over the future of the field and the dimensions and significance of a "digital" history in which written documents preserved in traditional formats are becoming increasingly rare.[1]

Although a full exploration of this debate is obviously beyond the scope of this epilogue, it also raises important questions about the future of the microhistorical documentary. The challenges of the digital turn have had a more immediate impact on historical documentaries than on written history, because it has affected not only the sources available and the research methods but also the format itself, particularly with the appearance of interactive documentaries (also known as i-docs or web documentaries), designed specifically for the Internet, using multimedia elements and nonlinear structures.[2] Documentary filmmakers have also begun experimenting with virtual reality (VR), a technology not yet fully developed for documentary making, but which might offer some original perspectives.[3] Also worthy of consideration are the possibilities offered by educational video games that focus on historical issues, although their specific objectives place them in the field of historical dissemination and they are aimed more explicitly at children and youth. Nevertheless, there are examples of video games that imitate elements of filmic styles and narratives, which at first glance appear to adopt something of a microhistorical approach. Such is the case with *1979 Revolution: Black Friday* (2016), which provides information on the events of the Iranian Revolution by turning the player into a protagonist, underscoring the centrality of human agency in the study of history.[4] Yet this could not be said to be a truly microhistorical approach, as the protagonist of the game is a fictional character that serves as a channel of access to the macrohistorical events of the revolution. The innovative feature, inherent in the dynamic of video games, is the way it connects historical knowledge to the player experience, as if the player is simply one more character in this public history, supported by links to short texts that provide the game play with historical context.[5] In any case, predicting the future of formats based on new technologies is no easy task in an era of such rapid changes. The fragile nature of multimedia platforms, in terms of both access (with so many websites becoming inaccessible after a few years) and software (whose designers may eventually stop maintaining it[6]), points to one of the serious problems affecting mainly interactive documentaries, a format that includes works of historiographical value, but whose promising future is often jeopardized when technological changes render these works inaccessible.

Beyond questions of accessibility, interactive documentaries offer some noteworthy narrative and expressive options that are not possible in linear documentaries, resulting in interesting approaches that can be described as microhistorical. This is the case, for example, of *A Polish Journey* (2016).[7] In this i-doc, the multimedia environment allows its creator, Julian Konczak, to bring together three different expressive channels (structured around seven episodes): the audiovisual pieces he has created (which can also be viewed together as a linear documentary on YouTube); a photo journal of the places he and his son visit, created by his son; and the macrohistorical context, explained in short texts, which can be expanded to a fourth level with links to these subjects on

Wikipedia (except for the first episode), telling us the history of the more than 200,000 Polish soldiers who fought alongside the British army, only to find at the end of the war that Poland was to be left under Stalin's control, forcing most of them to live the rest of their lives in exile. At the center of this i-doc are the audiovisual pieces, which have a clear autobiographical dimension, due not only to the filmmaker's autodiegetic narration but also to their central theme: the story of his father, a Pole who enlisted in the German army after his country was invaded, then deserted and fought with the Allies, and finally ended up in exile in Scotland, where he got married and lived the rest of his life. Konczak recounts the basic elements of this story, but he focuses more on the places and the feelings, imbuing his work with a powerfully poetic quality in keeping with the primacy of the personal mnemonic journey that characterizes his i-doc. His son's photo journal strays even further from a conventional historical approach to place the focus on the landscapes and his personal relationship with these locations. With such different approaches, *A Polish Journey* does not quite manage to integrate the microhistorical narrative, based on Konczak's journey into his father's past using filmic language, and the macrohistorical context, which is presented in standard written texts supported by historical explanations on Wikipedia. It is true that the i-doc begins with Konczak's discovery of his father's Nazi German army identity book (the *Soldbuch*), which constitutes a promising link between the two scales of observation; however, this connection turns out not to be as central as the spectator might expect, weakening the dialogue between the macro- and microhistorical scales.

Where i-docs may offer a more promising avenue for the microhistorical documentary is in the creation of collective portraits, because in such cases they can provide access to each of the protagonists and to their presentation together in a collective portrait on the same website—a possibility that linear documentaries cannot offer. A noteworthy example of this approach is *Hidden like Anne Frank* (2010), which explores the lives of Jewish children hidden during the Nazi occupation of the Netherlands. The project was also published as a book, compiling fourteen first-person testimonies.[8] As interactive documentary, it features twenty-two stories accessible via each person or via a map showing the routes taken by the children, who were often forced to change hiding places. Each personal history also combines text, photos, written documents, and short audiovisual pieces with the testimonies of the protagonists, illustrated with animation. Although its interactive structure is relatively simple, this project clearly offers an interesting microhistorical perspective on the Shoah, set in the same geographical location as *The Maelstrom*, but in this case through a collective portrait exploring the personal experiences of Jewish children, constructed using a range of sources and expressive forms, including the protagonists' own oral testimonies. In a creative decision that is undeniably surprising, the creators do not offer these testimonies in the form of filmed interviews, limiting our visual knowledge of the protagonists to a few pictures of their childhood and a contemporary photo that closes each story.

Another interactive documentary that offers a powerful collective portrait of a past era from a microhistorical perspective is *Jerusalem, We Are Here* (2016).[9] This i-doc offers a virtual tour around the streets of Katamon, a wealthy, predominantly Christian Arab neighborhood of Jerusalem, whose inhabitants fled or were expelled in the 1948 war. *Jerusalem, We Are Here* is presented more immediately as an exploration of the locations, shown on three different routes with different stops, and even including a map with the history of the buildings in the neighborhood. But each stop constitutes a foray into the past using different types of archival sources—photographs, home movies, press clips—complemented by contemporary oral or filmed testimonies. This creates a rich and complex palimpsest of archival sources, expressive elements, and historical scales, clearly dominated by a microhistorical approach, but always in dialogue with its macrohistorical context, as is also evidenced by the starting and ending points shared by all three routes: the former Regent Cinema (now operating as Lev Smadar Theater) and St. Simeon Monastery. Presented by three "tour guides" (two Palestinian and one Jewish, Dorit Naaman, who is also director and co-producer), the i-doc recounts the history of different places and houses of Katamon, and of the families who lived there in the past. These stories are always presented with a short text accompanied by audio or video, usually narrated by the former inhabitants of the homes or their descendants. In some cases, the videos show these descendants trying to visit their homes, although they are often refused access. Other videos depict the present situation of the former inhabitants, such as in the moving short piece (on "Route 3") made by Ranwa Stephan, which shows her father tending his garden, while in a voice-over she reflects on her status as an exile: "I inherited exile from my parents. . . . Palestinian, Christian, I was born in Beirut and raised in France. Nobody is like me. I have neither territory nor community." And, thinking of her father, she adds: "Nothing will bring back his Palestine, the lost paradise of his childhood, snatched away by history." This clearly echoes some of the themes analyzed in chapter 6, particularly in the film *A World Not Ours*, told from the point of view of the exilic condition of a Palestinian filmmaker, but also in *My Land Zion*, in relation to the "abandoned" Palestinian house near Motti Golani's mother's home.[10] On the whole, *Jerusalem, We Are Here* also manifests more fully than any linear microhistorical documentary the idea of a collage or mosaic made with "miniatures" to form societal patchwork structures, which is advocated by Alf Lüdtke for telling histories of everyday life, as explained in chapter 1.[11]

Parallel to the debate over the forms that the microhistorical documentary might take in coming years is the debate about the future of archives and, more specifically, family archives. Archivists are tackling the digital turn from various angles, although the discussion tends to center on the preservation of written documents and the consequences of their transformation to digitalized form, including the risk that documents that are not digitalized will be consigned to oblivion. Another important line of debate is related to preservation methods for native digital sources, whose future access raises many questions (as was mentioned above in relation to i-docs). These native digital sources range from public websites to personal correspondence, which has shifted almost entirely from written letters to emails or conversations on social media. This issue directly affects personal and family archives, which, as discussed in chapter 2, are very common sources for microhistorical documentaries. The speed and immediacy of personal communication in the digital era has undermined the document status acquired by written correspondence, which families once were often in the habit of preserving. The same phenomenon has affected the family snapshot. With the smartphone replacing the camera, photographs have lost their value as documents and have become images created mainly for sharing on social media. This has resulted in the progressive disappearance of family albums and photo collections (traditionally stored in shoeboxes, unclassified but always retrievable), in the confidence that all photos taken will be available forever at no charge in the "cloud," when in reality the latest commercial or technological turn could deprive families of access to that cloud or force them to pay for it.

In the specific area of home movies, technological changes have occurred extraordinarily quickly, especially since the 1980s with the mass distribution of VHS cameras, followed by camcorders using various formats (Video8, Hi8, Digital8, MiniDV, memory cards), and finally the current smartphones with their increasingly sophisticated cameras. The current proliferation of videos taken with cell phones has brought us into an age of mass reproduction of both private and public events, but the preservation of those recordings seems to be of little concern to nonprofessional users, once again naively confident that they will enjoy permanent access to whatever they have stored in the cloud. In this context, filmmakers who decide to take a microhistorical perspective on the recent past may have access to audiovisual family archives that are much more abundant than they ever were before. The unknown factor lies precisely in the accessibility of these audiovisual archives for future generations, which was more assured in the era of analog film and photography, despite the more limited nature of the material.

The omnipresence of smartphones as recording devices has also blurred the line between the private or family sphere and the public sphere. On the one hand, countless family images are shared on widely accessible social media platforms, while on the other hand, public events are constantly being recorded on smartphones, sometimes serving as whistleblowing tools. Ever since the infamous case of the arrest of Rodney King in Los Angeles in 1991, filmed on a neighbor's camera, home videos have become a common source of spontaneous news stories and have been used to denounce dictatorial regimes or expose human rights violations. One well-known example of the importance of cell phone recordings in the development of historical events was their use during the so-called Arab Spring, both for mobilizing local populations and for spreading news of the popular uprising and its subsequent repression to the outside world. It is interesting to note that part of the work of archiving and disseminating the audio/visual documents of the uprising has relied on multimedia platforms like the website Vox Populi, which describes itself as "archiving a revolution in the digital age." This website actually includes a specific section titled "Archives," which contains numerous photos, videos, press articles, works of graffiti, and legal documents, related mainly to the events of the 2011 Egyptian Revolution and its aftermath.[12]

These very same events are the subject of an interactive documentary created by Alisa Lebow in 2018, *Filming Revolution*, self-described as a "meta-documentary," based chiefly on interviews with Egyptian filmmakers, activists, and archivists who reflect on the role and meaning of making films in times of revolution, supplemented with short analytical reflections by Lebow herself, a well-known documentary scholar.[13] In the section titled "History + Memory," she suggests that "it was well understood that the material shot during the events of the revolution could one day be used to write that history. The Mosireen archive would be the prime vehicle for such a writing, and the history that would emerge will certainly tell a very different story than what the government has been attempting to recount."[14] But what she finds even more striking is that although the interviews were conducted one or two years after the events, "the impression was that history was alive in daily practice, as the materials from the archive actively participate in defining the terms of the present and the future." And referring to one of the projects examined, she points out that "the archive is not just a repository of memory, it is a tool for the intervention in history . . . that continually undermines the authoritarian methods in which dominant narratives are crafted, and takes the power out of the hands of the officials."[15] These assertions might be dismissed as somewhat utopian given the historical development of events in Egypt, where the popular uprising that ousted Mubarak from power was followed just three years later by the installment of a regime similar to Mubarak's, with another military strongman, Abdel Fattah el-Sisi, in the president's chair. Indeed, Lebow seems to acknowledge this when she concludes: "While this may appear to be an unrealized ideal, never fully accomplished by any one project, these archival projects when seen in aggregate do offer an alternative view of this history and many alternatives for its writing." The underlying idea is the possibility of writing a "crowd-sourced history," based on different recordings made both by professional filmmakers and by ordinary people. In this sense, this proposal could be interpreted as a literal case of "history from below," not only in terms of its objects of study but also in terms of the people recording and providing the archival material.

Lebow is pointing to a trend that Luke Tredinnick also identifies in his reflection on the making of history in the digital era, characterized by an immediacy that threatens to close the gap between the historical trace and the written history, which has always been such an inherent feature of any process of professional history: "In contemporary culture, the past and the present, the record and the history are converging. The past has saturated the present, and the two exhibit complex interaction in an already historicized present. This occurs because of the immediacy of the digital record."[16] Tredinnick applies this thesis to historical events such as the death of Princess Diana or the September 11 terrorist attacks, which became "instant history," characterized by "the immediacy of the interaction between media representation and public consumption."[17] This has effectively collapsed a distinction that was basic to the discipline, which requires a space between the original moment and its writing as history: "The immediacy of digital culture means that the record is already written in the moment of its experience, already understood as a property of mediation, already framed by the conventions of representation and narrative, and the conventions of history."[18]

Although both Lebow and Tredinnick offer a perhaps excessively polemical view of contemporary history in the digital era, the two authors share an understanding of history clearly in line with the "history of the present" explored in chapter 1, which to different degrees characterizes the microhistorical documentaries analyzed in this book. It is a history closely linked to the mnemonic experience of its protagonists, who are often still alive, and to the different records of their recent past. In this sense, it would seem reasonable to expect that microhistorical documentaries—whether they adopt linear or interactive formats— will become more prominent in the near future. They have the advantage of naturally allowing a stronger interaction between a diverse range of digital records (written, audio, photographic, and audiovisual; personal, family, and public), usually with a process of historicization undertaken quite soon after the events, as has been observed in the films analyzed in this book.

FILMOGRAPHY

5 Broken Cameras (خمس كاميرات محطمة). 2011. Emad Burnat and Guy Davidi

Angelos' Film. 1999. Péter Forgács

Another Land (תרחא ץרא). 1998. Amit Goren

The Bartos Family. 1988. Péter Forgács

A Bibó Reader. 2001. Péter Forgács

The Bishop's Garden. 2002. Péter Forgács

Bophana: A Cambodian Tragedy (*Bophana, une tragédie cambodgienne*). 1996. Rithy Panh

Bourgeois Dictionary. 1992. Péter Forgács

Carta a un padre. 2013. Edgardo Cozarinsky

Class Lot. 1997. Péter Forgács

The Danube Exodus. 1998. Péter Forgács

Diary (ומוי). 1983. David Perlov

The Diary of Mr. N. 1990. Péter Forgács

Dimona Twist (טסיווט הנומיד). 2016. Michal Aviad.

Duch: Master of the Forges of Hell (*Duch, le maître des forges de l'enfer*). 2011. Rithy Panh

Dusi & Jenő. 1988. Péter Forgács

El misterio de los ojos escarlata. 1993. Alfredo J. Anzola

El Perro Negro. 2005. Péter Forgács

Exile Family Movie. 2013. Arash T. Riahi

A Family Gathering. 1989. Lise Yasui and Ann Tegnell

Filming Revolution. 2018. Alisa Lebow

For My Children (ילש םידליל). 2002. Michal Aviad

Free Fall. 1996. Péter Forgács

From a Silk Cocoon. 2005. Stephen Holsapple, Emery Clay III, and Satsuki Ina

GermanUnity@Balaton. 2011. Péter Forgács

Hacer patria. 2007. David Blaustein

Hidden Like Anne Frank. 2010. Marcel Prins, Peter Henk Steenhuis, and Marcel van der Drift

History and Memory. 1991. Rea Tajiri

Hunky Blues. 2009. Péter Forgács

I Am Von Höfler. 2008. Péter Forgács

I for India. 2005. Sandhya Suri

Israel: A Home Movie (וניאר דכ). 2012. Eliav Lilti and Arik Bernstein

Jerusalem, We Are Here (يا قدس، نحن هنا). 2016. Dorit Naaman

Juan, como si nada hubiera sucedido. 1987. Carlos Echeverría

Kádár's Kiss. 1997. Péter Forgács

La línea paterna. 1994. José Buil and Marisa Sistach

Letter Without Words. 1998. Lisa Lewenz

Los rubios. 2003. Albertina Carri

Lost, Lost, Lost. 1976. Jonas Mekas

M. 2007. Nicolás Prividera

The Maelstrom. 1997. Péter Forgács

Meanwhile Somewhere . . . 1940–1943. 1994. Péter Forgács

Mémoire d'outremer. 1997. Claude Bossion

Miss Universe 1929. 2006. Péter Forgács

The Missing Picture (*L'image manquante*). 2014. Rithy Panh

My Brother (ילש חאה). 2007. Yulie Cohen

My Land Zion (יתמדא, וויצ). 2004. Yulie Cohen

My Terrorist (ילש לבחמה). 2002. Yulie Cohen

The Notebook of a Lady. 1994. Péter Forgács

Out of Love . . . Be Back Shortly (בושא וקית—הבהא שפחל יתאצי). 1997. Dan Katzir

Papá Iván. 2000. María Inés Roqué

Picturesque Epochs. 2016. Péter Forgács

A Polish Journey. 2016. Julian Konczak

Private Century (*Soukromé století*). 2006. Jan Kikl

Private Chronicles: Monologue (*Частные хроники. Монолог*). 1999. Vitaly Manskij

Rabbit in the Moon. 1999. Emiko and Chizu Omori

Reminiscences of a Journey to Lithuania. 1972. Jonas Mekas

S-21: The Khmer Rouge Killing Machine (*S21: La machine de mort Khmere rouge*). 2003. Rithy Panh

Simply Happy. 1993. Péter Forgács

Something Strong Within. 1994. Robert Nakamura and Karen L. Ishizuka

Updated Diary (וכדוׁעמ וׁמוׁי). 1999. David Perlov

Venom. 2016. Péter Forgács

Who's Going to Pay for These Donuts, Anyway? 1992. Janice Tanaka

Wittgenstein Tractatus. 1992. Péter Forgács

The Women Pioneers (תצולחה). 2013. Michal Aviad

A World Not Ours (عالمٌ ليس لنا). 2012. Mahdi Fleifel

Y in Vyborg (*Hetket jotka jäivät*). 2005. Pia Andell

Yidl in the Middle. 1999. Marlene Booth

Zahra. 2009. Mohammed Bakri

NOTES

ACKNOWLEDGMENTS

1. Efrén Cuevas, ed., *La casa abierta: El cine doméstico y sus reciclajes contemporáneos*, Madrid: Ocho y medio, 2010. The whole book as well as the original English texts of some of the chapters are available at https://efrencuevas.com/books.

2. Efrén Cuevas, "Microhistoria y cine documental: Puntos de encuentro," *Historia Social*, no. 91 (2018): 69–83; Efrén Cuevas, "Change of Scale: Home Movies as Microhistory in Documentary Films," in *Amateur Filmmaking: the Home Movie, the Archive, the Web*, ed. Laura Rascaroli, Gwenda Young, and Barry Monahan (London: Bloomsbury, 2014), 139–51; Efrén Cuevas, "Home Movies as Personal Archives in Autobiographical Documentaries," *Studies in Documentary Film* 17, no. 1 (2013): 17–29; Efrén Cuevas, "The Immigrant Experience in Jonas Mekas's Diary Films: A Chronotopic Analysis of *Lost, Lost, Lost*," *Biography* 29, no. 1 (2006): 55–73.

INTRODUCTION

1. Robert Rosenstone, *History on Film/Film on History* (Harlow, UK: Pearson Longman, 2006), 86.

2. The information on the number of monographs is mentioned by Robert Rosenstone in his article "Reflections on What the Filmmaker Historian Does (to History)," in *Film, History and Memory*, ed. Jennie M. Carlsten and Fearghal McGarry (London: Palgrave Macmillan, 2015), 188.

3. Tiziana M. Di Blasio, *Cinema e storia: Interferenze e confluenze tra due scritture* (Rome: Viella, 2014); Mia E. M. Treacey, *Reframing the Past: History, Film and Television* (London: Routledge, 2016). These monographs also reflect the effects of language

barriers: Di Blasio barely cites any works in English not translated into Italian, while Treacey similarly omits works not translated into English. These barriers are also evident in the exclusion from both monographs of research published in languages like Spanish. In the specific case of Spain, this field has developed significantly, particularly thanks to the work of José María Caparrós, who created the Centro de Investigación Film-Historia in 1983 and launched a journal with the same name in 1991.

4. Bolesław Matuszewski, "A New Source of History: The Creation of a Depository for Historical Cinematography," in *Film Manifestos and Global Cinema Cultures*, ed. Scott MacKenzie (Berkeley: University of California Press, 2014), 520. First published in French as *Une nouvelle source de l'histoire* (Paris: Imprimerie Noizette, 1898).

5. Marc Ferro, *Cinema and History* (Detroit: Wayne University Press, 1988), first published in French as *Cinema et histoire* (Paris: Denoël/Gonthier, 1977); Pierre Sorlin, *The Film in History: Restaging the Past* (Oxford: Basil Blackwell, 1980). A few years earlier, Sorlin had published another seminal work in this field, *Sociologie du Cinéma: Ouverture pour l'histoire de demain* (Paris: Aubier Montaigne, 1977).

6. Paul Smith, ed., *The Historian and Film* (Cambridge: Cambridge University Press, 2011); Rosenstone, *History on Film/Film on History*, with a second edition in 2012 published by Routledge.

7. See, for instance, chapter 3 in Rosenstone, *History on Film*, 32–49.

8. Sorlin, *Film in History*, 3.

9. John E. O'Connor and Martin A. Jackson, *American History/American Film: Interpreting the Hollywood Image*, 2nd ed. (New York: Continuum, 1991), xx.

10. Antoine de Baecque, *Camera Historica: The Century in Cinema* (New York: Columbia University Press, 2012), 356–59.

11. Robert B. Toplin, "The Filmmaker as Historian," *American Historical Review* 93, no. 5 (1988): 1226.

12. Robert Rosenstone, "History in Images/History in Words: Reflections on the Possibility of Really Putting History onto Film," *American Historical Review* 93, no. 5 (1988): 1173–85.

13. Rosenstone, *History on Film*, 37.

14. Rosenstone, *History on Film*, 159.

15. Rosenstone, *History on Film*, 160.

16. Hayden White, "Historiography and Historiophoty," *American Historical Review* 93, no. 5 (1988): 1193.

17. White, "Historiography and Historiophoty," 1194.

18. Jennie M. Carlsten and Fearghal McGarry, "Introduction," in *Film, History and Memory*, 6.

19. Marnie Hughes-Warrington, *History Goes to the Movies: Studying History on Film* (London: Routledge, 2007). The Toplin article cited above, "The Filmmaker as Historian," also focuses on documentary films in its brief analysis of different case studies.

20. See Bill Nichols, *Representing Reality: Issues and Concepts in Documentary* (Bloomington: Indiana University Press, 1991), 33–38.

21. There are various reasons for the interest that these films have aroused in film studies, but there is little evidence, at least in the more restricted field of documentary studies, of a keen interest in documentaries that have an exploration of the past as a central concern. Apart from specific studies of individual films, it is worth noting here the chapter by Ann Gray, "History Documentaries for Television," in *The Documentary Film Book*, ed. Brian Winston (London: BFI Publishing, 2013), and the special issue on documentary and history, edited by Marcius Freire and Manuela Penafria, in the Portuguese journal *Doc on-line*, no. 15 (2013), http://doc.ubi.pt/index15.html.

22. See Robert A. Rosenstone, "The Future of the Past: Film and the Beginnings of Postmodern History," in *The Persistence of History: Cinema, Television, and the Modern Event*, ed. Vivian Sobchack (London: Routledge, 1996), 201–18.

1. MICROHISTORY AND DOCUMENTARY FILM

1. The arguments presented in the middle part of this chapter were originally posited in a previous article of mine, published in Spanish, "Microhistoria y cine documental: Puntos de encuentro," *Historia Social*, no. 91 (2018): 69–83.

2. John Brewer, "Microhistory and the Histories of Everyday Life," *Cultural and Social History* 7, no. 1 (2010): 92.

3. Juan Gracia Cárcamo, "Microsociología e historia de lo cotidiano," *Revista Ayer*, no. 19 (1995): 189.

4. Ben Highmore, *Everyday Life and Cultural Theory* (London: Routledge, 2001), 19.

5. Highmore, *Everyday Life and Cultural Theory*, 21.

6. Highmore, *Everyday Life and Cultural Theory*, 24–25.

7. Highmore, *Everyday Life and Cultural Theory*, 27.

8. Brewer, "Microhistory and the Histories of Everyday Life"; and Harry D. Harootunian, *History's Disquiet: Modernity, Cultural Practice, and the Question of Everyday Life* (New York: Columbia University Press, 2000), particularly chapter 2, "The 'Mystery of the Everyday:' Everydayness in History."

9. Brewer, "Microhistory and the Histories of Everyday Life," 99.

10. Georg Simmel, *Sociology: Inquiries into the Construction of Social Forms* (Leiden: Brill, 2009), 33.

11. Georg Simmel, "Sociological Aesthetics," in *The Conflict in Modern Culture and Other Essays* (New York: Teachers College, 1968), 69.

12. David Frisby, *Fragments of Modernity: Theories of Modernity in the Work of Simmel, Kracauer and Benjamin* (Cambridge, MA: MIT Press, 1988), 271.

13. Brewer, "Microhistory and the Histories of Everyday Life," 99.

14. Walter Benjamin, *The Arcades Project* (Cambridge, MA: Belknap Press, 1999), 461, N2,6. Matti Peltonen explores this connection between Benjamin and microhistory in "Clues, Margins, and Monads: The Micro-Macro Link in Historical Research," *History and Theory* 40, no. 3 (2001): 353–55.

15. Highmore, *Everyday Life and Cultural Theory*, 71.

16. Harootunian, *History's Disquiet*, 105.

17. For a more detailed analysis of the role of cinema in Benjamin's thought, see Daniel Mourenza, *Walter Benjamin and the Aesthetics of Film* (Amsterdam: Amsterdam University Press, 2020).

18. Walter Benjamin, *Illuminations* (London: Fontana, 1982), 238.

19. Harootunian, *History's Disquiet*, 89.

20. For an analysis of these texts in the context of everyday life studies, see Nurçin Ileri, "The Distraction and Glamour of Everyday Life in *The Salaried Masses* and *The Mass Ornament*," *Journal of Historical Studies*, no. 5 (2007): 83–93.

21. Siegfried Kracauer, "The Mass Ornament," in *The Mass Ornament: Weimar Essays* (Cambridge, MA: Harvard University Press, 1995), 75.

22. Siegfried Kracauer, *Theory of Film: The Redemption of Physical Reality* (New York: Oxford University Press, 1960), 304.

23. Siegfried Kracauer, "The Structure of the Historical Universe," in *History, the Last Things Before the Last* (New York: Oxford University Press, 1969), 104–38.

24. Carlo Ginzburg, "Microhistory: Two or Three Things That I Know About It," *Critical Inquiry* 20, no. 1 (1993): 27.

25. Brewer, "Microhistory and the Histories of Everyday Life," 90.

26. Alf Lüdtke, ed., *History of Everyday Life: Reconstructing Historical Experiences and Ways of Life* (Princeton, NJ: Princeton University Press, 1995). The German edition was published the same year: *Alltagsgeschichte. Zur Rekonstruktion historischer Erfahrungen und Lebensweisen* (Frankfurt: Campus, 1995).

27. Giovanni Levi, *Inheriting Power: The Story of an Exorcist* (Chicago: University of Chicago Press, 1988). Originally published as *L'eredità immateriale: Carriera di un esorcista nel Piemonte del seicento* (Turin: Einaudi, 1985); Carlo Ginzburg, *The Cheese and the Worms: The Cosmos of a Sixteenth-Century Miller* (Baltimore: Johns Hopkins University Press, 1992). Originally published as *Il formaggio e i vermi: Il cosmo di un mugnaio del '500* (Turin: Einaudi, 1976).

28. Brad S. Gregory, "Is Small Beautiful? Microhistory and the History of Everyday Life," *History and Theory* 38, no. 1 (1999): 100.

29. Gregory, "Is Small Beautiful?," 103. These connections are even revealed in some of the titles of the publications, like the book edited by Winfried Schulze, *Sozialgeschichte, Alltagsgeschichte und Mikro-Historie* (Göttingen: Vandenhoeck und Ruprecht, 1994).

30. Jacques Revel, ed., *Jeux d'echelles: La micro-analyse à la expérience* (Paris: Seuil/Gallimard, 1996); Hans Medick, "Mikro-Historie," in Schulze, *Sozialgeschichte, Alltagsgeschichte, Mikro-Historie*, 40–53; Justo Serna and Anacleto Pons, *Como se escribe la microhistoria: Ensayo sobre Carlo Ginzburg* (Madrid Cátedra, 2000), which was revised and updated in a new edition published in 2019: *Microhistoria: Las narraciones de Carlo Ginzburg* (Granada: Comares); Carlos A. Aguirre, *Microhistoria italiana: Modo de empleo* (Caracas: Fundación Centro Nacional de Historia, 2009); Sigurður G. Magnússon and István Szíjártó, *What Is Microhistory? Theory and Practice* (London:

Routledge, 2013). For a more exhaustive bibliography of microhistory, see the website www.microhistory.eu.

31. Celso Medina, "Intrahistoria, cotidianidad y localidad," *Atenea*, no. 500 (2009): 123–39.

32. See E. P. Thompson, *The Making of the English Working Class* (New York: Vintage Books, 1963).

33. Clifford Geertz, *The Interpretation of Cultures* (New York: Basic Books, 1973), 21. Giovanni Levi questioned this approach for its relativism, which he argued is more obvious in the work of Geertz's followers than of Geertz himself. See Giovanni Levi, "On Microhistory," in *New Perspectives on Historical Writing*, ed. Peter Burke, 2nd ed. (Cambridge: Polity Press, 2001), 103–9; Levi, "I pericoli del geertzismo," *Quaderni storici* 20, no. 58 (1985): 269–77; Levi, "Antropologia y microhistoria: Conversación con Giovanni Levi," *Manuscrits*, no. 1 (1993): 22.

34. Brewer, "Microhistory and the Histories of Everyday Life," 100.

35. Emmanuel Le Roy, *Montaillou: Cathars and Catholics in a French Village 1294–1324* (London: Penguin, 2013). Originally published as *Montaillou, village occitan de 1294 à 1324* (Paris: Gallimard, 1975).

36. Edoardo Grendi, "Micro-analisi e storia sociale," *Quaderni Storici* 12, no. 35 (1977): 506–20. On Barth and microhistory, see Paul-André Rosetal's chapter, "Construire le 'macr' par le 'micro:' Fredrik Barth et la microstoria," in Revel, *Jeux d'echelles*, 141–59.

37. Carlo Ginzburg and Carlo Poni, "The Name and the Game: Unequal Exchange and the Historiographical Marketplace," in *Microhistory and the Lost Peoples of Europe*, ed. Edward Muir and Guido Ruggiero (Baltimore: Johns Hopkins University Press, 1991), 1–10. Originally published in *Quaderni storici*, no. 40 (1979), 181–90. With different nuances, discussion of this division between social and cultural microhistory can be found in Magnússon and Szíjártó, *What Is Microhistory?*, 17–18; Justo Serna and Anacleto Pons, "Formas de hacer microhistoria," *Agora: Revista de Ciencias Sociales*, no. 7 (2002), http://www.uv.es/~jserna/Fhm.htm; and Jacques Revel, "Micro-analyse et construction du social," in *Jeux d'echelles*, 19–30. An abridged English version of Revel's chapter can be found in "Microanalysis and the Construction of the Social," in *Histories: French Constructions of the Past*, ed. Jacques Revel and Lynn Hunt (New York: New Press, 1995), 492–502.

38. Peter Burke, ed., *New Perspectives on Historical Writing*, 2nd ed. (Cambridge: Polity Press, 2001), 115–17.

39. This outline of the basic features of microhistory is based on the works cited previously, and, in particular, for their comprehensive vision of the field, on Serna and Pons, *Como se escribe la microhistoria*; and Magnússon and Szíjártó, *What Is Microhistory?*

40. Revel, "Micro-analyse et construction du social," 19.

41. Paul Ricoeur, *Memory, History, Forgetting* (Chicago: University of Chicago Press, 2004), 212.

42. Magnússon and Szíjártó, *What Is Microhistory?*, 50–53. Here Szíjártó cites the expression "incidental analysis" coined by Darton in the *New York Review of Books* 51, no. 11 (June 24, 2004): 60–64.

43. Magnússon and Szíjártó, *What Is Microhistory?*, 63–64

44. Levi, "Antropologia y microhistoria," 17.

45. Levi, "Antropologia y microhistoria," 17.

46. Levi, "Antropologia y microhistoria," 18. Ginzburg poses a similar argument on the relationship between microhistory and local history in "Acerca de la historia local y la microhistoria," published in Spanish in *Tentativas* (Morelia, Mexico: Universidad Michoacana de San Nicolás de Hidalgo, 2003), 253–68. Originally published in Italian in 1985.

47. Ginzburg and Poni, "The Name and the Game," 5–8.

48. Levi, "On Microhistory," 110.

49. Levi, "On Microhistory," 111.

50. Carlo Ginzburg, "Morelli, Freud, and Sherlock Holmes: Clues and Scientific Method," *History Workshop Journal* 9, no. 1 (1980): 5–36. First published as "Spie: Radici di un paradigma indiziario," in *Crisi della ragione*, ed. Aldo Gargani (Turin: Einaudi, 1979).

51. Carlo Ginzburg, "Proofs and Possibilities: Postscript to Natalie Zemon Davis, *The Return of Martin Guerre*," in *Threads and Traces: True False Fictive* (Berkeley: University of California Press, 2012), 70. Originally published as an epilogue to the Italian edition of *The Return of Martin Guerre*, 1984. Davis's book was originally published in English by Harvard University Press, also in 1984.

52. Ginzburg explores this narrative dimension of history in his postscript to Davis's *The Return of Martin Guerre*. See "Proofs and Possibilities."

53. See, for example, Carlo Ginzburg, "Montrer et citer, La vérité de l'histoire," *Le Débat*, no. 56 (1989), 43–54; Ginzburg, "Just One Witness," in *Probing the Limits of Representation: Nazism and the 'Final Solution,'* ed. Saul Friedlander (Cambridge, MA: Harvard University Press, 1992), 82–96; and Ginzburg, "Microhistory," specifically point 15 (31–32). Levi makes similar arguments directed against relativism without actually labeling it as postmodernist. See, for example, his "On Microhistory" and "Antropologia y microhistoria."

54. Serna and Pons, *Como se escribe la microhistoria*, 223. The authors dedicate a whole chapter, titled "AntiWhite" (177–230), to analyzing Ginzburg's rejection of White's theories. In the recent updated version of that study, *Microhistoria: Las narraciones de Carlo Ginzburg*, the chapter has been retitled "Contra el escepticismo" ["Against Skepticism"] (75–98). This is a matter that is closely tied to the question of how to understand the role of narration in historiography. On this point, see, for example, Ann Rigney, "History as Text: Narrative Theory and History," in *The SAGE Handbook of Historical Theory*, ed. Nancy Partner and Sarah Foot (London: SAGE, 2013), 183–201.

55. Kracauer, *History, the Last Things Before the Last*, 122.

56. Revel, "Micro-analyse et construction du social," 36.

57. Natalie Z. Davis, *Slaves on Screen* (Cambridge, MA: Harvard University Press, 2000), 6.

58. Andrej Slávik, "Microhistory and Cinematic Experience: Two or Three Things I Know About Carlo Ginzburg," in *Microhistories*, ed. Magnus Bärtås and Andrej Slávik (Stockholm: Konstfack, 2016), 61.

59. Brewer, "Microhistory and the Histories of Everyday Life," 101.

60. Brewer, "Microhistory and the Histories of Everyday Life," 101.

61. Carlo Ginzburg, "Historia y microhistoria: Carlo Ginzburg entrevistado por Mauro Boarelli," *Pasajes: Revista de pensamiento contemporáneo*, no. 44 (2014): 91.

62. To be precise, Ginzburg refers on a few occasions to *The Triumph of the Will* in a talk he gave in 1982 on film as a historical source. Although this talk contains interesting references to the relationship between history and film, he does not specifically explore the relationship between microhistory and documentary film. See Ginzburg, "De todos los regalos que le traigo al Kaisare . . . Interpretar la película, escribir la historia," *Tentativas*, 197–215. Originally published in Italian as "Di tutti i doni che porto a Kaisire . . . Leggere il film scrivere la storia," *Storie e storia* 5, no. 9 (1983): 5–17.

63. See Bill Nichols, *Representing Reality: Issues and Concepts in Documentary* (Bloomington: Indiana University Press, 1991), 34–38.

64. Levi, "On Microhistory," 110. Ginzburg also identifies these features as microhistorical. See Ginzburg, "Microhistory," 32.

65. Dan Sipe, "The Future of Oral History and Moving Images," *Oral History Review* 19, no. 1–2 (1991): 75–87; Michel Frisch, *A Shared Authority: Essays on the Craft and Meaning of Oral and Public History* (New York: State University of New York Press, 1990), chaps. 6 and 7. In film studies, see Cahal McLaughlin, "What Happens When an Interview Is Filmed? Recording Memories from Conflict," *Oral History Review* 45, no. 2 (2018): 304–20.

66. Argentine documentary films, and more specifically those that deal with the victims of forced disappearances during the last dictatorship, are worthy of a case study of their own, as there are documentaries that have explored these issues with a wide range of approaches. Some examples include *Papá Iván* (María Inés Roqué, 2000), in which family letters play a central role, and *Los rubios* (Albertina Carri, 2003), which has a more performative and experimental approach.

67. Robert A. Rosenstone, "The Future of the Past: Film and the Beginnings of Postmodern History," in *The Persistence of History: Cinema, Television, and the Modern Event*, ed. Vivian Sobchack (London: Routledge, 1996), 201–18.

68. Rosenstone, "Future of the Past," 206.

69. Jeremy D. Popkin, *History, Historians, and Autobiography* (Chicago: University of Chicago Press, 2005).

70. Jaume Aurell, *Theoretical Perspectives on Historians' Autobiographies: From Documentation to Intervention* (London: Routledge, 2016).

71. See Ricoeur, *Memory, History, Forgetting*, 87, 386, 498.

72. Julio Arostegui, "Retos de la memoria y trabajos de la historia," *Pasado y memoria*, no. 3 (2004): 23–24. A reasonably comprehensive analysis of the relationship between memory and history can be found in chapter 2 of Geoffrey Cubitt, *History and Memory* (Manchester: Manchester University Press, 2007).

73. For a more detailed study of personal memory in film, see María del Rincón, Marta Torregrosa, and Efrén Cuevas, "La representación fílmica de la memoria personal: Las películas de memoria," *ZER* 22, no. 42 (2017): 175–88. We apply this approach to one of

Alan Berliner's films in "The Representation of Personal Memory in Alan Berliner's *First Cousin Once Removed*," *Studies in Documentary Film* 12, no. 1 (2018): 16–27.

74. See Gilles Deleuze, *Cinema 2: The Time-Image* (Minneapolis: University of Minnesota Press, 1989), 65–83.
75. Cubitt, *History and Memory*, 125.
76. This raises the complex question of how collective or social memory works, an issue that has called for greater attention since the first theories on social memory were proposed in the seminal works of Maurice Halbwachs, *Les cadres sociaux de la mémoire* (1925), and Frederic Bartlett, *Remembering: A Study in Experimental and Social Psychology* (1932).
77. See Jim Lane, *The Autobiographical Documentary in America* (Madison: University of Wisconsin Press, 2002), 95–119.
78. Alisa Lebow, *First Person Jewish* (Minneapolis: University of Minnesota Press, 2008), xii.
79. Lebow, *First Person Jewish*, xv.
80. Lane, *Autobiographical Documentary in America*, 96.
81. Juliette Goursat, *Mises en "je": Autobiographie et film documentaire* (Aix-en-Provence: Presses Universitaires de Provence, 2016), 145–90.
82. Goursat studies four Chilean documentaries more thoroughly in the chapter: *En algún lugar del cielo* (2003), *Mi vida con Carlos* (2009), *El edificio de los chilenos* (2010), and *Rue Santa Fe* (2007).
83. José Van Dijck, *Mediated Memories in the Digital Age* (Stanford, CA: Stanford University Press, 2007), 21.
84. See Marianne Hirsch, *The Generation of Postmemory: Writing and Visual Culture After the Holocaust* (New York: Columbia University Press, 2012), 29–54.
85. "History of the present" refers here to the concept proposed by historians like Henry Rousso and Julio Arostegui, which differs from the concept given the same name by Foucault, associated with his genealogical approach. For an explanation of the Foucauldian concept, see David Garland, "What Is a 'History of the Present'? On Foucault's Genealogies and their Critical Preconditions," *Punishment & Society* 16, no. 4 (2014): 365–84.
86. Julio Arostegui, "*Ver bien la propia época* (Nuevas reflexiones sobre el presente como historia)," *Sociohistórica*, nos. 9–10 (2001): 39.
87. Henry Rousso, *The Latest Catastrophe: History, the Present, the Contemporary* (Chicago: University of Chicago Press, 2016), 3.
88. See André Bazin, "The Ontology of the Photographic Image," in *What Is Cinema?*, vol. 1 (Berkeley: University of California Press, 1967), 14.

2. THE ARCHIVE IN THE MICROHISTORICAL DOCUMENTARY

1. Ann Laura Stoler, "Colonial Archives and the Arts of Governance," *Archival Science* 2, nos. 1–2 (2002): 93, 94.
2. Vicente Sánchez-Biosca, "Exploración, experiencia y emoción de archivo: A modo de introducción," *Aniki* 2, no. 2 (2015): 220.

3. Terry Cook, "Fashionable Nonsense or Professional Rebirth: Postmodernism and the Practice of Archives," *Archivaria*, no. 51 (2001): 27.
4. Marlene Manoff, "Theories of the Archive from Across the Disciplines," *portal: Libraries and the Academy* 4, no. 1 (2004): 14.
5. Cook, "Fashionable Nonsense or Professional Rebirth," 27.
6. George Didi-Huberman, *Images in Spite of All: Four Photographs from Auschwitz* (Chicago: University of Chicago Press, 2008), 100, 101.
7. Didi-Huberman, *Images in Spite of All*, 101. See Carlo Ginzburg, *Rapports de force: Historie, rhétorique, prevue* (Paris: Gallimard, 2003), 33–34.
8. Jeannette A. Bastian, "Moving the Margins to the Middle: Reconciling 'the Archive' with the Archives," in *Engaging with Records and Archives: Histories and Theories*, ed. Fiorella Foscarini et al. (London: Facet Publishing, 2016), 7.
9. Bastian, "Moving the Margins to the Middle," 7.
10. Ruth Rosengarten, *Between Memory and Document: The Archival Turn in Contemporary Art* (Lisbon: Museo Coleçao Berardo, 2012); Anna M. Guasch, *Arte y archivo 1920–2010: Genealogías, tipologías y discontinuidades* (Madrid: Akal, 2011); and Charles Merewether, ed., *The Archive: Documents of Contemporary Art* (London: Whitechapel, 2006). See also special issues of the journals *Visual Resources* (vol. 18, no. 2, 2002) and *Archives and Records* (vol. 36, no. 1, 2015).
11. Philip Rosen, "Document and Documentary: On the Persistence of Historical Concepts," in *Theorizing Documentary*, ed. Michael Renov (London: Routledge, 1993), 71.
12. Catherine Russell, *Archiveology: Walter Benjamin and Archival Film Practices* (Durham, NC: Duke University Press, 2018), 18.
13. Emma Cocker, "Ethical Possession: Borrowing from the Archives," in *Cultural Borrowings: Appropriation, Reworking, Transformation*, ed. Iain R. Smith (Nottingham, UK: Scope, 2009), 99–100.
14. Cocker, "Ethical Possession: Borrowing from the Archives," 100.
15. The growing importance of personal archives in archival studies has resulted in an increase in specialized publications. See, for instance, the special issues published in *Archivaria* in 2001 (no. 52) and 2013 (no. 76), the book edited by Christopher A. Lee, *I, Digital: Personal Collections in the Digital Era* (Chicago: Society of American Archivists, 2011), or Penny Summerfield's book *Histories of the Self: Personal Narratives and Historical Practice* (London: Routledge, 2018). Summerfield's book includes chapters dedicated to the analysis of letters, diaries, autobiographies, and oral histories as basic sources for histories of the self.
16. Anna Woodham et al., "We Are What We Keep: The 'Family Archive,' Identity and Public/Private Heritage," *Heritage & Society* 10, no. 3 (2017): 210. The authors point out an interesting distinction between the "collection," as a term more typical of institutional archives, and the family archive, which they explore through a bottom-up approach: "A family archive is not necessarily considered to be a typical collection, since its growth may be more fluid, informal and ad-hoc instead of a deliberate and 'active' process of acquisition and curation" (207).
17. See Richard Chalfen, *Snapshot Versions of Life* (Bowling Green, OH: Bowling Green State University Popular Press, 1987); James M. Moran, *There's No Place Like Home*

Video (Minneapolis: University of Minnesota Press, 2002), 44–63; Ryan Shand, "Theorizing Amateur Cinema: Limitations and Possibilities," *Moving Image* 8, no. 2 (2008): 51–57; and Tom Slootweg, "Home Mode, Community Mode, Counter Mode: Three Functional Modalities for Coming to Terms with Amateur Media Practices," in *Materializing Memories: Dispositifs, Generations, Amateurs*, ed. Susan Aasman, Andreas Fickers, and Joseph Wachelder (London: Bloomsbury, 2018), 208–9.

18. It is not my intention here to underplay the value of the contributions made to the specific study of snapshots, which include, apart from numerous articles in journals, books such as Jo Spence and Patricia Holland, eds., *Family Snaps: The Meanings of Domestic Photography* (London: Virago, 1991); Marianne Hirsch, ed., *The Familial Gaze* (Hanover, NH: University Press of New England, 1999); and Catherine Zuromskis, *Snapshot Photography: The Lives of Images* (Cambridge, MA: MIT Press, 2013). Zuromskis offers a good overview of research on snapshots in "Snapshot Photography: History, Theory, Practice and Aesthetics," in *A Companion to Photography*, ed. Stephen Bull (Chicester, UK: Wiley-Blackwell, 2020), 291–306.

19. José Van Dijck, *Mediated Memories in the Digital Age* (Stanford, CA: Stanford University Press, 2007), 115. The author is referring explicitly here to photographs taken with cell phones, but her argument could easily be extended to include contemporary home movies, also recorded with cell phones.

20. See Shand, "Theorizing Amateur Cinema," 51–57; Slootweg, "Home Mode, Community Mode, Counter Mode," 210–12.

21. For an exploration of the features of amateur film, see, for example, Ian Craven, ed., *Movies on Home Ground: Exploration in Amateur Cinema* (Newcastle, UK: Cambridge Scholar Publishing, 2009), particularly the introduction written by Craven, "A Very Fishy Tale: The Curious Case of Amateur Subjectivity." The boundaries with experimental film are hazier, as various experimental filmmakers, such as Maya Deren or Stan Brakhage, advocate amateur or home modes and small-gauge filming, although their films exhibit marked differences from amateur practices in terms of their creation and distribution processes.

22. This autobiographical dimension and the fruitful relationship between home movies and autobiographical films is analyzed in more detail in my chapter, "Del cine doméstico al autobiográfico: Caminos de ida y vuelta," in *Cineastas frente al espejo*, ed. Gregorio Martín Gutiérrez (Madrid: T&B, 2008), 101–20.

23. The development of digital technology, with the use of cell phones as cameras and the distribution of filmed content on social networks and websites, has somewhat blurred this distinction between home movies and amateur films. For an exploration of this issue, see Susan Aasman, "Everyday Complexities and Contradictions in Contemporary Amateur Practice," in *Amateur Media and Participatory Cultures: Film, Video, and Digital Media*, ed. Annamaria Motrescu-Mayes and Susan Aasman (London: Routledge, 2019), 44–64.

24. Charles Tepperman, *Amateur Cinema: The Rise of North American Moviemaking, 1923–1960* (Berkeley: University of California Press, 2014), 175, 191. The distinction between the two modes is even more pronounced in the films analyzed by Tepperman,

since he focuses his research mainly on what he calls "serious" or "advanced" amateur filmmakers, who compete in the main amateur film festivals.

25. Patricia R. Zimmermann, "The Home Movie Movement: Excavations, Artifacts," in *Mining the Home Movies: Excavations in Histories and Memories*, ed. Karen Ishizuka and Patricia R. Zimmermann (Berkeley: University of California Press, 2008), 5.

26. Zimmermann, "Home Movie Movement," 18.

27. Roger Odin, "Reflections on the Family Home Movie as Document: A Semio-pragmatic Approach," in Ishizuka and Zimmerman, *Mining the Home Movies*, 265–66.

28. Jacques Derrida, *Archive Fever* (Chicago: University of Chicago Press, 1997), 2.

29. Michel Foucault, *The Archaeology of Knowledge and the Discourse on Language* (New York: Pantheon Books, 1972), 130. Foucault touches on this idea a little earlier in the same book: "We have in the density of discursive practices, systems that establish statements as events (with their own conditions and domain of appearance) and things (with their own possibility and field of use). They are all these systems of statements (whether events or things) that I propose to call archive" (128).

30. Roland Barthes, *Camera Lucida: Reflections on Photography* (New York: Hill & Wang, 1982), 89.

31. A standard reference for this view of home movies as constructions imbued with a patriarchal gaze is the Michele Citron film *Daughter Rite* (1979), and her subsequent reflection on the film in the first chapter of her book *Home Movies and Other Necessary Fictions* (Minneapolis: University of Minnesota Press, 1998).

32. Alf Lüdtke, "What Is the History of Everyday Life and Who Are Its Practitioners?," in *History of Everyday Life: Reconstructing Historical Experiences and Ways of Life*, ed. Alf Lüdtke (Princeton, NJ: Princeton University Press, 1995), 21.

33. Lüdtke, "What Is the History of Everyday Life," 14.

34. Carolyn Steedman, "Something She Called a Fever: Michelet, Derrida, and Dust," *American Historical Review* 106, no. 4 (2001): 1177.

35. Didi-Huberman, *Images in Spite of All*, 101.

36. Didi-Huberman, *Images in Spite of All*, 167.

37. Carlo Ginzburg, "Morelli, Freud, and Sherlock Holmes: Clues and Scientific Method," *History Workshop Journal* 9, no. 1 (1980): 5–36.

38. This section takes up the main ideas outlined in an earlier article of mine: "Home Movies as Personal Archives in Autobiographical Documentaries," *Studies in Documentary Film* 17, no. 1 (2013): 17–29. In the final section of this chapter, I also occasionally return to some of the questions raised in that article.

39. Julia J. Noordegraaf and Elvira Pouw, "Extended Family Films: Home Movies in the State-sponsored Archive," *Moving Image* 9, no. 1 (2009): 97.

40. Jaimie Baron, *The Archive Effect: Found Footage and the Audiovisual Experience of History* (London: Routledge, 2014).

41. Baron, *Archive Effect*, 82. This is more obvious when the sense of transgression is foregrounded, as in the cases of *Capturing the Friedmans* or *Tarnation*, where the filmmakers are using controversial family footage. Baron's astute criticism of *Tarnation* fits very well into her analytical framework, suggesting that the openly voyeuristic approach of this film turns us into "archival peeping toms" (99).

42. Baron is also aware of the impact of this temporal disparity, which often produces not only an "archive *effect*" but also an "archive *affect*," an emotional effect linked to a feeling of loss (21) and to an awareness of the passage of time (128).

43. Rebecca Swender, "Claiming the Found: Archive Footage and Documentary Practice," *Velvet Light Trap*, no. 64 (2009): 3–10.

44. Swender, "Claiming the Found," 6.

45. Swender, "Claiming the Found," 7–8.

46. Swender, "Claiming the Found," 5–6.

47. Paul J. Eakin, *How Our Lives Become Stories: Making Selves* (Ithaca, NY: Cornell University Press, 1999), 175–82.

48. Odin, "Reflections on the Family Home Movie as Document," 263.

49. Lüdtke, "What Is the History of Everyday Life," 21.

50. Ben Highmore, "Questioning Everyday Life," in *Everyday Life Reader*, ed. Ben Highmore (London: Routledge, 2002), 24–26.

51. Rachael Langford, "Colonial False Memory Syndrome? The Cinémémoire Archive of French Colonial Films and *Mémoire d'Outremer*," *Studies in French Cinema* 5, no. 2 (2005): 107, 108.

52. Langford, "Colonial False Memory Syndrome?," 108.

53. Highmore, "Questioning Everyday Life," 24–26.

54. Lüdtke, "What Is the History of Everyday Life," 21.

55. Michel de Certeau, *The Practice of Everyday Life* (Berkeley: University of California Press, 1984), xiv.

56. Certeau, *Practice of Everyday Life*, xiv–xv.

57. Edward Muir, "Introduction: Observing Trifles," in *Microhistory and the Lost Peoples of Europe*, ed. Edward Muir and Guido Ruggiero (Baltimore: Johns Hopkins University Press, 1991), ix–x.

58. Van Dijck, *Mediated Memories in the Digital Age*, 21.

59. Carolyn Steedman, *Dust* (Manchester: Manchester University Press, 2001), 3.

60. Marianne Hirsch, *Family Frames: Photography, Narrative and Postmemory* (Cambridge MA: Harvard University Press, 1997), 93.

61. Hirsch, *Family Frames*, 22.

3. PÉTER FORGÁCS'S HOME MOVIE CHRONICLE
OF THE TWENTIETH CENTURY

1. Despite its wide distribution on institutional circuits, Forgács's work is not available on DVD (with the exception of *Hunky Blues*) or on online platforms.

2. Bill Nichols and Michael Renov, eds., *Cinema's Alchemist: The Films of Péter Forgács* (Minneapolis: University of Minnesota Press, 2011).

3. Michael Renov, "Domestic Ethnography and the Construction of the 'Other Self,'" in *Collecting Visible Evidence*, ed. Jane M. Gaines and Michael Renov (Minneapolis: University of Minnesota Press, 1999), 140–55.

4. Sven Spieker, "At the Center of Mitteleuropa: A Conversation with Peter Forgács," *ARTMargins*, April 21, 2002, https://artmargins.com/at-the-center-of-mitteleuropa-a -conversation-with-peter-forgacs/.

5. Scott MacDonald, *A Critical Cinema 4: Interviews with Independent Filmmakers* (Berkeley: University of California Press, 2005), 299. (Interview reprinted in Nichols and Renov, *Cinema's Alchemist*, 3–38.)

6. MacDonald, *Critical Cinema 4*, 300.

7. Jacques Revel, "Micro-analyse et construction du social," in *Jeux d'echelles: La micro-analyse à la expérience*, ed. Jacques Revel (Paris: Seuil/Gallimard, 1996), 19.

8. Roger Odin, "How to Make History Perceptible: The Bartos Family and the Private Hungary Series," in Nichols and Renov, *Cinema's Alchemist*, 139. Published originally as "La Famille Bartos de Péter Forgács, ou comment rendre l'histoire sensible," in *Cinéma hongrois: Le temps et l'histoire*, ed. Kristian Feigelson (Paris: Presses Sorbonne Nouvelle, 2003).

9. Ruth Balint, "Representing the Past and the Meaning of Home in Péter Forgács's Private Hungary," in *Amateur Filmmaking: The Home Movie, The Archive, The Web*, ed. L. Rascaroli, G. Young, and B. Monahan (London: Bloomsbury, 2014), 194; Balázs Varga, "Façades: The Private and the Public in Kádár's Kiss by Péter Forgács," in *Past for the Eyes: East European Representations of Communism in Cinema and Museums After 1989*, ed. Oksana Sarkisova and Péter Apor (Budapest: Central European University Press, 2008), 89. Kristian Feigelson also points to a related question in passing when he connects Forgács's films to a "history from below" in his article "*The Labyrinth*: A Strategy of Sensitive Experimentation, a Filmmaker of the Anonymous," *KinoKultura*, no. 7 (2008), http://www.kinokultura.com/specials/7/feigelson.shtml.

10. Julio Arostegui, "Ver bien la propia época (Nuevas reflexiones sobre el presente como historia)," *Sociohistórica*, nos. 9–10 (2001): 38–39.

11. Henry Rousso, *The Latest Catastrophe: History, the Present, the Contemporary* (Chicago: University of Chicago Press, 2016), 192.

12. Numerous authors have analyzed the stylistic and narrative features of Forgács's films. See, for example, Richard Kilborn's chapter, "'I Am a Time Archaeologist': Some Reflections on the Filmmaking Practice of Péter Forgács," in Rascaroli, Young, and Monahan, *Amateur Filmmaking*, 179–92.

13. Bill Nichols, "The Memory of Loss: Péter Forgács's Saga of Family Life and Social Hell," *Film Quarterly* 56, no. 4 (2003): 7. (Interview reprinted in Nichols and Renov, *Cinema's Alchemist*, 39–55.)

14. Miguel Ángel Hernández-Navarro, *Materializar el pasado: El artista como historiador (benjaminiano)* (Murcia: Micromegas, 2012), 19–21.

15. Hernández-Navarro, *Materializar el pasado*, 39–42. This author actually mentions Forgács's films explicitly as an example of the second strategy, although he does not delve into an analysis of his films.

16. See Hernández-Navarro's chapter, "Walter Benjamin y las imágenes de la historia," in *Materializar el pasado*, 45–76. These questions are discussed in various works by Benjamin, the main source being his *Arcades Project*.

17. Forgács would make another film with footage taken outside of Europe: *Venom*, which uses footage filmed in Brazil in the 1950s and 1960s.

18. The interviews are not conducted directly by Forgács; instead, the filmmaker uses interviews conducted in the early 1960s by Elemér Bakó, a Hungarian linguist living in the United States who at that time was able to interview the first generation of Hungarian immigrants—then in their twilight years—who had arrived in the country at the beginning of the century. Information provided by Péter Forgács in a personal interview on March 4, 2020.

19. The fact that the Shoah has been studied so extensively in contemporary historiography is also reflected in the amount of attention it has received in film studies, although fewer studies have been dedicated to its representation in documentaries. Among monographs published in English, only one focuses exclusively on documentary films: Brad Prager, *After the Fact: The Holocaust in Twenty-First Century Documentary Film* (London: Bloomsbury, 2015). Other books about the Holocaust in film include both fictional and documentary accounts: Annette Insdorf, *Indelible Shadows: Film and the Holocaust*, 3rd ed. (Cambridge: Cambridge University Press, 2003); Joshua Hirsch, *Afterimage: Film, Trauma, and the Holocaust* (Philadelphia: Temple University Press, 2003); Aaron Kerner, *Film and the Holocaust: New Perspectives on Dramas, Documentaries, and Experimental Films* (New York: Continuum, 2011); and Gerd Bayer and Oleksandr Kobrynskyy, eds., *Holocaust Cinema in the Twenty-First Century: Images, Memory, and the Ethics of Representation* (New York: Columbia University Press/ Wallflower Press, 2015).

20. Michael Renov, "Historical Discourses of the Unimaginable: Peter Forgacs' The Maelstrom," in Nichols and Renov, *Cinema's Alchemist*, 86. Originally published in German as "Historische Diskurse des Unvorstellbaren: Peter Forgacs' The Maelstrom," *Montage AV* 11, no. 1 (2002): 27–40.

21. Sigurður Gylfi Magnússon and István Szíjártó, *What Is Microhistory? Theory and Practice* (London: Routledge, 2013), 63–64.

22. Carlo Ginzburg and Carlo Poni, "The Name and the Game: Unequal Exchange and the Historiographic Marketplace," in *Microhistory and the Lost Peoples of Europe*, ed. Edward Muir and Guido Ruggiero (Baltimore: Johns Hopkins University Press, 1991), 1–10.

23. This is a strategy that he maintains throughout the film, even for the Seyss-Inquarts' home movies in black and white, which are also tinted blue. There is one curious exception in the blue-tinted sequence of a local swimming race filmed by Max, shown close to the start of the film. Footage in color, however, is shown without chromatic alterations.

24. A similar but inverted strategy is used a little later, when we see images from an NSB training camp, while in a voice-over we hear a speech by the Dutch queen in exile in London.

25. Hannah Arendt, *Eichmann in Jerusalem: A Report on the Banality of Evil* (New York: Viking Press, 1963).

26. Ernst Van Alphen, "Towards a New Historiography: Péter Forgács and the Aesthetics of Temporality," in *Resonant Bodies, Voices, Memories*, ed. Anke Bangma et al.

(Rotterdam: Piet Zwart Institute, 2008), 98. Reprinted in Nichols and Renov, *Cinema's Alchemist*, 59–74.

27. Spieker, "At the Center of Mitteleuropa."

28. Roland Barthes, *Camera Lucida: Reflections on Photography* (New York: Hill & Wang, 1982), 96. Emphasis in original.

29. Barthes, *Camera Lucida*, 96. Emphasis in original.

30. Jill Lepore, "Historians Who Love Too Much: Reflections on Microhistory and Biography," *Journal of American History* 88, no. 1 (2001): 133.

31. Péter Forgács, "*Wittgenstein Tractatus*: Personal Reflections on Home Movies," in *Mining the Home Movie: Excavations in Histories and Memories*, ed. Karen L. Ishizuka and Patricia Zimmermann (Berkeley: University of California Press, 2008), 55.

32. For this analysis I follow the methodology proposed by Gerard Genette for literary narratives in *Narrative Discourse: An Essay in Method* (Ithaca, NY: Cornell University Press, 1980) and *Narrative Discourse Revisited* (Ithaca, NY: Cornell University Press, 1988). Genette's methodology has been applied to film studies by André Gaudreault and François Jost, among others. See Gaudreault and Jost, *Le Récit cinématographique: Films et séries télévisées*, 3rd. rev. and exp. ed. (1990; Paris: Armand Colin, 2017).

33. Like other chapters of the Holocaust, the literature on the Hungarian case is extensive. A good introduction to it is offered on the website for the National Committee for Attending Deportees, at www.degob.org.

34. *Free Fall* also includes other related information, such as the expedition of Slovak Jews who crossed the Danube on their way to Palestine in 1940, a curious digression that actually offers a brief summary of the story that Forgács would tell two years later in his film *Danube Exodus*.

35. A contrast of time frames can also be seen in Forgács's documentaries that include interviews with the protagonists, which are combined with home movies of the past, such as *I Am Von Höfler* or *Miss Universe 1929*. But the effect is very different, as it is a conventional technique to support interviews with related archival footage, even though in this case it is an archive as unique as the interviewee's own home movies. A different case, closer to that of *Class Lot*, can be found in *The Notebook of a Lady*, as in this film the old home movies are contrasted with contemporary images of its protagonist walking through the gardens of her former palazzo while she speaks to us in a voice-over. The different time frames—visible in the change from black and white to color, and in the aging of the building and the protagonist—connect more clearly with the contrast in *Class Lot*, although the contemporary image is not an archival image but filmed specifically for the documentary.

36. See André Bazin, "The Ontology of the Photographic Image," in *What Is Cinema?*, vol. 1 (Berkeley: University of California Press, 1967), 15.

37. Ben Highmore, *Everyday Life and Cultural Theory* (London: Routledge, 2001), 21. For Michel de Certeau's theory, see *The Practice of Everyday Life* (Berkeley: University of California Press, 1984).

4. THE INCARCERATION OF JAPANESE
AMERICANS DURING WORLD WAR II

1. The literature on this era refers to both "internment camps" and "concentration camps." The second term has generated some controversy due to its association with the Nazi concentration camps. Karen L. Ishizuka defends its use with a detailed argument in its favor in the chapter "Coming to Terms," in her book/catalog *Lost and Found: Reclaiming the Japanese American Incarceration* (Champaign: University of Illinois Press, 2006), 154–72.

2. A quite exhaustive list can be found in *Densho Encyclopedia*, last updated April 2018, http://encyclopedia.densho.org/Documentary_films/videos_on_incarceration/.

3. Betty Bergland, "Representing Ethnicity in Autobiography: Narratives of Opposition," in *Yearbook of English Studies* 24 (1994): 93.

4. George Lipsitz, *Time Passages* (Minneapolis: University of Minnesota Press, 1990), 213.

5. Jun Xing, *Asian America Through the Lens: History, Representations, and Identity* (Walnut Creek, CA: AltaMira Press, 1998), 163. This view is partly contested by Taunya Lovell Banks, who identifies a tendency (albeit not intentional) in many of these documentaries to reinforce certain stereotypes related to Japanese Americans, thereby illustrating "the continuing conflict within the Japanese American community between embracing the model minority stereotype and connecting the internment to American institutional racism." Banks, "Outsider Citizen: Film Narratives About the Internment of Japanese Americans," *Suffolk University Law Review* 42, no. 4 (2009): 780.

6. Rocío G. Davis, *Relative Histories: Mediating History in Asian American Family Memoirs* (Honolulu: University of Hawai'i Press, 2011), 117. Davis's book analyzes family stories of Asian Americans mainly in literature, although she dedicates her sixth chapter to what she calls the "Asian American Family Portrait Documentary."

7. Ishizuka, *Lost and Found*, 127.

8. Alf Lüdtke, "What Is the History of Everyday Life and Who Are Its Practitioners?," in *History of Everyday Life: Reconstructing Historical Experiences and Ways of Life*, ed. Alf Lüdtke (Princeton, NJ: Princeton University Press, 1995), 21.

9. Karen L. Ishizuka, "Through Our Own Eyes: Making Movies with Japanese American Home Movies," in *La casa abierta: El cine doméstico y sus reciclajes contemporáneos*, ed. Efrén Cuevas (Madrid: Ocho y medio, 2010), 217. Available in English at http://dadun.unav.edu/handle/10171/18498?locale=en.

10. Robert Rosen, "*Something Strong Within* as Historical Memory," in *Mining the Home Movies: Excavations in Histories and Memories*, ed. Karen L. Ishizuka and Patricia R. Zimmermann (Berkeley: University of California Press, 2008), 119.

11. Ishizuka, "Through Our Own Eyes," 218.

12. Michel de Certeau and Luce Giard, "Envoi," in Michel de Certeau, Luce Giard, and Pierre Mayol, *The Practice of Everyday Life*, vol. 2, *Living and Cooking* (Minneapolis: University of Minnesota Press, 1998), 255.

13. Luce Giard, "Introduction to Volume 1: History of a Research Project," in Certeau, Giard, and Mayol, *Practice of Everyday Life*, 2:xxi.

14. See "Producer's Statement/About the Production," https://www.fromasilkcocoon.com /inastatement.html.

15. Letters and diaries are basic sources for the "histories of the self" posited by Penny Summerfield as historiographical practices. Summerfield analyzes these sources in the chapters "Historians' Use of Letters" and "Historians and the Diary" in her book *Histories of the Self: Personal Narratives and Historical Practice* (London: Routledge, 2018), 22–77.

16. In this case, the parents are actually *Nikkei*, people of Japanese descent born in North America but educated mainly in Japan.

17. Marianne Hirsch, *The Generation of Postmemory: Writing and Visual Culture After the Holocaust* (New York: Columbia University Press, 2012), 38.

18. Marianne Hirsch, *Family Frames: Photography, Narrative and Postmemory* (Cambridge, MA: Harvard University Press, 1997), 22.

19. Hirsch, *Family Frames*, 22.

20. Hirsch, *Family Frames*, 23.

21. In addition to the documentary and its scholarly commentary, two books deal with the story of the family: one written by the filmmaker's father, Robert Shu Yasui, *The Yasui Family of Hood River, Oregon* (self-pub., 1987); and another by Lauren Kessler, *Stubborn Twig: Three Generations in the Life of a Japanese American Family* (New York: Random House, 1993).

22. Alisa Lebow, *First Person Jewish* (Minneapolis: University of Minnesota Press, 2008), xii.

23. Cassandra Van Buren, "Family Gathering: Release from Emotional Internment," *Jump Cut*, no. 37, July 1992, https://www.ejumpcut.org/archive/onlinessays/JC37folder /FamilyGathering.html.

24. Peter X. Feng, *Identities in Motion* (Durham, NC: Duke University Press, 2002), 17.

25. Feng, *Identities in Motion*, 17.

26. Roger Odin, "Le film de famille dans l'institution familiale," in *Le film de famille: Usage privage, usage public*, ed. Roger Odin (Paris: Meridiens Klincksieck, 1995), 32–33. The invented nature of this memory based on home movies could be associated with the idea of prosthetic memory proposed by Alison Landsberg, although this author is referring more to the mass media and mainstream cinema, where there is no autobiographical relationship between the viewer and the content viewed. See Alison Landsberg, *Prosthetic Memory: The Transformation of American Remembrance in the Age of Mass Culture* (New York: Columbia University Press, 2004).

27. Terry Cook, "Fashionable Nonsense or Professional Rebirth: Postmodernism and the Practice of Archives," *Archivaria*, no. 51 (2001): 27.

28. Carlo Ginzburg, "Proofs and Possibilities: Postscript to Natalie Zemon Davis, *The Return of Martin Guerre*," in *Threads and Traces: True False Fictive* (Berkeley: University of California Press, 2012), 70.

29. Glen M. Mimura, "Antidote for Collective Amnesia? Rea Tajiri's Germinal Image," in *Countervisions: Asian American Film Criticism*, ed. Darrel Y. Hamamoto and Sandra Liu (Philadelphia: Temple University Press, 2000), 157.

30. See Robert A. Rosenstone, "The Future of the Past: Film and the Beginnings of Post-modern History," in *The Persistence of History: Cinema, Television, and the Modern Event*, ed. Vivian Sobchack (London: Routledge, 1996), 208–9.

31. Rosenstone, "Future of the Past," 206.

32. Mikhail Bakhtin's theory of dialogic polyphony in fact serves Peter X. Feng as a starting point for his analysis of documentaries on Japanese Americans in his chapter "Articulating Silence: Sansei and Memories of the Camps," in *Identities in Motion*, 68–100.

33. José Medina, "Toward a Foucaultian Epistemology of Resistance: Counter-Memory, Epistemic Friction, and *Guerrilla* Pluralism," *Foucault Studies*, no. 12 (2011): 15.

34. Michel Foucault, *Society Must Be Defended* (New York: Picador, 2003), 70.

35. *Yankee Doodle Dandy* is referenced one last time to reiterate—perhaps a little redundantly—this same contradiction: the scene shows a group of African Americans around the statue of Lincoln and a recitation of the end of his famous Gettysburg Address, which, in the midst of the Civil War, asserted the values of democracy and freedom as elements of the nation's identity, while a superimposed caption reminds us that the year that this Hollywood film was released, the mass internment of Japanese Americans was taking place just four hundred miles away.

36. See Robert Rosenstone, *History on Film/Film on History* (Harlow, UK: Pearson Longman, 2006); and Marc Ferro, *Cinema and History* (Detroit, MI: Wayne State University Press, 1988).

37. See Janet Walker, "The Traumatic Paradox: Autobiographical Documentary and the Psychology of Memory," in *Contested Pasts: The Politics of Memory*, ed. Katharine Hodgkin and Susannah Radstone (London: Routledge, 2003), 111, 113.

38. Walker, "Traumatic Paradox," 109. I will go no further in studying the film from the perspective of trauma studies than the brief references included here, as it is beyond the scope of this chapter, which is limited to an analysis of these documentaries as microhistory. For an exploration of the relationships between image and trauma, which include documentary films but also photography, fiction film, and other visual forms of expression, see, for example: Frances Guerin and Robert Hallas, eds., *The Image and the Witness: Trauma, Memory and Visual Culture* (London: Wallflower Press, 2007); E. Ann Kaplan, *Trauma Culture: The Politics of Terror and Loss in Media and Literature* (New Brunswick, NJ: Rutgers University Press, 2005); Nick Hodgin and Amit Thakkar, eds., *Scars and Wounds: Film and Legacies of Trauma* (London: Palgrave, 2017); and Caterina Albano, *Memory, Forgetting and the Moving Image* (London: Palgrave, 2016), especially its third chapter.

39. As noted in chapter 1, the concept of the "crystal-image" is taken from Gilles Deleuze, *Cinema 2: The Time-Image* (Minneapolis: University of Minnesota Press, 1989), 65–83.

40. One of the clearest examples of the frailty of the mother's memory is the scene where we are shown some images of the canteen at Salinas while she states that there was no such place at that camp (10').

41. Marita Sturken, "The Absent Images of Memory: Remembering and Reenacting the Japanese Internment," in *Perilous Memories: The Asia-Pacific Wars*, ed. T. Fujitani, Geoffrey M. White, and Lisa Yoneyama (Durham, NC: Duke University Press, 2001), 37.

5. RITHY PANH'S AUTOBIOGRAPHICAL NARRATIVE OF THE CAMBODIAN GENOCIDE

1. For an analysis of the presence of the character of Bophana in Rithy Panh's work, and especially in *Bophana* and *Duch*, see the article by Vicente Sánchez-Biosca, "¿Qué espera de mí esa foto? La *Perpetrator image* de Bophana y su contracampo: Iconografías del genocidio camboyano," *Aniki* 2, no. 2 (2015): 322–48. For a study of the mug shots taken at Tuol Sleng and their subsequent use (in archives, museums, etc.), see Michelle Caswell, *Archiving the Unspeakable: Silence, Memory, and the Photographic Record in Cambodia* (Madison: University of Wisconsin Press, 2014).

2. See Elisabeth Beker, "The Romance of Comrade Deth," in *When the War Was Over: Cambodia and the Khmer Rouge Revolution* (New York: Public Affairs, 1986), 212–25.

3. Carlo Ginzburg and Carlo Poni, "The Name and the Game: Unequal Exchange and the Historiographic Marketplace," in *Microhistory and the Lost Peoples of Europe*, ed. Edward Muir and Guido Ruggiero (Baltimore: Johns Hopkins University Press, 1991), 1–10.

4. Ginzburg and Poni, "Name and the Game," 8.

5. Sánchez-Biosca, "¿Qué espera de mí esa foto?," 332.

6. Leshu Torchin, "Mediation and Remediation: La Parole Filmée in Rithy Panh's *The Missing Picture* (L'image Manquante)," *Film Quarterly* 68, no. 1 (2014): 36.

7. Deirdre Boyle, "Shattering Silence: Traumatic Memory and Re-enactment in Rithy Panh's *S-21: The Khmer Rouge Killing Machine*," *Frameworks* 50, nos. 1–2 (2009): 98, 100.

8. Rithy Panh, *L'elimination*, with Christophe Bataille (Paris: Grasset, 2012). Published in English as *The Elimination* (New York: Other Press, 2013).

9. The film was screened at numerous film festivals, winning several important awards, including the Prix Un Certain Regard at Cannes (2013). It also was nominated for the Oscar for Best Foreign Language Film (2014).

10. Jill Lepore, "Historians Who Love Too Much: Reflections on Microhistory and Biography," *Journal of American History* 88, no. 1 (2001): 133.

11. I have simplified the outline of the narrative structure in the interests of keeping the analysis brief, as a more detailed description would digress from the main focus of this chapter. As was the case in chapter 3, the narratological terminology used here is taken from the methodology proposed by Gerard Genette, described in *Narrative*

Discourse: An Essay in Method (Ithaca, NY: Cornell University Press, 1980) and *Narrative Discourse Revisited* (Ithaca, NY: Cornell University Press, 1988), applied here to film.

12. The concept of "memory film" or "film of memory" has been proposed by various authors. See, for example, Astrid Erll, *Memory in Culture* (Basingstoke, UK: Palgrave Macmillan, 2011); and David MacDougall, "Films of Memory," in *Transcultural Cinema*, ed. David MacDougall (Princeton, NJ: Princeton University Press, 1998), 231–44.

13. See María del Rincón, Marta Torregrosa, and Efrén Cuevas, "La representación fílmica de la memoria personal: Las películas de memoria," *ZER* 22, no. 42 (2017): 175–88. For a briefer outline in English, subsequently applied to one of Alan Berliner's films, see María del Rincón, Efrén Cuevas, and Marta Torregrosa, "The Representation of Personal Memory in Alan Berliner's *First Cousin Once Removed*," *Studies in Documentary Film* 12, no. 1 (2018): 16–27.

14. Geoffrey Cubitt, *History and Memory* (Manchester, UK: Manchester University Press, 2007), 27.

15. See Henri Bergson, *The Creative Mind: An Introduction to Metaphysics* (New York: Citadel Press, 1946).

16. Frances Guerin and Robert Hallas, "Introduction," in *The Image and the Witness: Trauma, Memory and Visual Culture*, ed. Frances Guerin and Robert Hallas (London: Wallflower Press, 2007), 4.

17. As I noted in chapter 4 in relation to *History and Memory*, I do not explore the issues more closely related to trauma studies further here, as this would go beyond the scope of this analysis, which focuses on its microhistorical dimension and the consequent relationships between memory, history, and archives. In addition to the book edited by Guerin and Hallas mentioned here, in chapter 4 I identified other references that explore trauma and cinema, such as the books by E. Ann Kaplan, Nick Hodgin and Amit Thakkar, and Caterina Albano, which are included in the bibliography.

18. The debate between White and Ginzburg was also waged in an area much closer to the subject matter of Panh's films, the Jewish genocide, subsequently collected in two chapters of the book *Probing the Limits of Representation: Nazism and the "Final Solution,"* edited by Saul Friedlander (Cambridge, MA: Harvard University Press, 1992). James E. Young offers a very good summary of this debate and Saul Friedlander's mediation of it in his article "Toward a Received History of the Holocaust," *History and Theory* 36, no. 4 (1997): 21–43.

19. After showing the visit by the Chinese leaders mentioned earlier, Panh concludes this section by showing three consecutive dioramas (69') with no specific narrative anchor, as a visual synopsis of the dramatic consequences of the communist regime in the Cambodian population: the first pictures his whole family in a frontal pose, with the clothes they wore before the arrival of the Khmer Rouge; the second shows the same characters, but now in the black clothes worn by the deportees, some of them now looking emaciated; the third shows only six of the thirteen original family members, emaciated and woebegone.

20. See, for example, two key reference works on this topic: Douglas MacDowell, *Irony in Film* (London: Palgrave MacMillan, 2016); and Sarah Kozloff, *Invisible Storytellers: Voice-Over Narration in American Fiction Film* (Berkeley: University of California Press, 1989).

21. Carlo Ginzburg, "Proofs and Possibilities: Postscript to Natalie Zemon Davis, *The Return of Martin Guerre*," in *Threads and Traces: True False Fictive* (Berkeley: University of California Press, 2012), 70.

22. There is one scene, however, where this dynamic seems to be inverted, when Panh recalls his childhood hobby of going to film shoots, invited by a neighbor of his who was a filmmaker. The dioramas reconstruct these scenes, but suddenly there appears a film image of a female dancer, who seems to be dancing for the figurine of the boy Panh, like a fragment rescued from the collective shipwreck caused by the Khmer Rouge regime (37').

23. Vicente Sánchez-Biosca, "Challenging Old and New Images Representing the Cambodian Genocide: *The Missing Picture* (Rithy Panh, 2013)," *Genocide Studies and Prevention: An International Journal* 12, no. 2 (2018): 157. In this article, Sánchez-Biosca conducts a detailed analysis of the types of images that appear in *The Missing Picture*, with special attention to three scenes, including the one dealing with the death of the children.

24. Stephanie Bou, *L'image manquante: Un film de Rithy Panh* (Paris: ACRIF-CIP, 2016), 11. Bou suggests these six possible interpretations for the "missing picture": the archive of the crime; the lost picture of childhood; the truth of the event; the picture we don't want to see; the very life that was stolen; and the split image.

25. It is interesting to note the dual meaning of the film's title in Spanish, *La imagen perdida*, which could refer both to its physical absence or to its material spoilage; this dual meaning is missing from its title in French (*manquante*) and English (*missing*).

26. Curiously, before moving on to the next scene (at the hospital, filmed with dioramas), Panh inserts a brief shot of a documentary image of a sick girl (70'); a shocking image, because it could be interpreted as a visual rectification of the complaint that has just been expressed.

6. IDENTITIES AND CONFLICTS IN ISRAEL AND PALESTINE

1. For a broader study of memory and trauma in Israeli cinema (including both fiction and documentary films), see Raz Yosef and Boaz Hagin, eds., *Deeper Than Oblivion: Trauma and Memory in Israeli Cinema* (London: Bloomsbury, 2013).

2. It is worth mentioning here another documentary with a similar approach: *Private Album* (2018), directed by Kobi Farag. This film is based on seventeen short interviews with ordinary people in Israel, who recount scenes of significance to them arranged in chronological order, from the 1940s through to the present day. The most characteristic feature of the film is that all the interviews are related to snapshots that in one way

or another bring back memories of the past; hence the title *Private Album*. Although this points to a microhistorical intention underlying the premise of the film, its structure (made up of scenes with no connection between them) ends up offering a kaleidoscopic portrait that distances it from a microhistorical perspective.

3. The film also includes a few scenes that access public history through the perspective of professional journalism, such as when we see a television screen broadcasting the historic visit in 1979 of Egyptian president Anwar Sadat (90'). Two sequences with footage filmed by the television journalist Benya Binnun have a similar effect, especially the second one. The first (59'–62') shows a Jewish march in 1968 through the occupied territories, filmed by Binnun with an amateur style. The second (78'–82') shows footage of his coverage of the Yom Kippur War. This footage was not included in the TV news broadcasts, because, as he explains in a voice-over, his interest in showing close-ups of the combatants, to give the war a human face, clashed with the official image of the war that the broadcasters sought to convey.

4. Lauren Davidson, "The Selective Memory of 'Israel: A Home Movie,'" *The Tower Magazine*, no. 5, August 2013, http://www.thetower.org/article/the-selective-memory-of-israel-a-home-movie/.

5. Linda Dittmar, "In the Eye of the Storm: The Political Stake of Israeli i-Movies," in *The Cinema of Me: The Self and Subjectivity in First Person Documentary*, ed. Alisa Lebow (New York: Columbia University Press/Wallflower Press, 2012), 164.

6. See Jim Lane, *The Autobiographical Documentary in America* (Madison: University of Wisconsin Press, 2002), 48–93.

7. Philippe Lejeune, "How Do Diaries End?," *Biography* 24, no. 1 (2001): 99–112.

8. Quoted in Shai Tsur, "*Out of Love . . . Be Back Shortly*," *Jerusalem Post*, December 11, 1997.

9. Yaron Shemer explores this issue in Amit Goren's filmography in the context of his extensive study of Mizrahi cinema in Israel: *Identity, Place, and Subversion in Contemporary Mizrahi Cinema in Israel* (Ann Arbor: University of Michigan Press, 2013), 73–75.

10. Yael Munk, "Ethics and Responsibility: The Feminization of the New Israeli Documentary," *Israel Studies* 16, no. 2 (2011): 156.

11. Dittmar, "In the Eye of the Storm," 162.

12. Dittmar, "In the Eye of the Storm," 160. The author bases her study on the work, among others, of Israeli scholar Shmulik Duvdevani, which I have been unable to read as it is published only in Hebrew.

13. The best-known and most widely quoted revisionist historians, also recognized as pioneers of the movement, are Benny Morris, Ilan Pappé, Simha Flapan, and Avi Shlaim. A good outline of their position can be found in the article by Shlaim titled "La guerre des historiens israéliens," *Annales* 59, no. 1 (2004): 161–67. English translation at https://users.ox.ac.uk/~ssfc0005/The%20War%20of%20the%20Israeli%20Historians.html.

14. Lisa Polland, "Film Review: *My Terrorist* and *For My Children*," *Hawwa: Journal of Women of the Middle East and the Islamic World* 3, no. 2 (2005): 277.

15. The filmmaker is credited in *My Terrorist* as Yulie Gerstel, the surname of her husband at the time. They were divorced in 2004, and in her next two films her name appears as Yulie Cohen Gerstel. Since her website currently identifies her as Yulie Cohen, I have opted to use this name to refer to her here.

16. Yossi K. Halevi, "The Real Dispute Driving the Israeli-Palestinian Conflict," *The Atlantic*, May 14, 2018.

17. The impact of the Shoah on the State of Israel is not analyzed further here, as it is beyond the scope of this chapter. For an analysis of its influence on the Palestinian-Israeli conflict, see Andreas Musolff, "The Role of Holocaust Memory in the Israeli-Palestinian Conflict," in *The Israeli Conflict System: Analytic Approaches*, ed. Harvey Starr and Stanley Dubinsk (London: Routledge, 2015), 168–80.

18. Yosefa Loshitzky, "Veiling and Unveiling the Israeli Mediterranean: Yulie Cohen-Gerstel's *My Terrorist* and *My Land Zion*," in *Visions of Struggle in Women's Filmmaking in the Mediterranean*, ed. Flavia Laviosa (New York: Palgrave Macmillan, 2010), 14. While accepting the sincerity of the filmmaker's intentions, Loshitzky ultimately classifies both of Cohen's films as the product of a "narcissistic self that, despite its critical aim, remythologizes the Israeli collective political self and its Zionist core" (4).

19. There are also few publications dealing specifically with Palestinian documentary production. Notable among the few written in English is the chapter by Nurith Gertz and George Khleifi, "A Dead-End: Road Block Movies" (134–170), included in their book *Palestinian Cinema: Landscape, Trauma, and Memory* (Edinburgh: Edinburgh University Press, 2008). The book analyzes Palestinian film production up to 2003, with an epilogue that includes newer titles up to 2007, which means it does not include either *Zahra* or *A World Not Ours*, which I discuss here, nor does it provide any information hinting at other documentaries with microhistorical approaches.

20. Michael Renov, "Domestic Ethnography and the Construction of the 'Other Self,'" in *Collecting Visible Evidence*, ed. Jane M. Gaines and Michael Renov (Minneapolis: University of Minnesota Press, 1999), 140–55.

21. The film had its world premiere at the Toronto International Film Festival, and won the Berlinale Peace Prize, as well as the Yamagata, Edinburgh, and DOC NYC Grand Jury Prizes, among other awards.

22. Data from UNRWA, https://www.unrwa.org/who-we-are.

23. Fleifel's explanation continues: "Instead I wanted to create a feeling of nostalgia for the old childhood years. I also wanted to make the film like a long episode of *The Wonder Years*, a series that I grew up watching as a kid and loved very much. Also *Radio Days* by Woody Allen was a big influence. Hence the use of old jazz music." Personal interview with the author, February 20, 2020.

24. Hamid Naficy, *An Accented Cinema: Exilic and Diasporic Filmmaking* (Princeton, NJ: Princeton University Press, 2001), 4.

25. The "transnational family" is a concept that has aroused growing academic interest in the current era of globalization. Debora F. Bryceson and Ulla Vuorela have defined it as "families that live some or most of the time separated from each other, yet hold together and create something that can be seen as a feeling of collective welfare and unity,

namely 'familyhood,' even across national borders." *The Transnational Family: New European Frontiers and Global Networks* (Oxford: Berg, 2002), 3. *Exile Family Movie*, directed by Arash T. Riahi, portrays his family divided between Austria and Iran, using home videos and Skype conversations. In *I for India*, Sandhya Suri offers a portrait of her family based largely on the home movies that her father and his relatives exchanged between England and India. I explore these types of films, and more specifically *I for India*, in Cuevas, "The Filmic Representation of Home in Transnational Families: The Case of *I for India*," *NECSUS*, Autumn 2016, https://necsus-ejms.org/the -filmic-representation-of-home-in-transnational-families-the-case-of-i-for-india/.

26.   The canonical longitudinal documentary is made up of a series, that is, episodes about the same protagonists at set intervals over a long period of time. One of the best-known examples is Michael Apted's *Up* series, which documents the lives of fourteen Britons every seven years from their childhood (1964) through to their old age (the last film was released in 2019). However, the concept can also be applied without stretching the definition to individual documentaries presenting the same protagonists in different periods. For a study of the longitudinal documentary and its best-known examples, see Richard Kilborn, *Taking the Long View: A Study of Longitudinal Documentary* (Manchester, UK: Manchester University Press, 2010).

7. THE IMMIGRANT EXPERIENCE IN JONAS MEKAS'S *LOST, LOST, LOST*

1.   This chapter is based in part on an analysis I conducted previously of *Lost, Lost, Lost* based on Bakhtin's theories, but which did not include a study of the film's microhistorical dimension: "The Immigrant Experience in Jonas Mekas's Diary Films: A Chronotopic Analysis of *Lost, Lost, Lost*," *Biography* 29, no. 1 (2006): 55–73. Mikhail Bakhtin describes his chronotopic approach in "Forms of Time and of the Chronotope in the Novel," in *The Dialogic Imagination: Four Essays* (Austin: University of Texas Press, 1981), 84–258.

2.   According to the 1980 U.S. census, there were 743,000 people of Lithuanian descent living in the country. For a detailed study of this question, see Alfonsas Eidintas, *Lithuanian Emigration to the United States, 1868–1950* (Vilnius: Mokslo ir Enciklopediju Leidybos Institutas, 2005).

3.   Mekas's written diary was published in 1991 by Black Thistle Press, under the title *I Had Nowhere to Go*. A new edition was published by Spector Books in 2017.

4.   Penny Summerfield, *Histories of the Self: Personal Narratives and Historical Practice* (London: Routledge, 2018), 50–77.

5.   Vahé Tachjian, *Daily Life in the Abyss: Genocide Diaries, 1915–1918* (New York: Berghahn Books, 2017).

6.   Katherine Pickering Antonova, *An Ordinary Marriage: The World of a Gentry Family in Provincial Russia* (New York: Oxford University Press, 2013).

7. Paul J. Eakin, "Breaking Rules: The Consequences of Self-Narration," *Biography* 24, no. 1 (2001): 115.

8. For a study of the relationships between documentary and the avant-garde in autobiographical films, see my chapter "Diálogo entre el documental y la vanguardia en clave autobiográfica," in *Documental y vanguardia*, ed. Mirito Torreiro and Josetxo Cerdán (Madrid: Cátedra, 2005), 219–50.

9. Jean Rousset, *Le lecteur intime: De Balzac au journal* (Paris: Librairie José Corti, 1986), 158.

10. David E. James, "Film Diary/Diary Film: Practice and Product in *Walden*," in *To Free the Cinema: Jonas Mekas and the New York Underground*, ed. David E. James (Princeton, NJ: Princeton University Press, 1992), 144–79. James's categorization refers to Mekas's *Walden* but can be extended to his other diary films.

11. James, "Film Diary/Diary Film," 161.

12. For a more detailed exploration of the relationship between diary films and home movies, see Roger Odin, "Du film de famille au journal filmé," in *Je Filme*, ed. Yann Beauvais and Jean-Michel Bouhours (Paris: Editions du Centre Pompidou, 1995), 1951–44; and Laurence Allard, "Une reencontre entre film de famille et film expérimental: Le cinéma personnel," in *Le filme de famille: Usage privé, usage public*, ed. Roger Odin (Paris: Meridiens Klincksieck, 1995), 113–25.

13. Susana Egan, *Mirror Talk: Genres of Crisis in Contemporary Autobiography* (Chapel Hill: University of North Carolina Press, 1999), 97. Egan is talking here about the work of Jim Lane and Tom Joslin.

14. Jonas Mekas, "The Diary Film (A Lecture on the Reminiscences of a Journey to Lithuania)," in *The Avant-Garde Film: A Reader of Theory and Criticism*, ed. P. Adam Sitney (New York: Anthology Film Archives, 1987), 191.

15. Mekas, "The Diary Film," 192.

16. Quoted from an interview of Jonas Mekas by Jérôme Sans, published in *Just Like a Shadow*, ed. Jérôme Sans (Paris: Patrick Remy Studio, 2000). The book has no pagination.

17. Mekas, "The Diary Film," 193.

18. Maureen Turim, "*Reminiscences*, Subjectivities, and Truths," in James, *To Free the Cinema*, 209. Italics in the original.

19. Philippe Lejeune, *L'autobiographie en France* (Paris: Armand Colin, 2003), 24.

20. Hamid Naficy, *An Accented Cinema: Exilic and Diasporic Filmmaking* (Princeton, NJ: Princeton University Press, 2001), 141. Naficy addresses the diary films of Jonas Mekas specifically (141–46) as what he calls "letter-films," presenting them as "an exemplar of exilic filmmaking," not only because they depict "exile, displacement, and longing," but also because they are "exilically accented" in their style, structure, and mode of production (141).

21. Turim, "*Reminiscences*, Subjectivities, and Truths," 209.

22. The titles in Mekas's films, usually written in capital letters, are expressed here in the same format used by Mekas.

23. Sau-Ling Cynthia Wong, "Immigrant Autobiography: Some Questions of Definition and Approach," in *American Autobiography: Retrospect and Prospect*, ed. Paul John Eakin (Madison: University of Wisconsin Press, 1991), 149.

24. James, "Film Diary/Diary Film," 163.

25. William Boelhower, *Autobiographical Transactions in Modernist America: The Immigrant, the Architect, the Artist, the Citizen* (Udine, Italy: Del Bianco Editore, 1992), 28–40.

26. See Michael V. Montgomery, *Carnival and Commonplaces: Bakhtin's Chronotope, Cultural Studies, and Film* (New York: Peter Lang, 1993); Vivian Sobchack, "Lounge Time: Postwar Crises and the Chronotope of Film Noir," in *Refiguring American Film Genres: History and Theory*, ed. Nick Browne (Berkeley: University of California Press, 1998), 129–70; and Naficy, *An Accented Cinema* (chaps. 5 and 6). Two other scholars should be mentioned in this context: Robert Stam, who has also applied Bakhtin to cinema in *Subversive Pleasures: Bakhtin, Cultural Criticism, and Film* (Baltimore: Johns Hopkins University Press, 1989), although he focuses on issues such as language, heteroglossia, carnival, and dialogism; and James M. Moran, who studies the "home mode" in video and television as a chronotope in chapter 4 of his book *There's No Place Like Home Video* (Minneapolis: University of Minnesota Press, 2002).

27. Bakhtin, *Dialogic Imagination*, 250. As Sobchack points out, it is important to note that for Bakhtin these chronotopes were not a mere backdrop to the plot, as they provide specific markers for the development of the story, limiting its narrative variations, shaping characterization, and establishing the most significant axiological sites of the work. Sobchack, "Lounge Time," 151.

28. Stam refers to this transfer of Bakhtin's ideas to cinema in a brief comment on *The Dialogic Imagination*: "Although Bakhtin once again does not refer to cinema, his category seems ideally suited to it. . . . Bakhtin's description of the novel as the place where time 'thickens, takes on flesh, becomes artistically visible' . . . seems in some ways more appropriate to film than to literature, for whereas literature plays itself out within a virtual, lexical space, the cinematic chronotope is quite literal, splayed out concretely across a screen with specific dimensions and unfolding in literal time." Stam, *Subversive Pleasures*, 11.

29. Boelhower, *Autobiographical Transactions in Modernist America*, 23.

30. Bakhtin, *Dialogic Imagination*, 247.

31. According to Mekas's website (jonasmekas.com), the total duration of the film is 178'. But the French version on DVD (the one available in Europe) lasts only 165'. This is the one I have used. It was also used by Francesco Mazzaferro for the discussion in his article "Jonas Mekas, Between Experimental Cinema and Art Literature: Part Two," *Letteratura artistica: Cross-cultural Studies in Art History Sources*, latest version April 2019, https://letteraturaartistica.blogspot.com/2018/03/jonas-mekas27.html.

32. Mekas, *I Had Nowhere to Go*; Jonas Mekas, *There Is No Ithaca* (New York: Black Thistle Press, 1996).

33. See Bakhtin, *Dialogic Imagination*, 243–45.

34. Henry Rousso, *The Latest Catastrophe: History, the Present, the Contemporary* (Chicago: University of Chicago Press, 2016), 3.

35. Rousso, *Latest Catastrophe*, 3.

36. Betty Bergland, "Postmodernism and the Autobiographical Subject: Reconstructing the 'Other,'" in *Autobiography and Postmodernism*, ed. Kathleen Ashley, Leigh Gilmore, and Gerald Peters (Amherst: University of Massachusetts Press, 1994), 159.

37. Several authors have studied autobiography from the point of view of "narrative recovery." See, for instance, Suzette A. Henke, who explains it as pivoting "on a double entendre meant to evoke both the recovery of the past experience through narrative articulation and the psychological reintegration of a traumatically shattered subject." Henke, *Shattered Subjects: Trauma and Testimony in Women's Life-Writing* (New York: St. Martin's Press, 1998), xxii.

38. Bergland, "Postmodernism and the Autobiographical Subject," 160.

39. Bakthin, *Dialogic Imagination*, 244.

40. Bakthin, *Dialogic Imagination*, 243, 245.

41. Bakthin, *Dialogic Imagination*, 224, 227.

42. Bakthin, *Dialogic Imagination*, 226.

43. James, "Film Diary/Diary Film," 158.

44. See, for instance, Jonas Mekas, "8 mm Cinema as Folk Art," in *Movie Journal: The Rise of the New American Cinema 1959–1971*, 2nd ed. (New York: Columbia University Press, 2016), 89.

45. James, "Film Diary/Diary Film," 159.

46. Jeffrey Rouf, "Home Movies of the Avant-Garde: Jonas Mekas and the New York Art World," in James, *To Free the Cinema*, 295.

47. Allard, "Une reencontre entre film de famille et film expérimental," 113–25.

48. A personal anecdote corroborates this family air that Allard associates with Mekas's films. In 2001, I was on a short research stay at the Anthology Film Archives. Mekas had recently finished *As I Was Moving Ahead Occasionally I Saw Brief Glimpses of Beauty* and organized a private screening, to which he invited me. As the film is almost five hours long, halfway through the screening Mekas interrupted it and invited the five audience members to a meal, based on the argument that "anyone who watches my films I consider my friend."

49. A similar case involves a rather atypical character in this context, Tiny Tim, who appears at the beginning of Reel 6, in the early 1960s, singing and playing the ukulele, also years before he became famous for his appearances on American television.

50. Reel 6 also includes a scene with a celebrity: a meeting with Salvador Dalí organized by Professor Oster, which took place in January 1964.

51. James, "Film Diary/Diary Film," 159.

52. Scott MacDonald, "Lost, Lost, Lost over *Lost, Lost, Lost*," *Cinema Journal* 25, no. 2 (1986): 32.

EPILOGUE

1. In the extensive literature on these questions, it is worth highlighting two anthologies: Jack Dougherty and Kristen Nawrotzki, eds., *Writing History in the Digital Age* (Ann

Arbor: University of Michigan Press, 2013); and Tony Weller, ed., *History in the Digital Age* (London: Routledge, 2013).

2. Regarding i-docs, see, for example: Judith Aston, Sandra Gaudenzi, and Mandy Rose, eds., *I-Docs: The Evolving Practices of Interactive Documentary* (New York: Columbia University Press/Wallflower, 2017); Judith Aston and Stefano Odorico, "The Poetics and Politics of Polyphony: Towards a Research Method for Interactive Documentary," *Alphaville: Journal of Film and Screen Media*, no. 15 (2018): 63–93.

3. It is worth noting, however, one "VR documentary" that seems in tune with microhistorical approaches: *Easter Rising: Voice of a Rebel* (2016), which reconstructs the Irish 1916 Easter Rising from the perspective of Willie McNeive, a young supporter of Irish independence from Britain. This VR experience, visually constructed using animation, is built on McNeive's eyewitness account, a recording of which lay undiscovered for decades. The project is presented as offering "a very personal insight into this a key moment in European history . . . an artistic journey into the memory of an ordinary man who was swept up into an extraordinary event." https://vrtov.com/projects/easter -rising-voice-of-a-rebel/, accessed February 5, 2021.

4. For a more detailed description of the video game, see its Wikipedia entry: https://en .wikipedia.org/wiki/1979_Revolution:_Black_Friday.

5. Another video game that could be described as taking a microhistorical approach is *Jewish Time Jump: New York* (2013). In this game, the player becomes a reporter who travels a century back in time to learn more about Jewish life in Greenwich Village in the 1900s. But in addition to being a location-based augmented reality (AR) game only playable in New York City, its focus is clearly didactic, aimed primarily at school students, and with supplementary teaching materials available at https://jwa.org/teach /jewishtimejump. For more on this project, see Owen Gottlieb, "Who Really Said What? Mobile Historical Situated Documentary as Liminal Learning Space," *Gamevironments*, no. 5 (2016): 237–57.

6. A clear example of this phenomenon is the large number of i-docs designed using Flash Player software, which Adobe stopped supporting at the end of 2020, rendering the documentaries inaccessible from one day to the next. A similar fate befell products made using the ARIS platform, which has also ceased to function. This was the platform used to create *Jewish Time Jump: New York* (mentioned above) and other historical i-docs such as *Dow Day*.

7. For a more detailed analysis of this i-doc, see "A Polish Journey—A Web-Doc About Migration and Its Legacy," http://i-docs.org/a-polish-journey-a-web-doc-about-migration -and-its-legacy/, accessed March 3, 2021.

8. Marcel Prins and Peter Henk Steenhuis, eds., *Hidden Like Anne Frank: 14 True Stories of Survival* (New York: Scholastic, 2014). The interactive project was made by Marcel Prins, Peter Henk Steenhuis, and Marcel van der Drift. Available at https:// hiddenlikeannefrank.com/, accessed March 10, 2021.

9. "About JWRH," *Jerusalem, We Are Here: An Interactive Documentary*, 2018, https:// info.jerusalemwearehere.com/, accessed February 20, 2021

10. *Jerusalem, We Are Here* also connects with the trilogy made by the well-known Israeli filmmaker Amos Gitai about a house that was abandoned by its Palestinian owner in 1948 and occupied by different Israeli tenants over the years. Gitai made the first film, *House*, in 1980, the second, *A House in Jerusalem*, in 1998, and the third, *News from Home/News from House*, in 2005, creating a sort of longitudinal documentary with the physical space of the house as the element of continuity.

11. Alf Lüdtke, "What Is the History of Everyday Life and Who Are Its Practitioners?," in *History of Everyday Life: Reconstructing Historical Experiences and Ways of Life*, ed. Alf Lüdtke (Princeton, NJ: Princeton University Press, 1995), 21.

12. Lara Baladi, Vox Populi, http://tahrirarchives.com/, accessed February 12, 2021.

13. Alisa Lebow, *Filming Revolution*, Stanford University, 2018, https://www.filmingrevolution.org, accessed February 10, 2021.

14. All Alisa Lebow's quotes in this paragraph are taken from the text included in the "History + Memory" link of her i-doc.

15. A similar idea is expressed by the scholar Luke Tredinnick when he reflects on the transformation of the archive in the digital era: "If history was once inscribed in the archive before it was inscribed in the historical account, if presence in the archive was once tantamount to presence in history, then now the archive itself is as much the site of popular contestation and participation as the histories it generates." See Luke Tredinnick, "The Making of History: Remediating Historicised Experience," in *History in the Digital Age*, ed. Tony Weller (London: Routledge, 2012), 56.

16. Tredinnick, "Making of History," 47.

17. Tredinnick, "Making of History," 52.

18. Tredinnick, "Making of History," 57.

BIBLIOGRAPHY

Aguirre, Carlos A. *Microhistoria italiana: Modo de empleo*. Caracas: Fundación Centro Nacional de Historia, 2009.

Albano, Caterina. *Memory, Forgetting and the Moving Image*. London: Palgrave, 2016.

Allard, Laurence. "Une reencontre entre film de famille et film expérimental: Le cinéma personnel." In Odin, *Le filme de famille*, 113–25.

Antonova, Katherine Pickering. *An Ordinary Marriage: The World of a Gentry Family in Provincial Russia*. New York: Oxford University Press, 2013.

Arendt, Hannah. *Eichmann in Jerusalem: A Report on the Banality of Evil*. New York: Viking Press, 1963.

Arostegui, Julio. "Retos de la memoria y trabajos de la historia." *Pasado y memoria*, no. 3 (2004): 23–24.

Arostegui, Julio. "Ver bien la propia época (Nuevas reflexiones sobre el presente como historia)." *Sociohistórica*, nos. 9–10 (2001): 13–43.

Aasman, Susan. "Everyday Complexities and Contradictions in Contemporary Amateur Practice." In Motrescu-Mayes and Aasman, *Amateur Media and Participatory Cultures*, 44–64.

Aston, Judith, Sandra Gaudenzi, and Mandy Rose, eds. *I-Docs: The Evolving Practices of Interactive Documentary*. New York: Columbia University Press/Wallflower Press, 2017.

Aston, Judith, and Stefano Odorico. "The Poetics and Politics of Polyphony: Towards a Research Method for Interactive Documentary." *Alphaville: Journal of Film and Screen Media*, no. 15 (2018): 63–93.

Aurell, Jaume. *Theoretical Perspectives on Historians' Autobiographies: From Documentation to Intervention*. London: Routledge, 2016.

Bakhtin, Mikhail. *The Dialogic Imagination: Four Essays*. Austin: University of Texas Press, 1981.

Balint, Ruth. "Representing the Past and the Meaning of Home in Péter Forgács's Private Hungary." In Rascaroli, Young, and Monahan, *Amateur Filmmaking*, 193–206.

Banks, Taunya Lovell. "Outsider Citizen: Film Narratives About the Internment of Japanese Americans." *Suffolk University Law Review* 42, no. 4 (2009): 769–94.

Baron, Jaimie. *The Archive Effect: Found Footage and the Audiovisual Experience of History.* London: Routledge, 2014.

Barthes, Roland. *Camera Lucida: Reflections on Photography.* New York: Hill & Wang, 1982.

Bartlett, Frederic. *Remembering: A Study in Experimental and Social Psychology.* Cambridge: Cambridge University Press, 1995. Originally published 1932.

Bastian, Jeannette A. "Moving the Margins to the Middle: Reconciling 'the Archive' with the Archives." In *Engaging with Records and Archives: Histories and Theories*, edited by Fiorella Foscarini, Heather MacNeil, Bonnie Mak, and Gillian Oliver, 3–19. London: Facet Publishing, 2016.

Bayer, Gerd, and Oleksandr Kobrynskyy, eds. *Holocaust Cinema in the Twenty-First Century: Images, Memory, and the Ethics of Representation.* New York: Columbia University Press/ Wallflower Press, 2015.

Bazin, André. *What Is Cinema?* Vol. 1. Berkeley: University of California Press, 1967. Originally published as *Qu'est-ce que le cinéma?* Paris: Editions du Cerf, 1958.

Beker, Elisabeth. *When the War Was Over: Cambodia and the Khmer Rouge Revolution.* New York: Public Affairs, 1986.

Benjamin, Walter. *The Arcades Project.* Cambridge, MA: Belknap Press, 1999.

Benjamin, Walter. *Illuminations.* London: Fontana, 1982.

Bergland, Betty. "Postmodernism and the Autobiographical Subject: Reconstructing the 'Other.'" In *Autobiography and Postmodernism*, edited by Kathleen Ashley, Leigh Gilmore, and Gerald Peters, 130–66. Amherst: University of Massachusetts Press, 1994.

Bergland, Betty. "Representing Ethnicity in Autobiography: Narratives of Opposition." *Yearbook of English Studies* 24 (1994): 67–93.

Bergson, Henri. *The Creative Mind: An Introduction to Metaphysics.* New York: Citadel Press, 1946.

Boelhower, William. *Autobiographical Transactions in Modernist America: The Immigrant, the Architect, the Artist, the Citizen.* Udine, Italy: Del Bianco Editore, 1992.

Boelhower, William. *Immigrant Autobiography in the United States: Four Versions of the Italian American Self.* Verona: Essedue, 1982.

Bou, Stephanie. *L'image manquante: Un film de Rithy Panh.* Paris: ACRIF-CIP, 2016.

Boyle, Deirdre. "Shattering Silence: Traumatic Memory and Re-enactment in Rithy Panh's *S-21: The Khmer Rouge Killing Machine.*" *Frameworks* 50, nos. 1–2, (2009): 95–106.

Breakell, Sue, ed. "Archival Practices and the Practice of Archives in the Visual Arts." Special Issue, *Archives and Records* 36, no. 1 (2015).

Brewer, John. "Microhistory and the Histories of Everyday Life." *Cultural and Social History* 7, no. 1 (2010): 87–109.

Bryceson, Debora F., and Ulla Vuorela, eds. *The Transnational Family: New European Frontiers and Global Networks.* Oxford: Berg, 2002.

Burke, Peter, ed. *New Perspectives on Historical Writing*. 2nd ed. Cambridge: Polity Press, 2001.

Carlsten, Jennie M. and Fearghal McGarry, eds. *Film, History and Memory*. London: Palgrave Macmillan, 2015.

Caswell, Michelle. *Archiving the Unspeakable: Silence, Memory, and the Photographic Record in Cambodia*. Madison: University of Wisconsin Press, 2014.

Certeau, Michel de. *The Practice of Everyday Life*. Berkeley: University of California Press, 1984.

Certeau, Michel de, Luce Giard, and Pierre Mayol. *The Practice of Everyday Life*. Vol. 2, *Living and Cooking*. Minneapolis: University of Minnesota Press, 1998.

Chalfen, Richard. *Snapshot Versions of Life*. Bowling Green, OH: Bowling Green State University Popular Press, 1987.

Citron, Michele. *Home Movies and Other Necessary Fictions*. Minnesota: University of Minnesota Press, 1998.

Cocker, Emma. "Ethical Possession: Borrowing from the Archives." In *Cultural Borrowings: Appropriation, Reworking, Transformation*, edited by I. R. Smith, 92–110. Nottingham, UK: Scope, 2009.

Cook, Terry. "Fashionable Nonsense or Professional Rebirth: Postmodernism and the Practice of Archives." *Archivaria*, no. 51 (2001): 14–35.

Craven, Ian, ed. *Movies on Home Ground: Exploration in Amateur Cinema*. New Castle, UK: Cambridge Scholar Publishing, 2009.

Cubitt, Geoffrey. *History and Memory*. Manchester, UK: Manchester University Press, 2007.

Cuevas, Efrén. "Change of Scale: Home Movies as Microhistory in Documentary Films." In Rascaroli, Young, and Monahan, *Amateur filmmaking*, 139–51.

Cuevas, Efrén. "Del cine doméstico al autobiográfico: Caminos de ida y vuelta." In *Cineastas frente al espejo*, edited by Gregorio Martín Gutiérrez, 101–20. Madrid: T&B, 2008.

Cuevas, Efrén. "Diálogo entre el documental y la vanguardia en clave autobiográfica." In *Documental y vanguardia*, edited by Mirito Torreiro and Josetxo Cerdán, 219–50. Madrid: Cátedra, 2005.

Cuevas, Efrén. "The Filmic Representation of Home in Transnational Families: The Case of *I for India*." *NECSUS*, Autumn 2016. https://necsus-ejms.org/the-filmic-representation-of-home-in-transnational-families-the-case-of-i-for-india/.

Cuevas, Efrén. "Home Movies as Personal Archives in Autobiographical Documentaries." *Studies in Documentary Film* 17, no. 1 (2013): 17–29.

Cuevas, Efrén. "The Immigrant Experience in Jonas Mekas's Diary Films: A Chronotopic Analysis of *Lost, Lost, Lost*." *Biography* 29, no. 1 (2006): 55–73.

Cuevas, Efrén, ed. *La casa abierta: El cine doméstico y sus reciclajes contemporáneos*. Madrid: Ocho y medio, 2010.

Cuevas, Efrén. "Microhistoria y cine documental: Puntos de encuentro." *Historia Social*, no. 91 (2018): 69–83.

Davidson, Lauren, "The Selective Memory of 'Israel: A Home Movie.'" *The Tower Magazine*, no. 5, August 2013. http://www.thetower.org/article/the-selective-memory-of-israel-a-home-movie/.

Davis, Natalie Z. *The Return of Martin Guerre*. Cambridge, MA: Harvard University Press, 1984.

Davis, Natalie Z. *Slaves on Screen*. Cambridge, MA: Harvard University Press, 2000.

Davis, Rocío G. *Relative Histories: Mediating History in Asian American Family Memoirs*. Honolulu: University of Hawai'i Press, 2011.

De Baecque, Antoine. *Camera Historica: The Century in Cinema*. New York: Columbia University Press, 2012.

Del Rincón, María, Efrén Cuevas, and Marta Torregrosa. "The Representation of Personal Memory in Alan Berliner's *First Cousin Once Removed*." *Studies in Documentary Film* 12, no. 1 (2018): 16–27.

Del Rincón, María, Marta Torregrosa, and Efrén Cuevas. "La representación fílmica de la memoria personal: Las películas de memoria." *ZER* 22, no. 42 (2017): 175–88.

Deleuze, Gilles. *Cinema 2: The Time-Image*. Minneapolis: University of Minnesota Press, 1989.

Derrida, Jacques. *Archive Fever*. Chicago: University of Chicago Press, 1997.

Di Blasio, Tiziana M. *Cinema e storia: Interferenze e confluenze tra due scritture*. Rome: Viella, 2014.

Didi-Huberman, George. *Images in Spite of All: Four Photographs from Auschwitz*. Chicago: University of Chicago Press, 2008.

Dittmar, Linda. "In the Eye of the Storm: The Political Stake of Israeli i-Movies." In Lebow, *The Cinema of Me*, 158–79.

Dougherty, Jack, and Kristen Nawrotzki, eds. *Writing History in the Digital Age*. Ann Arbor: University of Michigan Press, 2013.

Eakin, Paul J. "Breaking Rules: The Consequences of Self-Narration." *Biography* 24, no. 1 (2001): 113–27.

Eakin, Paul J. *How Our Lives Become Stories: Making Selves*. Ithaca, NY: Cornell University Press, 1999.

Egan, Susana. *Mirror Talk: Genres of Crisis in Contemporary Autobiography*. Chapel Hill: University of North Carolina Press, 1999.

Eidintas, Alfonsas. *Lithuanian Emigration to the United States, 1868–1950*. Vilnius: Mokslo ir Enciklopediju Leidybos Institutas, 2005.

Erll, Astrid. *Memory in Culture*. Basingstoke, UK: Palgrave Macmillan, 2011.

Feigelson, Kristian. "*The Labyrinth*: A Strategy of Sensitive Experimentation, a Filmmaker of the Anonymous." *KinoKultura*, no. 7, 2008, http://www.kinokultura.com/specials/7/feigelson.shtml.

Feng, Peter X. *Identities in Motion*. Durham, NC: Duke University Press, 2002.

Ferro, Marc. *Cinema and History*. Detroit, MI: Wayne State University Press, 1988. First published in French as *Cinema et histoire*. París: Denoël/Gonthier, 1977.

Fisher, Michael. "Ethnicity and the Postmodern Arts of Memory." In *Writing Culture: The Poetics and Politics of Ethnography*, edited by J. Clifford and G. E. Marcus, 194–233. Berkeley: University of California Press, 1986.

Forgács, Péter. "*Wittgenstein Tractatus*: Personal Reflections on Home Movies." In Ishizuka and Zimmermann, *Mining the Home Movies*, 47–56.

Foucault, Michel. *The Archaeology of Knowledge and the Discourse on Language.* New York: Pantheon Books, 1972.

Foucault, Michel. *Society Must Be Defended.* New York: Picador, 2003.

Freire, Marcius, and Manuela Penafria, eds. "Documentário e história." Special Issue, *Doc on-line,* no. 15 (2013). http://doc.ubi.pt/index15.html.

Friedlander, Saul, ed. *Probing the Limits of Representation: Nazism and the "Final Solution."* Cambridge, MA: Harvard University Press, 1992.

Frisby, David. *Fragments of Modernity: Theories of Modernity in the Work of Simmel, Kracauer and Benjamin.* Cambridge, MA: MIT Press, 1988.

Frisch, Michel. *A Shared Authority: Essays on the Craft and Meaning of Oral and Public History.* New York: State University of New York Press, 1990.

Garland, David. "What Is a 'History of the Present'? On Foucault's Genealogies and Their Critical Preconditions." *Punishment & Society* 16, no. 4 (2014): 365–84.

Gaudreault, André, and François Jost. *Le Récit cinématographique: Films et séries télévisées.* 3rd rev. and exp. ed. Paris: Armand Colin, 2017. Originally published 1990.

Geertz, Clifford. *The Interpretation of Cultures.* New York: Basic Books, 1973.

Genette, Gerard. *Narrative Discourse: An Essay in Method.* Ithaca, NY: Cornell University Press, 1980. First published as *Figures III.* Paris: Editions du Seuil, 1972.

Genette, Gerard. *Narrative Discourse Revisited.* Ithaca, NY: Cornell University Press, 1988. First published as *Nouveau discours du récit.* Paris: Editions du Seuil, 1983.

Gertz, Nurith, and George Khleifi. *Palestinian Cinema: Landscape, Trauma, and Memory.* Edinburgh: Edinburgh University Press, 2008.

Ginzburg, Carlo. "Acerca de la historia local y la microhistoria." In *Tentativas,* 253–68. Moralia, Mexico: Universidad Michoacana de San Nicolás de Hidalgo, 2003. Originally published as "Intorno a storia locale e microstoria." In *La memoria lunga: Le raccolte di storia locale dall'erudizione alla documentazione,* edited by P. Bertolucci and R. Pensato, 15–25. Milan: Bibliográfica, 1985.

Ginzburg, Carlo. *The Cheese and the Worms: The Cosmos of a Sixteenth-Century Miller.* Baltimore: Johns Hopkins University Press, 1992. Originally published as *Il formaggio e i vermi: Il cosmo di un mugnaio del '500.* Turin: Einaudi, 1976.

Ginzburg, Carlo. "De todos los regalos que le traigo al Kaisare . . . Interpretar la película, escribir la historia." In *Tentativas,* 197–215. Moralia: Universidad Michoacana de San Nicolás de Hidalgo, 2003. Originally published as "Di tutti i doni che porto a Kaisire . . . Leggere il film scrivere la storia." *Storie e storia* 5, no. 9 (1983): 5–17.

Ginzburg, Carlo. "Historia y microhistoria: Carlo Ginzburg entrevistado por Mauro Boarelli." *Pasajes: Revista de pensamiento contemporáneo,* no. 44 (2014): 89–101.

Ginzburg, Carlo. "Just One Witness." In Friedlander, *Probing the Limits of Representation,* 82–96.

Ginzburg, Carlo. "Microhistory: Two or Three Things That I Know About It." *Critical Inquiry* 20, no. 1 (1993): 10–34.

Ginzburg, Carlo. "Montrer et citer, La vérité de l'histoire." *Le Débat,* no. 56 (1989): 43–54.

Ginzburg, Carlo. "Morelli, Freud, and Sherlock Holmes: Clues and Scientific Method." *History Workshop Journal* 9, no. 1 (1980): 5–36. Originally published as "Spie: Radici di un paradigma indiziario." In *Crisi della ragione*, edited by Aldo Gargani, 57–106. Turin: Einaudi, 1979.

Ginzburg, Carlo. "Proofs and Possibilities: Postscript to Natalie Zemon Davis, *The Return of Martin Guerre*." In *Threads and Traces: True False Fictive*, 54–71. Berkeley: University of California Press, 2012.

Ginzburg, Carlo. *Rapports de force: Historie, rhétorique, prevue*. Paris: Gallimard, 2003.

Ginzburg, Carlo, and Carlo Poni. "The Name and the Game: Unequal Exchange and the Historiographic Marketplace." In Muir and Ruggiero, *Microhistory and the Lost Peoples of Europe*, 1–10. Originally published in *Quaderni storici* 14, no. 40 (1979): 181–90.

Gottlieb, Owen. "Who Really Said What? Mobile Historical Situated Documentary as Liminal Learning Space." *Gamevironments*, no. 5 (2016): 237–57.

Goursat, Juliette. *Mises en "je": Autobiographie et film documentaire*. Aix-en-Provence: Presses Universitaires de Provence, 2016.

Gracia Cárcamo, Juan. "Microsociología e historia de lo cotidiano." *Revista Ayer*, no. 19 (1995): 189–222.

Gray, Ann. "History Documentaries for Television." In *The Documentary Film Book*, edited by Brian Winston, 328–36. London: British Film Institute Publishing, 2013.

Gregory, Brad S. "Is Small Beautiful? Microhistory and the History of Everyday Life." *History and Theory* 38, no. 1 (1999): 100–110.

Grendi, Edoardo. "Micro-analisi e storia sociale." *Quaderni Storici* 12, no. 35 (1977): 506–20.

Guasch, Anna M. *Arte y archivo 1920-2010: Genealogías, tipologías y discontinuidades*. Madrid: Akal, 2011.

Guerin, Frances, and Robert Hallas, eds. *The Image and the Witness: Trauma, Memory and Visual Culture*. London: Wallflower Press, 2007.

Halbwachs, Maurice. *Les cadres sociaux de la mémoire*. Paris: Éditions Albin Michel, 1994. Originally published 1925.

Halevi, Yossi K. "The Real Dispute Driving the Israeli-Palestinian Conflict." *The Atlantic*, May 14, 2018.

Harootunian, Harry D. *History's Disquiet: Modernity, Cultural Practice, and the Question of Everyday Life*. New York: Columbia University Press, 2000.

Henke, Suzette A. *Shattered Subjects: Trauma and Testimony in Women's Life-Writing*. New York: St. Martin's Press, 1998.

Hernández-Navarro, Miguel Ángel. *Materializar el pasado: El artista como historiador (benjaminiano)*. Murcia: Micromegas, 2012.

Highmore, Ben. *Everyday Life and Cultural Theory*. London: Routledge, 2001.

Highmore, Ben, ed. *Everyday Life Reader*. London: Routledge, 2002.

Hirsch, Joshua. *Afterimage: Film, Trauma, and the Holocaust*. Philadelphia: Temple University Press, 2003.

Hirsch, Marianne, ed. *The Familial Gaze*. Hanover, NH: University Press of New England, 1999.

Hirsch, Marianne. *Family Frames: Photography, Narrative and Postmemory*. Cambridge, MA: Harvard University Press, 1997.

Hirsch, Marianne. *The Generation of Postmemory: Writing and Visual Culture After the Holocaust*. New York: Columbia University Press, 2012.

Hodgin, Nick, and Amit Thakkar, eds. *Scars and Wounds: Film and Legacies of Trauma*. London: Palgrave, 2017.

Hughes-Warrington, Marnie. *History Goes to the Movies: Studying History on Film*. London: Routledge, 2007.

Ileri, Nurçin. "The Distraction and Glamour of Everyday Life in *The Salaried Masses* and *The Mass Ornament*." *Journal of Historical Studies*, no. 5 (2007): 83–93.

Insdorf, Annette. *Indelible Shadows: Film and the Holocaust* 3rd ed. Cambridge: Cambridge University Press, 2003.

Ishizuka, Karen L. *Lost and Found: Reclaiming the Japanese American Incarceration*. Champaign: University of Illinois Press, 2006.

Ishizuka, Karen L. "Through Our Own Eyes: Making Movies with Japanese American Home Movies." In Cuevas, *La casa abierta*, 207–23.

Ishizuka, Karen, and Patricia R. Zimmermann, eds. *Mining the Home Movies: Excavations in Histories and Memories*. Berkeley: University of California Press, 2008.

James, David E., ed. *To Free the Cinema: Jonas Mekas and the New York Underground*. Princeton, NJ: Princeton University Press, 1992.

Kaplan, E. Ann. *Trauma Culture: The Politics of Terror and Loss in Media and Literature*. New Brunswick, NJ: Rutgers University Press, 2005.

Kerner, Aaron. *Film and the Holocaust: New Perspectives on Dramas, Documentaries, and Experimental Films*. New York: Continuum, 2011.

Kessler, Lauren. *Stubborn Twig: Three Generations in the Life of a Japanese American Family*. New York: Random House, 1993.

Kilborn, Richard. "'I Am a Time Archaeologist': Some Reflections on the Filmmaking Practice of Péter Forgács." In Rascaroli, Young, and Monahan, *Amateur Filmmaking*, 179–92.

Kilborn, Richard. *Taking the Long View: A Study of Longitudinal Documentary*. Manchester, UK: Manchester University Press, 2010.

Kozloff, Sarah. *Invisible Storytellers: Voice-Over Narration in American Fiction Film*. Berkeley: University of California Press, 1989.

Kracauer, Siegfried. *From Caligari to Hitler: A Psychological History of the German Film*. Princeton: Princeton University Press, 2004.

Kracauer, Siegfried. *History, the Last Things Before the Last*. New York: Oxford University Press, New York, 1969.

Kracauer, Siegfried. *The Mass Ornament: Weimar Essays*. Cambridge, MA: Harvard University Press, 1995.

Kracauer, Siegfried. *Theory of Film: The Redemption of Physical Reality*. New York: Oxford University Press, 1960.

Landsberg, Alison. *Prosthetic Memory: The Transformation of American Remembrance in the Age of Mass Culture*. New York: Columbia University Press, 2004.

Lane, Jim. *The Autobiographical Documentary in America*. Madison: University of Wisconsin Press, 2002.

Langford, Rachael. "Colonial False Memory Syndrome? The Cinémémoire Archive of French Colonial Films and *Mémoire d'Outremer.*" *Studies in French Cinema* 5, no. 2 (2005): 99–110.

Lebow, Alisa, ed. *The Cinema of Me: The Self and Subjectivity in First Person Documentary.* New York: Columbia University Press/Wallflower Press, 2012.

Lebow, Alisa. *First Person Jewish.* Minneapolis: University of Minnesota Press, 2008.

Lee, Christopher A., ed. *I, Digital: Personal Collections in the Digital Era.* Chicago: Society of American Archivists, 2011.

Lejeune, Philippe. "How Do Diaries End?" *Biography* 24, no. 1 (2001): 99–112.

Lejeune, Philippe. *L'autobiographie en France.* Paris: Armand Colin, 2003.

Lepore, Jill. "Historians Who Love Too Much: Reflections on Microhistory and Biography." *Journal of American History* 88, no. 1 (2001): 129–44.

Le Roy, Emmanuel. *Montaillou: Cathars and Catholics in a French Village 1294–1324.* London: Penguin, 2013. Originally published as *Montaillou, village occitan de 1294 à 1324.* Paris: Gallimard, 1975.

Levi, Giovanni. "Antropología y microhistoria: Conversación con Giovanni Levi." *Manuscrits* no. 1 (1993): 15–28.

Levi, Giovanni. "I pericoli del geertzismom." *Quademi storici* 20, no. 58 (1985): 269–77.

Levi, Giovanni. *Inheriting Power: The Story of an Exorcist.* Chicago: University of Chicago Press, 1988. Originally published as *L'eredità immateriale: Carriera di un esorcista nel Piemonte del seicento.* Turin: Einaudi, 1985.

Levi, Giovanni. "On Microhistory." In Burke, *New Perspectives on Historical Writing,* 97–119.

Lipsitz, George. *Time Passages.* Minneapolis: University of Minnesota Press, 1990.

Loshitzky, Yosefa. "Veiling and Unveiling the Israeli Mediterranean: Yulie Cohen-Gerstel's *My Terrorist* and *My Land Zion.*" In *Visions of Struggle in Women's Filmmaking in the Mediterranean,* edited by Flavia Laviosa, 3–19. London: Palgrave Macmillan, 2010.

Lüdtke, Alf, ed. *History of Everyday Life: Reconstructing Historical Experiences and Ways of Life.* Princeton, NJ: Princeton University Press, 1995. Published in German as *Alltagsgeschichte. Zur Rekonstruktion historischer Erfahrungen und Lebensweisen.* Frankfurt: Campus, 1995.

Lüdtke, Alf. "What Is the History of Everyday Life and Who Are Its Practitioners?" In Lüdtke, *History of Everyday Life,* 3–40.

MacDonald, Scott. *A Critical Cinema 4: Interviews with Independent Filmmakers.* Berkeley: University of California Press 2005.

MacDonald, Scott. "Lost, Lost, Lost over *Lost, Lost, Lost.*" *Cinema Journal* 25, no. 2 (1986): 20–34.

MacDougall, David, ed. *Transcultural Cinema.* Princeton, NJ: Princeton University Press, 1998.

MacDouwell, Douglas. *Irony in Film.* London: Palgrave Macmillan, 2016.

Magnússon, Sigurður G., and István Szíjártó. *What Is Microhistory? Theory and Practice.* London: Routledge, 2013.

Manoff, Marlene. "Theories of the Archive from Across the Disciplines." *portal: Libraries and the Academy* 4, no. 1 (2004): 9–25.

Matuszewski, Bolesław. "A New Source of History: The Creation of a Depository for Historical Cinematography." In *Film Manifestos and Global Cinema Cultures*, edited by Scott
MacKenzie, 520–23. Berkeley: University of California Press, 2014.

McLaughlin, Cahal. "What Happens When an Interview Is Filmed? Recording Memories
from Conflict." *Oral History Review* 45, no. 2 (2018): 304–20.

Medick, Hans. "Mikro-Historie." In *Sozialgeschichte, Alltagsgeschichte, Mikro- Historie*,
edited by Winfried Schulze, 40–53. Göttingen: Vandenhoeck und Ruprecht, 1994.

Medina, Celso. "Intrahistoria, cotidianidad y localidad." *Atenea*, no. 500 (2009): 123–39.

Medina, José. "Toward a Foucaultian Epistemology of Resistance: Counter-Memory, Epistemic Friction, and *Guerrilla* Pluralism." *Foucault Studies*, no. 12 (2011): 9–35.

Mekas, Jonas. "The Diary Film (A Lecture on the Reminiscences of a Journey to Lithuania)."
In *The Avant-Garde Film: A Reader of Theory and Criticism*, edited by P. Adam Sitney,
190–98. New York: Anthology Film Archives, 1987.

Mekas, Jonas. *I Had Nowhere to Go*. New York: Spector Books, 2017.

Mekas, Jonas. *Movie Journal: The Rise of a New American Cinema 1959–1971*. 2nd ed. New
York: Columbia University Press, 2016. Originally published by Macmillan, 1972.

Mekas, Jonas. *There Is No Ithaca*. New York: Black Thistle Press, 1996.

Merewether, Charles, ed. *The Archive: Documents of Contemporary Art*. London: Whitechapel, 2006.

Mimura, Glen M. "Antidote for Collective Amnesia? Rea Tajiri's Germinal Image." In *Countervisions: Asian American Film Criticism*, edited by Darrel Y. Hamamoto and Sandra
Liu, 150–62. Philadelphia: Temple University Press, 2000.

Montgomery, Michael V. *Carnival and Commonplaces: Bakhtin's Chronotope, Cultural Studies, and Film*. New York: Peter Lang, 1993.

Moran, James M. *There's No Place like Home Video*. Minneapolis: University of Minnesota
Press, 2002.

Motrescu-Mayes, Annamaria, and Susan Aasman, eds. *Amateur Media and Participatory
Cultures: Film, Video, and Digital Media*. London: Routledge, 2019.

Mourenza, Daniel. *Walter Benjamin and the Aesthetics of Film*. Amsterdam: Amsterdam
University Press, 2020.

Muir, Edward, and Guido Ruggiero, eds. *Microhistory and the Lost Peoples of Europe*. Baltimore: Johns Hopkins University Press, 1991.

Munk, Yael. "Ethics and Responsibility: The Feminization of the New Israeli Documentary."
Israel Studies 16, no. 2 (2011): 151–64.

Munk, Yael. "Motherhood as an Oppositional Standpoint: on Michal Aviad's *For My Children*." In *Gender in Conflicts: Palestine-Israel- Germany*, edited by Christina von Braun
and Ulrike Auga, 143–48. Berlin: LIT Verlag, 2007.

Musolff, Andreas. "The Role of Holocaust Memory in the Israeli–Palestinian Conflict." In
The Israeli Conflict System: Analytic Approaches, edited by Harvey Starr and Stanley
Dubinsk, 168–80. London: Routledge, 2015.

Naficy, Hamid. *An Accented Cinema: Exilic and Diasporic Filmmaking*. Princeton, NJ: Princeton University Press, 2001.

Nichols, Bill. "The Memory of Loss: Péter Forgács's Saga of Family Life and Social Hell." *Film Quarterly* 56, no. 4 (2003): 2–12.

Nichols, Bill. *Representing Reality: Issues and Concepts in Documentary*. Bloomington: Indiana University Press, 1991.

Nichols, Bill, and Michael Renov, eds. *Cinema's Alchemist: The Films of Péter Forgács*. Minneapolis: University of Minnesota Press, 2011.

Noordegraaf, Julia J., and Elvira Pouw. "Extended Family Films: Home Movies in the State-sponsored Archive." *Moving Image* 9, no. 1 (2009): 83–103.

O'Connor, John E., and Martin A. Jackson. *American History/American Film: Interpreting the Hollywood Image*. 2nd ed. New York: Continuum, 1991.

Odin, Roger. "Du film de famille au journal filmé." In *Le Je Filme*, edited by Yann Beauvais and Jean-Michel Bouhours, 1951–44. Paris: Editions du Centre Pompidou, 1995.

Odin, Roger. "How to Make History Perceptible: The Bartos Family and the Private Hungary Series." In Nichols and Renov, *Cinema's Alchemist: The Films of Péter Forgács*, 137–58. Published originally as "La Famille Bartos de Péter Forgács, ou comment rendre l'histoire sensible." In *Cinéma hongrois: Le temps et l'histoire*, edited by Kristian Feigelson. Paris: Presses Sorbonne Nouvelle, 2003.

Odin, Roger, ed. *Le film de famille: Usage privé, usage public*. Paris: Meridiens Klincksieck, 1995.

Odin, Roger. "Reflections on the Family Home Movie as Document: A Semio-pragmatic Approach." In Ishizuka and Zimmermann, *Mining the Home Movies*, 255–71.

Panh, Rithy. *The Elimination*. With Christophe Bataille. Translated by John Cullen. New York: Other Press, 2013. Originally published in French in 2012 as *L'elimination*. Paris: Grasset.

Peltonen, Matti. "Clues, Margins, and Monads: The Micro-Macro Link in Historical Research." *History and Theory* 40, no. 3 (2001): 347–59.

Polland, Lisa. "Film Review. *My Terrorist* and *For My Children*." *Hawwa: Journal of Women of the Middle East and the Islamic World* 3, no. 2 (2005): 272–78.

Popkin, Jeremy D. *History, Historians, and Autobiography*. Chicago: University of Chicago Press, 2005.

Prager, Brad. *After the Fact: The Holocaust in Twenty-first Century Documentary Film*. London: Bloomsbury, 2015.

Prins, Marcel, and Peter Henk Steenhuis, eds. *Hidden Like Anne Frank: 14 True Stories of Survival*. New York: Scholastic, 2014.

Rascaroli, Laura, Gwenda Young, and Barry Monahan, eds. *Amateur Filmmaking: The Home Movie, the Archive, the Web*. London: Bloomsbury, 2014.

Renov, Michael. "Domestic Ethnography and the Construction of the 'Other Self.'" In *Collecting Visible Evidence*, edited by Jane M. Gaines and Michael Renov, 140–55. Minneapolis: University of Minnesota Press, 1999.

Renov, Michael. "Historical Discourses of the Unimaginable: Peter Forgacs' The Maelstrom." In Nichols and Renov, *Cinema's Alchemist*, 86. Originally published in German as "Historische Diskurse des Unvorstellbaren: Peter Forgacs' The Maelstrom." *Montage AV* 11, no. 1 (2002): 27–40.

Revel, Jacques, ed. *Jeux d'echelles: La micro-analyse à la expérience*. Paris: Seuil/Gallimard, 1996.

Revel, Jacques. "Microanalysis and the Construction of the Social." In *Histories: French Constructions of the Past*, edited by Jacques Revel and Lynn Hunt, 492–502. New York: New Press, 1995.

Ricoeur, Paul. *Memory, History, Forgetting*. Chicago: University of Chicago Press, 2004.

Rigney, Ann. "History as Text: Narrative Theory and History." In *The SAGE Handbook of Historical Theory*, edited by Nancy Partner and Sarah Foot, 183–201. London: SAGE, 2013.

Rosen, Philip. "Document and Documentary: On the Persistence of Historical Concepts." In *Theorizing Documentary*, edited by Michael Renov, 58–89. Routledge: London, 1993.

Rosen, Robert. "*Something Strong Within* as Historical Memory." In Ishizuka and Zimmermann, *Mining the Home Movies*, 107–21.

Rosengarten, Ruth. *Between Memory and Document: The Archival Turn in Contemporary Art*. Lisboa: Museo Coleçao Berardo, 2012.

Rosenstone, Robert A. "The Future of the Past: Film and the Beginnings of Postmodern History." In *The Persistence of History: Cinema, Television, and the Modern Event*, edited by Vivian Sobchack, 201–18. London: Routledge, 1996.

Rosenstone, Robert A. "History in Images/History in Words: Reflections on the Possibility of Really Putting History onto Film." *American Historical Review* 93, no. 5 (1988): 1173–85.

Rosenstone, Robert A. *History on Film/Film on History*. Harlow, UK: Pearson Longman, 2006. Second edition, London: Routledge, 2012.

Rosenstone, Robert A. "Reflections on What the Filmmaker Historian Does (to History)." In *Film, History and Memory*, edited by J. M. Carlsten and F. McGarry, 183–97. London: Palgrave Macmillan, 2015.

Rosetal, Paul-André. "Construire le 'macr' par le 'micro:' Fredrik Barth et la microstoria." In Revel, *Jeux d'echelles*, 141–59.

Rouf, Jeffrey. "Home Movies of the Avant-Garde: Jonas Mekas and the New York Art World." In James, *To Free the Cinema*, 294–312.

Rousset, Jean. *Le lecteur intime: De Balzac au journal*. Paris: Librairie José Corti, 1986.

Rousso, Henry. *The Latest Catastrophe: History, the Present, the Contemporary*. Chicago: University of Chicago Press, 2016.

Russell, Catherine. *Archiveology: Walter Benjamin and Archival Film Practices*. Durham, NC: Duke University Press 2018.

Sánchez-Biosca, Vicente. "Challenging Old and New Images Representing the Cambodian Genocide: *The Missing Picture* (Rithy Panh, 2013)." *Genocide Studies and Prevention: An International Journal* 12, no. 2 (2018): 140–64.

Sánchez-Biosca, Vicente. "Exploración, experiencia y emoción de archivo: A modo de introducción." *Aniki* 2, no. 2 (2015): 220–23.

Sánchez-Biosca, Vicente. "¿Qué espera de mí esa foto? La *Perpetrator image* de Bophana y su contracampo. Iconografías del genocidio camboyano." *Aniki* 2, no. 2 (2015): 322–48.

Sans, Jérôme, ed. *Just Like a Shadow*. Paris: Patrick Remy Studio, 2000.

Schulze, Winfried, ed. *Sozialgeschichte, Alltagsgeschichte und Mikro-Historie*. Göttingen: Vandenhoeck und Ruprecht, 1994.

Serna, Justo, and Anacleto Pons. *Cómo se escribe la microhistoria: Ensayo sobre Carlo Ginzburg*. Madrid: Cátedra, 2000.

Serna, Justo, and Anacleto Pons. "Formas de hacer microhistoria." *Agora: Revista de Ciencias Sociales*, 7 (2002): 220–47.

Serna, Justo, and Anacleto Pons. *Microhistoria: Las narraciones de Carlo Ginzburg*. Granada: Comares, 2019.

Shand, Ryan. "Theorizing Amateur Cinema: Limitations and Possibilities." *Moving Image: The Journal of the Association of Moving Image Archivists* 8, no. 2 (2008): 36–60.

Shemer, Yaron. *Identity, Place, and Subversion in Contemporary Mizrahi Cinema in Israel*. Ann Arbor: University of Michigan Press, 2013.

Shlaim, Avi. "La guerre des historiens israéliens." *Annales* 59, no. 1 (2004): 161–67.

Simmel, Georg. *The Conflict in Modern Culture and Other Essays*. New York: Teachers College, 1968.

Simmel, Georg. *Sociology: Inquiries into the Construction of Social Forms*. Leiden: Brill, 2009.

Simon, Cheryl, ed. "Following the Archival Turn: Photography, the Museum, and the Archive." Special Issue, *Visual Resources: An International Journal on Images and Their Uses* 18, no. 2 (2002).

Sipe, Dan. "The Future of Oral History and Moving Images." *Oral History Review* 19, no. 1–2 (1991): 75–87.

Slávik, Andrej. "Microhistory and Cinematic Experience: Two or Three Things I Know About Carlo Ginzburg." In *Microhistories*, edited by Magnus Bärtås and Andrej Slávik, 40–69. Stockholm: Konstfack, 2016.

Slootweg, Tom. "Home Mode, Community Mode, Counter Mode: Three Functional Modalities for Coming to Terms with Amateur Media Practices." In *Materializing Memories: Dispositifs, Generations, Amateurs*, edited by Susan Aasman, Andreas Fickers, and Joseph Wachelder, 203–16. London: Bloomsbury, 2018.

Smith, Paul, ed. *The Historian and Film*. Cambridge: Cambridge University Press, 2011.

Sobchack, Vivian. "Lounge Time: Postwar Crises and the Chronotope of Film Noir." In *Refiguring American Film Genres: History and Theory*, edited by Nick Browne, 129–70. Berkeley: University of California Press, 1998.

Sorlin, Pierre. *The Film in History: Restaging the Past*. Oxford: Basil Blackwell, 1980.

Sorlin, Pierre. *Sociologie du Cinéma: Ouverture pour l'histoire de demain*. Paris: Aubier Montaigne, 1977.

Spence, Jo, and Patricia Holland, eds. *Family Snaps: The Meanings of Domestic Photography*. London: Virago, 1991.

Spieker, Sven. "At the Center of Mitteleuropa, A Conversation with Peter Forgács." *ARTMargins*, April 21, 2002. https://artmargins.com/at-the-center-of-mitteleuropa-a-conversation-with-peter-forgacs/.

Stam, Robert. *Subversive Pleasures: Bakhtin, Cultural Criticism, and Film*. Baltimore: Johns Hopkins University Press, 1989.

Steedman, Carolyn. *Dust*. Manchester, UK: Manchester University Press, 2001.

Steedman, Carolyn. "Something She Called a Fever: Michelet, Derrida, and Dust." *American Historical Review* 106, no. 4 (2001): 1159–80.

Stoler, Ann Laura. "Colonial Archives and the Arts of Governance." *Archival Science* 2, nos. 1–2 (2002): 87–109.

Sturken, Marita. "The Absent Images of Memory: Remembering and Reenacting the Japanese Internment." In *Perilous Memories: The Asia-Pacific Wars*, edited by T. Fujitani, Geoffrey M. White, and Lisa Yoneyama, 33–49. Durham, NC: Duke University Press, 2001.

Summerfield, Penny. *Histories of the Self: Personal Narratives and Historical Practice*. London: Routledge, 2018.

Swender, Rebecca. "Claiming the Found: Archive Footage and Documentary Practice." *Velvet Light Trap*, no. 64 (2009): 3–10.

Tachjian, Vahé. *Daily Life in the Abyss: Genocide Diaries, 1915–1918*. New York: Berghahn Books, 2017.

Tepperman, Charles. *Amateur Cinema: The Rise of North American Moviemaking, 1923–1960*. Berkeley: University of California Press, 2014.

Toplin, Robert B. "The Filmmaker as Historian." *American Historical Review* 93, no. 5 (1988): 1210–27.

Torchin, Leshu. "Mediation and Remediation: La Parole Filmée in Rithy Panh's *The Missing Picture* (L'image Manquante)." *Film Quarterly* 68, no. 1 (2014): 32–41.

Treacey, Mia E. M. *Reframing the Past: History, Film and Television*. London: Routledge, 2016.

Tredinnick, Luke. "The Making of History: Remediating Historicised Experience." In *History in the Digital Age*, edited by Toni Weller, 39–60. London: Routledge, 2012.

Turim, Maureen. "*Reminiscences*, Subjectivities, and Truths." In James, *To Free the Cinema*, 193–212.

Van Alphen, Ernst. "Towards a New Historiography: Péter Forgács and the Aesthetics of Temporality." In *Resonant Bodies, Voices, Memories*, edited by Anke Bangma, Deirdre M. Donoghue, Lina Issa, and Katarina Zdjelar, 90–113. Rotterdam: Piet Zwart Institute, 2008.

Van Buren, Cassandra. "Family Gathering: Release from Emotional Internment." *Jump Cut*, no. 37 (1992): 65–63.

Van Dijck, José. *Mediated Memories in the Digital Age*. Stanford, CA: Stanford University Press, 2007.

Varga, Balázs. "Façades: The Private and the Public in Kádár's Kiss by Péter Forgács." In *Past for the Eyes: East European Representations of Communism in Cinema and Museums After 1989*, edited by Oksana Sarkisova and Péter Apor, 81–101. Budapest: Central European University Press, 2008.

Walker, Janet. "The Traumatic Paradox: Autobiographical Documentary and the Psychology of Memory." In *Contested Pasts: The Politics of Memory*, edited by Katharine Hodgkin and Susannah Radstone, 104–19. London: Routledge, 2003.

Weller, Tony, ed. *History in the Digital Age*. London: Routledge, 2012.

White, Hayden. "Historiography and Historiophoty." *American Historical Review* 93, no. 5 (1988): 1193–99.

Wong, Sau-Ling Cynthia. "Immigrant Autobiography: Some Questions of Definition and Approach." In *American Autobiography: Retrospect and Prospect*, edited by Paul J. Eakin, 142–70. Madison: University of Wisconsin Press, 1991.

Woodham, Anna, Laura King, Liz Gloyn, Vicky Crewe, and Fiona Blair. "We Are What We Keep: 'The "Family Archive.' Identity and Public/Private Heritage." *Heritage & Society* 10, no. 3 (2017): 203–20.

Xing, Jun. *Asian America Through the Lens: History, Representations, and Identity.* Walnut Creek, CA: AltaMira Press, 1998.

Yasui, Robert Shu. *The Yasui Family of Hood River, Oregon.* Self-published, 1987.

Yosef, Raz, and Boaz Hagin, eds. *Deeper Than Oblivion: Trauma and Memory in Israeli Cinema.* London: Bloomsbury, 2013.

Young, James E. "Toward a Received History of the Holocaust." *History and Theory* 36, no. 4 (1997): 21–43.

Zimmermann, Patricia R. "The Home Movie Movement: Excavations, Artifacts." In Ishizuka and Zimmermann, *Mining the Home Movies*, 1–28.

Zuromskis, Catherine. *Snapshot Photography: The Lives of Images.* Cambridge, MA: MIT Press, 2013.

Zuromskis, Catherine. "Snapshot Photography: History, Theory, Practice and Aesthetics." In *A Companion to Photography*, edited by Stephen Bull, 291–306. Chicester, UK: Wiley-Blackwell, 2020.

INDEX

autobiographical approach: family archives and, 63–64; in *A Family Gathering* (Yasui and Tegnell, 1989), 104, 108–15, *111*; in *History and Memory* (Tajiri, 1991), 104, 124–26; home movies and, 48, 54, 63; in *Lost, Lost, Lost* (Mekas, 1976), 189–90, 191, 198–201, 209–11, 216, 218; microhistorical documentary and, 30–31, 32, 33, 34–39, 104, 222; in *The Missing Picture* (Panh, 2013), 132–39, 150; in *My Brother* (Cohen, 2007), 172–73; in *For My Children* (Aviad, 2002), 153, 160–61, 165; in *My Land Zion* (Cohen, 2004), 153, 160–61, 165, 172–73, 177–78, 179–80; in *My Terrorist* (Cohen, 2002), 153, 160–61, 172–75, 177–78; postmemory and, 107–8; in *Private Chronicles: Monologue* (Manskij, 1999), 60–61; in *Reminiscences of a Journey to Lithuania* (Mekas, 1972), 195–97; in *From a Silk Cocoon* (Holsapple, Clay, and Ina, 2005), 104–8, 109; soundtracks and, 63–64; in *A World Not Ours* (Fleifel, 2012), 180–87; in *Yidl in the Middle* (Booth, 1999), 57

autobiographical studies, 96

Aviad, Michal, 165; *Dimona Twist* (2016), 165, 166; *The Women Pioneers* (2013), 165–66. See also *For My Children* (Aviad, 2002)

Avshalom-Dahan, Avigail, 157–58

Bad Day at Black Rock (Sturges, 1955), 119, 120–21, 125

Baecque, Antoine de, 3–4

Bakhtin, Mikhail, 15, 120, 188, 199, 211

Bakó, Elemér, 246n18

Bakri, Mohammed: *1948* (1999), 180; *Zahra* (2009), 180

Balint, Ruth, 67

banality of evil, 79

Banks, Taunya Lovell, 248n5

Baron, Jaimie, 53–54

Barth, Fredrick, 23

Barthes, Roland, 51, 82–83

Bartos Family, The (Forgács, 1988), 65, 67, 68, 69, 73, 75

Bastian, Jeannette, 43

Bataille, Christophe, 132–33, 142–43

Baudelaire, Charles, 18

Bazin, André, 39, 51, 90, 160

Beker, Elisabeth, 128

Benjamin, Walter, 15, 16–19, 71–72

Bergland, Betty Ann, 96, 209

Bergson, Henri, 136

Bernstein, Arik: *Israel: A Home Movie* (with Lilti, 2012), 49, 58, 153–60, *157–58*

Bibó Reader (Forgács, 2001), 67–68

Binnun, Benya, 157–58, 159, 254n3

biography, 83–84, 133

Bishop's Garden, The (Forgács, 2002), 69

Blaustein, David: *Hacer patria* (2007), 33

Blow-up (Antonioni, 1966), 27–28

Boelhower, William, 199–200

Booth, Marlene: *Yidl in the Middle* (1999), 57

Bophana: A Cambodian Tragedy (Panh, 1996), 46, 127–30, *129*, 132, 133

Bossion, Claude: *Mémoire d'outremer* (1997), 58–60

Bou, Stéphane, 149

Bourgeois Dictionary (Forgács, 1992), 67–68

Boyle, Deirdre, 131

Brakhage, Stan, 242n21

Brecht, Bertolt, 18

Brewer, John, 15, 16–18, 21, 22, 28

Breznay, József, 74

Brigante, Louis, 217

Bryceson, Debora F., 255–56n25

Buil, José: *La línea paterna* (with Sistach, 1994), 55, 56–57

Burke, Peter, 23

Burnat, Emad: *5 Broken Cameras* (with Davidi, 2011), 161, 164

Cambodian genocide (1975–1979), 127. *See also* Panh, Rithy

Camera Lucida (Barthes), 51, 82–83

microhistorical documentary: concept and characteristics of, 1–2, 6–7, 14, 27–34, 39–40, 221; archival sources and, 6–7, 31–32, 38, 41–49; autobiographical approach and, 30–31, 32, 33, 34–39, 104, 222; everyday life studies and, 14–20, 72; future trends in, 222–26; human agency in, 221; postmodernism and, 33–34. *See also* home movies; *specific documentaries*

microhistory and *microstoria* school, 21–27, 128, 133, 138, 144. *See also* Ginzburg, Carlo; Levi, Giovanni

Mihyi, Fahad, 173, 174

Mimura, Glen M., 118

Mining the Home Movie (Zimmermann), 49–50

Miss Universe 1929 (Forgács, 2006), 68, 69, 75, 247n35

Missing Picture, The (Panh, 2013): absence of images of the genocide and, 149–51; archival sources in, 133, *146–47*; autobiographical approach of, 132–39, 150; dioramas in, 135–37, 143, 145–51, *146–47*; fiction films in, 45, 144; macrohistorical dimension in, 137–43; as memory film, 134–37; as microhistorical documentary, 127; music in, 139, 141–42, 148; newsreels and propaganda films in, 45, 138–49; voice-over narration in, 133, 134–35, 139–43, 144, 145, 146–48

misterio de los ojos escarlata, El (Anzola, 1993), 55, 56–57

mnemonic objects: archival materials as, 187; in *A Family Gathering* (Yasui and Tegnell, 1989), 112; family photographs as, 38, 107–8; in *History and Memory* (Tajiri, 1991), 47, 116, 117–18; home movies as, 38, 47, 70, 72, 112–15; in *The Missing Picture* (Panh, 2013), 137; in *From a Silk Cocoon* (Holsapple, Clay, and Ina, 2005), 107–8

Mograbi, Avi: *Happy Birthday, Mr. Mograbi* (1999), 152–53

Montaillou (Le Roy), 23

Montgomery, Michael V., 199

Moran, James M., 47

mug shots, 129–30, *129*, 132, 137, 144

Munk, Yael, 165

music and soundtracks: archival sources and, 44; autobiographical approach and, 63–64; in *Class Lot* (Forgács, 1997), 90, 91–93; in *A Family Gathering* (Yasui and Tegnell, 1989), 111–12; in Forgács's films, 71; in *Israel: A Home Movie* (Lilti and Bernstein, 2012), 154; in *Lost, Lost, Lost* (Mekas, 1976), 201, 203, 204, 215; in *The Maelstrom* (Forgács, 1997), 75, 80, 88; in *Mémoire d'outremer* (Bossion, 1997), 59; in microhistorical documentary, 32; in *The Missing Picture* (Panh, 2013), 139, 141–42, 148; in *From a Silk Cocoon* (Holsapple, Clay, and Ina, 2005), 106; in *Something Strong Within* (Nakamura and Ishizuka, 1994), 98, 100; in *A World Not Ours* (Fleifel, 2012), 183, 186

My Brother (Cohen, 2007), 165, 172–73

My Land Zion (Cohen, 2004): autobiographical approach of, 153, 160–61, 165, 172–73, 177–78, 179–80; interviews in, 176–77; *Jerusalem, We Are Here* (Naaman, 2016) and, 226; macrohistorical dimension in, 176–77, *177*, 178–79; voice-over narration in, 178; *A World Not Ours* (Fleifel, 2012) and, 187

My Terrorist (Cohen, 2002), 153, 160–61, 165, 172–75, 177–78

Naaman, Dorit: *Jerusalem, We Are Here* (2016), 225

Naficy, Hamid, 183, 194, 199

Nakamura, Robert. See *Something Strong Within* (Nakamura and Ishizuka, 1994)

Nanook of the North (Flaherty, 1927), 29

narrative identity, 191

narrative recovery, 209

New American Cinema movement, 215

New Historians, 169